*"In taking us straight to the hea...
us magnificently. We so need t...
Scriptures get into us. The fact t...
such submission to Biblical reve...
helped to be shaped...*

– Te...

"Phil makes the deep truths of Scripture alive and accessible. If you want to grow in your understanding of each book of the Bible, then buy these books and let them change your life!"

– PJ Smyth – *GodFirst Church, Johannesburg, South Africa*

"Most commentaries are dull. These are alive. Most commentaries are for scholars. These are for you!"

– Canon Michael Green

"These notes are amazingly good. Lots of content and depth of research, yet packed in a Big Breakfast that leaves the reader well fed and full. Bible notes often say too little, yet larger commentaries can be dull - missing the wood for the trees. Phil's insights are striking, original, and fresh, going straight to the heart of the text and the reader! Substantial yet succinct, they bristle with amazing insights and life applications, compelling us to read more. Bible reading will become enriched and informed with such a scintillating guide. Teachers and preachers will find nuggets of pure gold here!"

– Greg Haslam – *Westminster Chapel, London, UK*

"The Bible is living and dangerous. The ones who teach it best are those who bear that in mind – and let the author do the talking. Phil has written these studies with a sharp mind and a combination of creative application and reverence."

– Joel Virgo – *Leader of Newday Youth Festival*

"Phil Moore's new commentaries are outstanding: biblical and passionate, clear and well-illustrated, simple and profound. God's Word comes to life as you read them, and the wonder of God shines through every page."

– Andrew Wilson – *Author of* Incomparable *and* GodStories

For more information about the Straight to the Heart series, please go to **www.philmoorebooks.com**.

Moses

60 BITE-SIZED INSIGHTS FROM EXODUS, LEVITICUS, NUMBERS AND DEUTERONOMY

Phil Moore

MONARCH
BOOKS

Oxford, UK & Grand Rapids, Michigan, USA

First published in the UK in 2011 by Monarch Books
(a publishing imprint of Lion Hudson plc)
Wilkinson House, Jordan Hill Road, Oxford OX2 8DR, England
Tel: +44 (0)1865 302750 Fax: +44 (0)1865 302757
Email: monarch@lionhudson.com
www.lionhudson.com

ISBN 978 0 85721 056 2 (print)
ISBN 978 0 85721 181 1 (epub)
ISBN 978 0 85721 180 4 (Kindle)
ISBN 978 0 85721 182 8 (PDF)

Distributed by:
UK: Marston Book Services, PO Box 269, Abingdon, Oxon, OX14 4YN
USA: Kregel Publications, PO Box 2607, Grand Rapids, Michigan 49501

British Library Cataloguing Data
A catalogue record for this book is available from the British Library.

Printed and bound in the UK by Clays Ltd, St Ives plc.

This book is for my nephews and nieces:
Susanna, Rebekah, Elisabeth, Daniel, Cassia and Naomi;
Elijah, Theo, Winter, Bella and Afia.
May you enjoy the thrill of following the God
who wants to be seen through his People.

CONTENTS

LEVITICUS: GOD THE HOLY ONE

NUMBERS: GOD THE FAITHFUL ONE

DEUTERONOMY: GOD THE COVENANT KEEPER

About the *Straight to the Heart* Series

On his eightieth birthday, Sir Winston Churchill dismissed the compliment that he was the "lion" who had defeated Nazi Germany in World War Two. He told the Houses of Parliament that *"It was a nation and race dwelling all around the globe that had the lion's heart. I had the luck to be called upon to give the roar."*

I hope that God speaks to you very powerfully through the "roar" of the books in the *Straight to the Heart* series. I hope they help you to understand the books of the Bible and the message which the Holy Spirit inspired their authors to write. I hope that they help you to hear God's voice challenging you, and that they provide you with a springboard for further journeys into each book of Scripture for yourself.

But when you hear my "roar", I want you to know that it comes from the heart of a much bigger "lion" than me. I have been shaped by a whole host of great Christian thinkers and preachers from around the world, and I want to give due credit to at least some of them here:

Terry Virgo, David Stroud, John Hosier, Adrian Holloway, Greg Haslam, Lex Loizides and all those who lead the Newfrontiers family of churches. Friends and encouragers, such as Stef Liston, Joel Virgo, Stuart Gibbs, Scott Taylor, Nick Sharp, Nick Derbridge, Phil Whittall, and Kevin and Sarah Aires. Tony Collins, Jenny Ward and Simon Cox at Monarch Books. Malcolm Kayes and all the elders of The Coign Church, Woking. My fellow elders and church members here at Queens Road Church, Wimbledon.

My great friend Andrew Wilson – without your friendship, encouragement and example, this series would never have happened.

I would like to thank my parents, my brother Jonathan, and my in-laws, Clive and Sue Jackson. Dad – your example birthed in my heart the passion that brought this series into being. I didn't listen to all you said when I was a child, but I couldn't ignore the way you got up at five o'clock every morning to pray, read the Bible and worship, because of your radical love for God and for his Word. I'd like to thank my children – Isaac, Noah and Esther – for keeping me sane when publishing deadlines were looming. But most of all, I'm grateful to my incredible wife, Ruth – my friend, encourager, corrector and helper.

You all have the lion's heart, and you have all developed the lion's heart in me. I count it an enormous privilege to be the one who was chosen to sound the lion's roar.

So welcome to the *Straight to the Heart* series. My prayer is that you will let this roar grip your own heart too – for the glory of the great Lion of the Tribe of Judah, the Lord Jesus Christ!

Introduction: God Wants to Be Seen Through His People

Then the Lord said: "I am making a covenant with you. Before all your people I will do wonders never before done in any nation in all the world. The people you live among will see how awesome is the work that I, the Lord, will do for you."

(Exodus 34:10)

God is invisible. That's a problem. It was a problem in ancient Egypt and it's still a problem today. In a world where people tend to worship what they can see and feel and taste and touch, an invisible God is all too easy to ignore.

Take, for example, John Lennon's boast to a reporter in March 1966 that *"We're more popular than Jesus now."* Although many Christians found his tactless comment quite offensive, it was difficult for them to deny the raw facts behind his claim. The Beatles had just held the largest music concert in human history, filling a New York City stadium with 55,000 screaming fans. In the nine days since the release of their new album they had sold 1.2 million copies in America alone. In contrast five weeks later, *Time Magazine* ran a cover story which asked the provocative question *"Is God Dead?"* Quoting from a spoof obituary, it speculated from the shrinking congregations of most Western churches that: *"God, creator of the universe, principal deity of the world's Jews, ultimate reality of Christians and most eminent of all divinities, died late yesterday during major surgery undertaken to correct a massive diminishing influence.*"[1] That's the basic problem: Even a visible human can draw more worship than an invisible God.

Got that? Then you are ready for the books which Moses wrote in the desert.[2] The Pentateuch (the word is simply Greek for *five-volume story*[3]) recounts the invisible God's master plan to make himself seen. More glorious than the gods of Egypt; more powerful than the gods of Canaan; more satisfying than the gods of the twenty-first-century Western world – the invisible God would be seen through his People.

Another book in this series covers volume one of the Pentateuch, Genesis, in which the Lord began to make himself visible. Paul reflects on those early chapters in Romans 1: *"What may be known about God is plain to [all people], because God has made it plain to them. For since the creation of the world God's invisible qualities – his eternal power and divine nature – have been clearly seen, being understood from what has been made, so that men are without excuse."* Yet because humans sin and close their eyes to this revelation, the Lord executes a plan which makes him impossible to ignore. He chooses Abraham and his family to make the rulers of the nations exclaim that *"God is with you in everything you do"*, and *"Can we find anyone like this man, one in whom is the Spirit of God?"*[4] The great finale of Genesis sees him moving the seventy members of Abraham's family

14

---

[1] *Time Magazine* ran this cover story on 8th April 1966, only five weeks after John Lennon made his boast in an interview with the London *Evening Standard*.

[2] Although some scholars question whether Moses was the author of the Pentateuch, they make too much of a late editorial insertions and ignore the united testimony of the Pentateuch, Jesus, both Old and New Testaments, and 3,000 years of Judaeo-Christian consensus. See Exodus 17:14; 24:4; 34:27, Deuteronomy 1:5; 31:9; 31:24; Joshua 8:31; 1 Kings 2:3; Mark 7:10; 10:3–5; 12:26; Luke 2:22–23; John 4:46–47; Acts 7:37–38.

[3] The Pentateuch was originally one book which was divided into five scrolls for ease of reading.

[4] Genesis 21:22; 41:38.

to Egypt with a missionary calling to make him visible to the greatest superpower nation of their day.[5] Sure enough, many Egyptians are saved through Israel's God, and the curtain falls for a 300-year-long interval before the start of volume two.[6]

Exodus 1 therefore comes as a colossal disappointment. The Egyptians are still worshipping their idols as before, and have so oppressed Abraham's family that their faith in Yahweh starts to fail. The distant promises of Israel's patriarchal past are so at odds with the painful realities of the present that the Hebrews are either worshipping their invisible God in private or else giving up on him entirely to serve the bold, brash and visible gods of the Egyptians they were sent to save.[7] By the time Moses challenges Pharaoh to let God's People go, the Lord has become so invisible that Pharaoh sneers, *"Who is the Lord, that I should obey him and let Israel go? I do not know the Lord and I will not let Israel go."*[8] The scene is set for the greatest showdown of the Old Testament. The invisible God is about to be seen through his People.

In Exodus 1–18 the Lord displays that he is *God the Saviour*, laughing at the overwhelming odds to free his down-and-out Hebrews from the stranglehold of slavery. In Exodus 19–40 he reveals that he did this because he is *God the Indweller*, who brought them to Mount Sinai in order to camp among them in his Tabernacle home. This leads into the message of Leviticus that he is *God the Holy One* who wants to be seen through his holy People and, when they refuse to live up to this calling in Numbers, into the revelation that he is *God the Faithful One* as he leads and protects them for forty years in the hostile desert.

---

[5] The Septuagint adds the children of Ephraim and Manasseh to make *seventy-five* in Genesis 46:27 and Exodus 1:5 (as quoted in Acts 7:14). However, it leaves the total as *seventy* in Deuteronomy 10:22.

[6] The Hebrews spent 430 years in Egypt (Exodus 12:40). Joseph died after seventy years and Moses was born eighty years before their end (Genesis 41:46; 45:6; 50:26; Exodus 7:7).

[7] Joshua 24:14; Ezekiel 20:7–8.

[8] Exodus 5:2.

In Deuteronomy he displays that he is *God the Covenant Keeper*, who remains true to the promises he made to their fathers even when they fail him and provoke him to anger. The Lord wants to be seen through his People, and Moses tells us that nothing can thwart him in his plan.

I have written this book because God still pursues the same strategy with us as he did in the pages of Exodus, Leviticus, Numbers and Deuteronomy. In a world where "The Beatles" are still googled more often than "Jesus", God wants to be seen through his People.[9] In a world which still echoes with the cry of Psalm 42 – *"My foes taunt me, saying to me all day long, 'Where is your God?'"* – God wants to be seen through his People. In a world which largely ignores the true yet invisible God, we must not skim read these books as if they were written for somebody other than ourselves.

I want to bring the pages of the Pentateuch to life for you, so that you can be like the Hebrews who *"saw the great power the Lord displayed...and put their trust in him".*[10] I want to help you reveal the invisible God to those around you, so that they exclaim like the foreigners in the Pentateuch that *"Now I know that the Lord is greater than all other gods".*[11]

So let's journey through the pages of the Pentateuch together, learning how the Lord wants to use us to capture the attention of the world. The same invisible God who was seen through the Israelites has not changed his strategy today. It is 3,500 years since Moses wrote the Pentateuch, but God still wants to be seen through his People.

---

[9] The British *Daily Telegraph* reported this on 21st September 2009 under the headline *"The Beatles 'bigger than Jesus' on Google"*.

[10] Exodus 14:31.

[11] Jethro, a Midianite worshipper of the Lord, says this in Exodus 18:11. The *'ēreb* – Hebrew for a *mixed-race crowd* – come to a similar conclusion in 12:38 and turn their backs on Egypt to follow Israel's God.

Exodus 1–18:

God the Saviour

God's Prison Break
(1:1–2:10)

But the more they were oppressed, the more they multiplied and spread.

(Exodus 1:12)

When God wants to be seen through his People, there is simply no obstacle strong enough to stop him. If you were impressed by Michael Schofield's elaborate plans to escape from Fox River State Penitentiary in the TV series *Prison Break*, you will love what happens in Exodus 1 and 2. The Greek word *Exodus* means literally *exit* or *way out*, and these chapters form the prelude to the Old Testament's great escape story.

Make no doubt about it, Egypt in the fifteenth century BC was the world's largest prison. The seventy Hebrews had gone there in obedience to the Lord's promise in Genesis 46 that he would turn them into a mighty nation in Egypt and bring them back to Canaan as conquerors of the land. Almost four centuries later, such promises looked like pipe dreams, and the Devil's agenda to keep the Lord invisible looked more successful than the plotting of a clever prison guard on any television show.

First, the Hebrews lost their privileged status in the nation. Joseph had saved Egypt from disaster under the Twelfth Dynasty of pharaohs, and his family had been rewarded with possession of Goshen, the most fertile fields in the land. Pharaoh appointed Joseph as his royal vizier and mummified his body when he died as if he were one of his own. But shortly after Joseph's death, the Twelfth Dynasty fell and five new dynasties came and went during two turbulent centuries known as the Second

Intermediate Period. Pharaoh Ahmose I of the Eighteenth Dynasty founded the New Kingdom by expelling the Canaanite Hyksos, but this made him naturally suspicious of the Hebrews who remained.[1] Hadn't these foreigners originally come from Canaan? Were they not natural allies to the Hyksos if they reappeared with a new army? So he enslaved them and forced them to build great monuments which shouted to the world that Egypt's new regime was here to stay.[2] Pharaoh turned their Goshen into his Gulag.

But the plan backfired, spectacularly. Moses tells us in 1:12 that *"the more they were oppressed, the more they multiplied and spread."* He uses five separate Hebrew verbs in 1:7 alone to describe the ensuing Hebrew baby boom.[3] Alarmed by the Egyptians' open hatred towards them, Jacob's family tried to multiply and soon became a seven-figure nation.[4] God had promised Abraham this would happen in Egypt in Genesis 15, and he was at work behind the Devil's clumsy scheming. *"The Lord made his people very fruitful; he made them too numerous for their foes,* **whose hearts he turned to hate his people.**"[5]

The Devil tried a second strategy. He incited Pharaoh's heart to order the Hebrew midwives to murder every baby boy

---

[1] This is why Stephen chooses a Greek word in Acts 7:18 which emphasizes that this ruler was not *another similar* (*allos*) Pharaoh, but *another different* (*heteros*) Pharaoh, from a completely new dynasty.

[2] Don't be confused by the reference to Rameses in 1:11. Some scholars put this together with Galatians 3:17 (where Paul is humouring a Septuagint mistranslation) to argue that the Exodus took place in the thirteenth century BC under Pharaoh Rameses II, but Genesis 15:13, Exodus 12:40 and the chronology of Judges show us that this must be a later editorial update to the place name, like the one in Genesis 14:14. That also means that Exodus 6:16–20 must give only a selective, abridged genealogy.

[3] He tells us literally that the Hebrews *were fruitful, teemed, multiplied, grew very numerous* and *filled* the land.

[4] As a result, although the word *Israelite* is only used twice in Genesis, it is used over 100 times in Exodus.

[5] Psalm 105:24–25. We will look in more detail in the chapter "Hardened" at how God's sovereignty works.

at birth. Future Hebrew slave-girls were useful to Egypt, but boys were potential insurrectionists and must not be allowed to live. Again this fresh attempt to thwart God's plan backfired, as it galvanized the flagging faith of the dispirited Hebrews to put their hope in him. Spurred on by Pharaoh's threats of murder and the Hebrew midwives' brave defiance, Moses tells us in 1:20 that *"the people increased and became even more numerous."*

Satan's third strategy was increasingly desperate, provoking Pharaoh to order that every Hebrew baby boy be drowned in the River Nile. This time the Lord's response outshines the very best of Michael Schofield, as he turns Satan's worst into the centrepiece of his plan. *"One weak link can break the chain of a mighty dynasty,"* worries Pharaoh in the animated movie *The Prince of Egypt*.[6] He had no idea that the Lord was smarter by far and could even use infanticide as a way to smuggle his deliverer into Pharaoh's palace.

Pharaoh's decree forces two Hebrew parents to take their baby boy down to the river and hide him in a basket among the reeds. They pray to the Lord for a miracle, and he reveals himself as God the Saviour when Pharaoh's very own daughter finds the baby and adopts him as her son. By God's power, he had not been overheard crying during his three months in hiding, but now he cries at the right moment to move Pharaoh's daughter to compassion. His sister Miriam is hiding and appears in time for the Lord to use her to make Pharaoh *pay* Moses' mother to look after his enemy![7] The Lord runs rings around his would-be opponent Satan. He is smarter by far and will let nothing foil his plan.

Even now, God hasn't finished. He has another trump card left to play. The baby grows up with a dual nationality which is epitomized by his name. *Moses* means *Drawn-Out* in Hebrew, but it also means *Born* in Egyptian and sounds like the names

---

[6] *The Prince of Egypt* (Dreamworks Pictures, 1998).

[7] Miriam is not named in chapter 2, but she reappears in the story by name from Exodus 15:20–21 onwards.

of Pharaohs *Ahmoses* and *Thutmoses*.[8] Moses is therefore given a royal education in Egypt's wisdom, and gains unparalleled know-how of the inner workings of Pharaoh's court, yet his primary spiritual influence remains his mother so that *"when he had grown up, he refused to be known as the son of Pharaoh's daughter. He chose to be mistreated along with the people of God rather than to enjoy the pleasures of sin for a short time."*[9]

The Devil's three strategies to thwart God's great prison break had failed, because God wants to be seen through his People. All those strategies did was create a larger, more unified, more devout Hebrew nation, which cried out to God for a deliverer and found one forged in the furnace which the Devil had stoked against them.

The story of God's great escape is even cleverer than Michael Schofield's *Prison Break* at its most fanciful. This baby in the basket grew up and went on to write Exodus as his personal account of the Lord as God the Saviour. He smiles at us through these opening verses and assures us that nothing can stop the Lord from succeeding in his plan. He is going to be seen through his People.

---

[8] *Ahmoses* means *Born-to-Aah* (the moon-god) and *Thutmoses* means *Born-to-Thoth* (the magic-god). Both names usually lose the final "s" in English. The name of Nineteenth-Dynasty Pharaoh *Rameses* means *Born-to-Ra* (the sun-god).

[9] Hebrews 11:24–25. This is why Moses flouted Egyptian convention by refusing to marry even at forty. Forbidden from marrying a Hebrew, he refused to marry an Egyptian girl instead. The Lord rewards him with Zipporah in a scene that deliberately echoes Jacob meeting Rachel in Genesis 29:10.

Waiting is Not Wasting
(2:11–25)

During that long period, the king of Egypt died. The Israelites groaned in their slavery and cried out, and their cry for help because of their slavery went up to God.

(Exodus 2:23)

God wants to be seen through his People, but it certainly didn't feel that way to the Hebrew slaves in Egypt. They had none of the hindsight we enjoy today to reassure them that he was working in secret on his prison break. Many of them began to doubt whether he actually wanted to be seen through them at all. We can all feel the same during our own periods of waiting.

If you have been a Christian for any length of time, you will have discovered that God is not in a hurry. Like Gandalf in the film *The Fellowship of the Ring*, he *"is never late; nor is he early. He always arrives precisely when he means to"* – but even so, the Christian life involves a lot of waiting. A marriage partner, a job search, the conception of a baby, the salvation of a friend – whatever it is, he is invariably the God *"who acts on behalf of those who wait for him"*.[1] As I write this, I am entering a second year of trying to sell my house, which doesn't make sense when I have told all my neighbours that I serve the God who answers his People's prayers. Situations like these can make us doubt whether the Lord truly wants to be seen as much as the Pentateuch suggests. That's why Exodus begins with an

---

[1] Isaiah 64:4.

encouragement that "waiting is not wasting", because the Lord can be seen through his People even as they wait.

During Israel's darkest night, the Lord still used them to reveal himself as *God the Faithful One*. When Pharaoh commanded the Hebrew midwives to murder every newborn baby boy, they were tempted to put their faith to one side and to compartmentalize their working lives. Pharaoh demanded that his subjects address him as *"My King, my Lord, my God, my Sun, the Sun in the sky"*,[2] and he had power to execute any health worker who refused to obey his edicts straight away. When the midwives *"feared God and did not do what the king of Egypt had told them to do"*, they gave the Lord an opportunity to demonstrate his faithfulness through their lives. Moses tells us that *"because the midwives feared God, he gave them families of their own."* In fact, although he does not even bother to identify the pharaoh who gave the order,[3] he makes sure to record the names of Shiphrah and Puah because they made God's faithfulness visible through their courage while they waited.[4]

In the midst of delay, the Lord also revealed himself as *God the Saviour*. Moses tells us in 6:20 that his parents were named Jochebed and Amram, meaning *Yahweh is Glorious* and *The People are Exalted*. This implies they were a family who still believed that God wanted to be seen through his People despite the confusingly long delay. They kept such faith in the Lord that he describes himself to Moses in 3:6 as *"the God of your father"*

---

[2] Yapahu of Gezer calls Pharaoh this repeatedly in one of the *Amarna Letters* written shortly after the Exodus.

[3] Since 1 Kings 6:1 tells us that the Exodus took place in c.1446 BC, it was probably Ahmose I or Amenhotep I, but even the best Egyptologists cannot agree over the precise dates of each pharaoh.

[4] Their two Hebrew names mean *Beauty* and *Splendid*, appropriate names for those who made God's glory visible. They refused to compartmentalize their work and private lives, defying the law of the land to prevent babies being terminated. They were not lying to Pharaoh, because the essence of his problem was that the Hebrew women truly were more fertile than their Egyptian counterparts.

(not *the God of your fathers*), and they saw something in their newborn baby boy that made them trust God to save him and give him a role in delivering his People.[5] We can see this even more clearly if we understand a bit of Hebrew, since the word *tēbāh* is used in only two places in the Bible: twenty-six times to refer to Noah's Ark and twice here to refer to Moses' basket in the Nile. By faith, Jochebed copied Noah and coated a papyrus basket with waterproof pitch,[6] then took her baby down to the very riverbank where Pharaoh ordered that he be drowned. When she trusted the Lord to save him from the floodwaters and bring him to rest on an "Ararat" of his own, her unflinching trust in her unseen Lord made him visible as God the Saviour.

When the grown-up Moses refused to wait any longer, the Lord was even able to reveal himself as *God the Indweller* through his sin. The New Testament tells us that he hoped to give the Lord a helping hand, assuming that *"his own people would realize that God was using him to rescue them, but they did not."*[7] It only took one nasty comment from a Hebrew to send Moses running into forty years of exile in the desert. He learned the hard way that man-made solutions always fail, but he *"persevered because he saw him who is invisible"*.[8] When the Lord met him at the burning bush and sent him back to Egypt with a promise that this time *"I will be with you"* (3:12), he made God visible to the rest of Egypt too. The man who was spooked by a Hebrew slave on his own, could stand up to Pharaoh when accompanied by his God.

Finally, those forty years of delay enabled the Lord to

---

[5] Acts 7:20 and Hebrews 11:23 quote from the Septuagint translation of Exodus 2:2 to tell us that his parents did not merely fall in love with their *"fine child"*. They sensed he had a role to play in God's prison break.

[6] Genesis 6:14.

[7] Stephen was inspired by the Holy Spirit to give this commentary on Exodus 2 in Acts 7:25.

[8] Hebrews 11:27. This verse also tells us that Moses did not flee primarily out of fear. He could have gained a pardon through his adoptive mother, but preferred to live as the Lord's outcast than as Egypt's prince.

reveal himself as *God the Covenant Keeper*. Moses married into a family of Midianites, the descendants of Abraham through his concubine Keturah. Unlike most Midianites, they still followed Abraham's God and offered sacrifices based on the covenant he had made with their forefather many centuries before.[9] Moses was a failed-schemer-turned-shepherd like the patriarch Jacob before him, but Jethro's family out-Israeled Israel and modelled a covenant-keeping community for him to follow. They inspired him to name his first son Gershom, or *Alien*, out of homesickness for his Hebrew countrymen, and to name his second son Eliezer out of confidence that *God Is My Helper*.[10] That's why Moses ends chapter 2 by telling us that *"God heard their groaning and he remembered his covenant with Abraham, with Isaac and with Jacob."* The Lord *had* heard. The Lord *had* remembered. The Lord *had* looked on his waiting People with concern.

All this should encourage us in our own times of waiting and confusion. If the Lord could be seen through the Hebrews as God the Saviour, God the Indweller, God the Faithful One and God the Covenant Keeper, even during the darkest midnights of their lives, then he will also make himself visible through our own lives if we trust him while we wait.

Will our lives be full of delays and disappointments and dismay? Yes, probably. But waiting is never wasting when we follow the God who wants to be seen through his People.

---

[9] Genesis 25:2. Jethro means *His Remnant*, and his other name Reuel means *Friend of God*. He showed Moses and Aaron how to offer sacrifices in 18:12 and helped Moses to organize a nation under God. Exodus 2:17 suggests that the pagan Midianites hated this little God-fearing community in their midst.

[10] Exodus 2:22; 18:4. Moses refers to the Hebrews twice in 2:11 literally as *"his own brothers"*.

Seeing and Believing
(3:1–4:31)

This will be the sign to you that it is I who have sent you: When you have brought the people out of Egypt, you will worship God on this mountain.

(Exodus 3:12)

Seeing is believing. That's what many people assume anyway, and they use it as a reason to ignore the living-yet-invisible God. At the other end of the scale, some Christians treat faith as a blind leap in the dark and look down on those who want signs and evidence to believe. That's why we all need to understand what God taught Moses in these two chapters about what it means to put our faith in the invisible. Exodus 3 and 4 are not just an introduction to the four books which took Israel from Egypt to the Promised Land. They are also a description of the kind of faith we need in order to make a similar spiritual journey of our own.

Notice how the Lord starts by capturing Moses' attention with something visible. He has shepherded his father-in-law Jethro's flocks for forty years,[1] which means that he has probably been to Mount Horeb a hundred times before. He assumes this thorny patch of mountainous wasteland is nothing more than *"the backside of the desert"*, but when he has a visible encounter with the Lord he discovers that the mountain has been holy all along. It is *"the mountain of God"* and therefore *"holy ground"*, but

---

[1] Acts 7:30 tells us that forty years passed between Exodus 2:15 and 3:1. Numbers 14:33 and Deuteronomy 8:2 imply that God used this to prepare Moses to lead Israel through forty more years in the desert.

it took a burning bush that was not consumed by fire in order to convince him to take off his sandals and listen to the Lord.[2] *"I will go over and see this strange sight – why the bush does not burn up,"* Moses said, but when he came close he *"hid his face, because he was afraid to look at God"*. The Lord appeared to the patriarchs to help them believe, and now he appears to Moses in a similar fashion.[3] It seems that God is more comfortable than many Christians with the idea that "seeing is believing".

But that is only half of the story. Moses asks the Lord for proof that his plan to rescue Israel will be successful, and the Lord starts to teach him that "believing is seeing" too. *"This will be the sign to you that it is I who have sent you: When you have brought the people out of Egypt, you will worship God on this mountain."* Frankly, that's not the sign Moses was after. God's proof required Moses to act in faith over something that would only be visible *after* he went in faith! He had to trust the Lord with what he couldn't see on the basis of what he could, because "seeing is believing" is meant to be a launch pad into "believing is seeing".

God was not teaching Moses a one-off lesson. The message of the Bible is that God *"has provided proof to everyone"*, in order that we can be *"sure of what we hope for and certain of what we do not see"*.[4] He caught the attention of Bethlehem's shepherds by sending them an angel, but then told them in Luke 2:12 to trust him on that basis because *"This will be a sign to you: You will find a baby wrapped in cloths and lying in a manger."* They would only know for sure if they left their precious sheep behind and went, because "seeing is believing" must catapult us on to "believing is seeing". Jesus performed miraculous signs which

---

[2] *Horeb* means *Desolate* and the mountain's other name, *Sinai*, means *Full of Thorns*. Although the Hebrew of 3:1 simply means the *"far side"* of the desert, I like the King James Version's *"backside"*.

[3] These chapters echo God's appearances to the patriarchs, where he appeared as *the Angel of the Lord* so that they could see him and survive.

[4] Acts 17:31 (New English Translation) and Hebrews 11:1.

captivated every Jew in Israel, but then warned them in John 7:17 to use these signs to trust him further, because *"If anyone chooses to do God's will, he will find out whether my teaching comes from God or whether I speak on my own."* The Lord gives us evidence because "seeing is believing", but then calls us to trust him with what we can't see on the basis of what we can. We need to graduate to "believing is seeing" if we want to shake the world like Moses.

Moses responds with five different excuses for not trusting God and going back to Egypt: *I am too weak, too ignorant, too unconvincing, too tongue-tied and too ordinary for the job.*[5] The Lord responds by performing more miracles for Moses in these two chapters than he did for any the patriarchs. He calls them *signs* five times in chapter 4, and urges Moses to let them build his faith to trust him with his unseen future. He turns Moses' staff into a snake and back again, strikes him with leprosy then cures him, and promises even to turn Nile water into blood. When Moses still refuses to trust him, he provokes the Lord to anger because "seeing is believing" must always lead to "believing is seeing" too. God gives us visible evidence to help us have faith to step out and take risks over the invisible.

The Israelites are exemplary in the way that they do this when Moses finally arrives back in Egypt at the end of chapter 4.[6] *"This is so that they may believe that the Lord...has appeared to you,"* God had told Moses when he taught him to perform miracles in 4:5, so he doesn't try to convince them through energetic preaching or through testimony alone. He trusts God to do what he also did for the apostles in Acts 14:3 when they found he *"confirmed the message of his grace by enabling them to do miraculous signs and wonders."* Pharaoh was still on the throne and the Hebrews were still his slaves, but the visible miracles gave them faith that appearances were deceiving. They

[5] Exodus 3:11, 13; 4:1, 10, 13.

[6] We will examine the strange episode of 4:24–26 in the later chapter, "Second Love Language: Obedience".

"bowed down and worshipped" because "believing is seeing". We must bow down and worship with them instead of hardening our hearts to God's visible proof like Pharaoh.

So if you are not sure if you believe in the God of the Bible, these chapters contain some good news for you. They tell you that God knows that "seeing is believing", and he gives plenty of evidence to show you he is real. The life and death of Jesus, as recorded in the gospels; the resurrection, which even atheist historians cannot explain away; the changed lifestyle of people who have trusted him ahead of you – all these should give you confidence to trust the Lord with what you cannot see, and spur you on to find that "believing is seeing" when you do.

If you are a Christian, these chapters are also good news for you. They encourage you to give non-Christians proof that the Gospel is true – through discussion, through godly lifestyle, through answered prayer and through miracles performed by the Holy Spirit.[7]

The invisible God says "seeing is believing", but then asks you to trust him that "believing is seeing" too. *"Did I not tell you that if you believed, you would see the glory of God?"* asked Jesus in John 11:40. He is still asking us the same question today.

---

[7] Paul warns us in Romans 15:19 that we only fully preach the Gospel when we perform miracles to prove it.

YHWH (3:13–15)

God said to Moses, "I AM WHO I AM. This is what you are to say to the Israelites: 'I AM has sent me to you'."

(Exodus 3:14)

When Moses struggled to trust him at the burning bush, the Lord said a four-letter word.[1] *YHWH* was the covenant name by which the Lord revealed himself to his People. It would be enough to answer their doubts and fears during the Exodus, and it will be enough to answer all our own challenges as well.

The Israelites understood the power of this name. When Jews read Scripture aloud, even today, they read *Adonai* instead of YHWH, for fear of inadvertently breaking the Third Commandment and taking the Lord's name in vain. When the Masorete Jews added the symbols indicating vowels to the Hebrew text of the Old Testament in the ninth century AD, they wrote the vowels for Adonai above and below YHWH, and this led medieval scholars to misread it as *Jehovah*. Only in the nineteenth century did scholars spot what they had done and start to pronounce his covenant name more accurately as *Yahweh*. This should remind us how immeasurably holy this name has been viewed by generations of Hebrews. It should warn us not to gloss over the power of God's promise when he told Moses to go and rally Israel to Yahweh.

Some readers assume that Yahweh was a new name that the Lord gave to Moses at the burning bush. They point to 6:2–3,

---

[1] Theologians call this the *tetragrammaton*, which is simply Greek for *four-letter word*.

which can be translated as *"I am Yawheh [the Lord]. I appeared to Abraham, to Isaac and to Jacob as El-Shaddai [God Almighty], but by my name Yahweh I did not make myself known to them."* The problem with this view is that Abraham, Isaac and Jacob address the Lord as Yahweh throughout the book of Genesis,[2] and that Moses' own mother was called *Jochebed*, which means *Yahweh is Glorious*. We should probably translate 6:3 as *"and by my name Yahweh did I not make myself known to them?"* The Lord was not so much revealing a new name to Moses at the burning bush as urging him to call Israel back to living in the light of a name they already knew.

He used his name to remind them he was the God of Israel's *past*. That's why he reminds Moses in verse 14 that it comes from the Hebrew verb "to be". It means *"The Eternal One"* or "The One Who Really Is", and is why God refers to this verse in Revelation 1:8 when he calls himself the one *"who is, and who was, and who is to come"*.[3] Although most English Bibles follow the lead of the Jewish translators of the Septuagint and translate Yahweh as if it should read *Adonai*, or *Lord*, we must not forget the depth of its meaning.[4] Some English Bibles try to differentiate between Yahweh and Adonai by translating it as *"LORD"* in capital letters. It is the name of the eternal God who was seen through the patriarchs, through Moses and the Israelites, and who still wants to be seen through us today.

God used his name to make sense of the Hebrew slaves' troubled past. If their God were truly the Eternal One – the same yesterday, today and forever – then they could trust in all the promises he had made centuries earlier to the patriarchs.

---

[2] See Genesis 22:14; 26:22; 49:18. The Lord reveals himself to them as Yahweh in 15:7 and 28:13, and even their pagan friends know that the Hebrew God is named Yahweh in 26:28–29.

[3] The Septuagint translates *"I AM WHO I AM"* in Exodus 3:14 as *egō eimi ho ōn*. This forms the first part of God's statement in Revelation 1:8 that he is the one *"who is, and who was, and who is to come"*.

[4] French Bibles translate the name Yahweh more accurately as *"the Eternal One"*.

Pharaoh might tell them they were his slaves forever and the Canaanites might build ever-stronger walls to keep them out, but they couldn't resist the promise of The One Who Really Is to lead them out of Egypt and into the Promised Land.[5] It didn't matter that the Hebrews' recent past was full of disappointment and despair. Moses could remind them that they were the descendants of Abraham, Isaac and Jacob, who were chosen by God. His message must be that *"Yahweh says: Israel is my firstborn son"*,[6] and that nothing could stop the eternal God from shaping history in accordance with his plan.

God used his name to give the Hebrews faith for their present. Four centuries of knock-backs, disappointment and oppression suddenly began to make sense in the light of the eternal, unchangeable God. We read in Genesis 15:13–14 that *"Yahweh said to Abraham, 'Know for certain that your descendants will be strangers in a country not their own, and they will be enslaved and ill-treated four hundred years. But I will punish the nation they serve as slaves, and afterwards they will come out with great possessions.'"* Moses could remind the Israelites that their slave life in Egypt was not a tragic twist of ill fortune, but something which had been predicted by The One Who Really Is. If the first half of his promise felt painfully real, they could trust that the second half would certainly come true.

God therefore used his name to give the Hebrews confidence for their *future*. Pharaoh, whose rule was depicted by a cobra on his crown, was a Johnny-come-lately pretender before Israel's eternal God. He demonstrated this to Moses by turning his staff into a cobra and then teaching him to grab it by the tail without being harmed. As the prophet of The One Who Really Is, he had power to go to Egypt and shatter the hardest of human hearts.[7] Pharaoh depended on the River Nile for his kingdom to prosper,

---

[5] Genesis 15:18–21; 26:2–4; 48:3–4; 50:24.

[6] Exodus 4:22.

[7] Although 4:3 simply tells us that the staff became a *snake*, we will see in chapter 7 that it was in fact a cobra.

but Moses would turn the river's water to blood to demonstrate that Yahweh depended on nothing. Whatever tomorrow threw at Moses and God's People, the Eternal God of Israel was more than ready for the fight.

This explains why God's tone changes towards Moses at the end of chapter 4. Moses addresses him as *Adonai* in verses 10 and 13, and throws back five objections which all focus on his human limitation instead of on his God. He has been stripped of the self-confidence he displayed in chapter 2, but has not yet learned to replace it with the faith that comes when we fix our gaze on the God whose name is Yahweh.

It always angers the Lord when his People are more struck by the size of their own weakness than by the size of his great strength. When we worship him as a weak and faded shadow of the God who revealed himself to Moses, we surely can't be too surprised that he is not more visible through us, his unbelieving People.

"What's in a name?" asked Shakespeare's Juliet in her famous balcony scene with Romeo.[8] The answer when it comes to *Yahweh*, Moses tells us, is absolutely everything. *YHWH* is far more than just a four-letter word. It is the essence of the eternal God who wants to be seen through his People.

---

[8] William Shakespeare, *Romeo and Juliet*, Act II, Scene II.

God is Not Like Pharaoh
(5:1–7:7)

You are no longer to supply the people with straw
for making bricks; let them go and gather their own
straw. But require them to make the same number
of bricks as before; don't reduce the quota. They are
lazy.

(Exodus 5:7–8)

By far the hottest morning of my life was spent in the Valley of the Kings, across the Nile from Luxor, exploring the tombs of Tutankhamen and the other pharaohs of the Eighteenth Dynasty. I visited them at six in the morning to try to avoid the heat of the day, but by the time I reached the tomb of Rekhmire, I knew I couldn't have survived as one of Pharaoh's Hebrew slaves.

Rekhmire was vizier for Thutmose III and Amenhotep II in the middle of the fifteenth century BC. He was in charge of the slave-labour force at the time of the Exodus and, sure enough, I was greeted by a magnificent fresco on the wall inside his tomb. Above a picture of slaves putting mud and chopped straw into brick moulds to bake in the sun, there is a fading inscription in Egyptian hieroglyphics. It records Rekhmire's words to the slave workers of Egypt: *"The taskmaster says to the builders, 'The rod is in my hand; do not be lazy!'"*

Pharaoh was unimpressed by Moses' command from Yahweh to let his People go. Although he calls him Yahweh twice in 5:2, he failed to take him seriously as The One Who Really Is. He decided to teach the restless Hebrew slaves a lesson, and told his vizier Rekhmire to say the words that are written on the wall of his tomb. No longer would his officers provide the slaves with straw to mix with mud from the Nile in order to make bricks. They would have to forage for their own straw, but their brick quotas would remain the same. Pharaoh gave them orders he knew could not be obeyed, in the hope that removing what little free time they had would silence their idle chatter about freedom.

It may sound strange to put it this way, but many people picture God a bit like Pharaoh. They think he gives us a book full of difficult rules then complains when we fall short of his impossible standard. Jesus warned that many turn these four books of Moses into the divine equivalent of Rekhmire's harsh instruction. *"They tie up heavy loads and put them on men's shoulders,"* Jesus pointed out in Matthew 23:4, *"but they themselves are not willing to lift a finger to move them."* He warned Christian leaders not to drive their congregations like Rekhmire or the Pharisees, and he told naïve believers not to listen to them and get weighed down by unnecessary guilt and frustration. *"I was afraid of you, because you are a hard man. You take out what you did not put in and reap what you did not sow,"* cowered one man in Luke 19:21. God therefore uses Pharaoh's example in these chapters to teach us what it is really like to follow him.

It's not that following the Lord is ever easy. He told Moses to *"Go, tell Pharaoh king of Egypt to let the Israelites go out of his country"*, and to *"Bring the Israelites out of Egypt"*. He told him to *"Tell the Israelites to move on"* when the Red Sea was in the way![1] Compared to the mission the Lord gave to Moses, Pharaoh's brick quota actually looked quite restrained. There was a reason why the Hebrews turned on Moses and Aaron in 5:20–21, and why they refused to listen to them because of their discouragement in 6:9. Even Moses began to doubt the Lord for

---

[1] Exodus 6:11, 26; 14:15.

a moment in 5:22–23, and in 6:12 and 30.[2] That is always what happens to church leaders and their people when they think the Bible is a list of dos and don'ts, and therefore that their God is like Pharaoh.

What they fail to notice is that in 6:1–8 and 7:1–5 the Lord says the words *I* and *my* over thirty times in only thirteen verses. Sure, he calls us to an impossible mission, but he only does so because he also promises to do the heavy lifting for us. *"I will do…because of **my** mighty hand… I have remembered **my** covenant… I will bring you out… I will free you… I will redeem you… I will take you… I will give you."* The Lord wants to be seen as God the Saviour through his People, and he does so by calling us to do the impossible so that he can rush to help us in our simple acts of faith. Listen to his strategy in 7:5: *"The Egyptians will know that **I** am The One Who Really Is when **I** stretch out **my** hand against Egypt and bring the Israelites out of it."* The Lord is not looking for helpers but for faith-filled receivers. He is far too powerful to need to act like Pharaoh.

Moses made him visible as God the Saviour when he ordered Pharaoh to let the Hebrews go, trusting God to work the impossible on his behalf. Jesus did the same when he commanded a man with a shrivelled hand to stretch it out – the very thing he knew he could not do! – in faith that the Father's supernatural power would flow into the man's body to heal him as soon as he attempted the impossible.[3] He did so again when he commissioned his disciples to *"Go and make disciples of all nations"*, knowing full well that they would rather lock the doors and hide in Jerusalem.[4] He sent them to win the Roman Empire to Christ by telling blind people to *"see!"*, deaf people to *"hear!"*, lame people to *"walk!"*, and stubborn sinners to *"repent!"*, because he was confident that his Father would

---

[2] The Lord had actually already warned Moses to expect this setback in 3:19 and 4:21.

[3] Mark 3:1–6.

[4] Matthew 28:19; John 20:19.

accompany them with *"signs, wonders and various miracles, and gifts of the Holy Spirit distributed according to his will."*[5]

This understanding is what stops church leaders from being Rekhmires, and what stops Christians from serving a slave-driver God like Pharaoh. In case we miss it here, God tells us again in 14:14 that *"The Lord will fight for you; you need only to be still"*. If we still miss it, he thinks it's so important that he repeats it throughout the rest of the Pentateuch by ordering his People to enjoy a Sabbath rest. Don't be surprised when the Lord sets impossible challenges before you. He simply loves to be seen through his weak and helpless People.

Peter summarized this message in one of his letters after decades of following Jesus: *"If anyone serves, **he should do it with the strength God provides**, so that in all things God may be praised through Jesus Christ."*[6]

So remember that your Saviour-God is not at all like the slave-driver Pharaoh. He commands you to do the impossible today, then promises to come to your aid as you do. He makes impossible tasks possible for anyone who believes.

---

[5] Hebrews 2:4.

[6] 1 Peter 4:11. 2 Peter 1:3 also promises *"his divine power has given us everything we need for life and godliness"*.

Hardened (7:3–5)

But I will harden Pharaoh's heart, and though I
multiply my miraculous signs and wonders in Egypt,
he will not listen to you.

(Exodus 7:3–4)

One day in the fifteenth century BC, Pharaoh's younger son went hunting. He reached the Great Pyramids of Giza at noon, and decided to shelter from the heat of the day in the shade of a rock that jutted out of the sand. He fell asleep, and in his dream one of the Egyptian gods appeared to him with a promise. He told him that the rock was the tip of the long-forgotten Great Sphinx of Giza, neglected and buried under many years of sand. The gods had chosen him to dig out and restore the Sphinx to its former glory, and in return they promised to make him Pharaoh when his father died.

So reads the *Dream Stele of Thutmose IV*, the stone inscription that still stands today between the front paws of the Great Sphinx of Giza. It makes little difference that the story was probably invented by Thutmose in his early years as Pharaoh to legitimize his unexpected reign. The fact that the story was invented at all is proof that Thutmose cannot have been his father's firstborn son, which becomes very interesting when we consider that his father may well have been the Pharaoh of the Exodus.[1] Did the crown prince die in the tenth plague against the firstborn and pave the way for the unexpected accession of his younger brother? We cannot know for sure, but the Dream Stele

---

[1] Although 1 Kings 6:1 pinpoints the Exodus to around 1446 BC,
Egyptologists cannot agree on the dates of the Eighteenth-Dynasty pharaohs.
Amenhotep II died any time from 1450 to 1397 BC.

shows us that the Ancient Egyptians thought very differently to us about how rulers come to sit on the throne. They saw the hand of the gods behind the reign of every king, and we must not forget this context when we read about the battle between Yahweh and Pharaoh in these chapters.

Modern readers of the Pentateuch are often offended by the raw sovereignty of God. How can God tell Pharaoh in 9:16 that *"I have raised you up for this very purpose, that I might show you my power and that my name might be proclaimed in all the earth"*? How can he have been just in judging Pharaoh if Exodus tells us repeatedly that *"the Lord hardened Pharaoh's heart"*?[2] It is fine to ask such questions if we remember not to divorce them from the culture in which these chapters were written. No Hebrew or Egyptian was offended by the idea that the gods raised up and cast down their kings. Their only question was which of the gods was powerful enough to control the throne of the great superpower Egypt. Remember, this was a culture where Pharaoh retained a group of court magicians to help shape his public policy through miracles and omens.[3] Both the Egyptians and the Israelites took it for granted that a god was in control of Pharaoh's reign. All that surprised them in these chapters was which God it actually was.

The God who raised up Pharaoh was *more gracious* than they dared imagine. The Egyptians lived in mortal fear of their idols, and their religion was an anxious attempt to keep each of the gods in their pantheon happy. They felt like human pawns in their gods' power games, so they wouldn't have been offended to read ten times in these chapters that God hardened Pharaoh's heart.[4] What would surprise them was to read ten times more that God also granted Pharaoh freedom to decide to harden his own heart towards him.[5] He gave Pharaoh a genuine

---

[2] Even first-century readers raised this objection in Romans 9:17–24.

[3] 2 Timothy 3:8 names two of these magicians as *Jannes and Jambres*.

[4] Exodus 4:21; 7:3; 9:12; 10:1, 20, 27; 11:10; 14:4, 8, 17.

[5] Exodus 7:13, 14, 22; 8:15, 19, 32; 9:7, 34, 35; 13:15.

opportunity to obey, but then confirmed his stubborn choice and handed him over to a path of destruction.[6] Our secular mindset may object that God has no right to intervene at all, but in their proper context these chapters speak of a grace and mercy unknown to any of the gods of Egypt.

The God who raised up Pharaoh was also *more patient* than they dared imagine. He warned Pharaoh before unleashing each of the Ten Plagues, sometimes giving him as long as a week to repent and avert the disaster before it came.[7] When God turned the River Nile to blood, he spared the underground water table so the Egyptians could dig wells and not die of thirst. When he sent a plague of hail, he told them the exact time it would come so they could save their flocks and herds by bringing them inside. He even destroyed the plague of locusts by drowning them in the Red Sea as a prophecy of what would happen to Pharaoh's army if they mistook his patient grace for weakness. Finally, he used the plague of darkness to force the Egyptians to spend three days reflecting at home before the tenth and deadliest plague struck their unrepentant nation.[8] The God who decided the destiny of each pharaoh was far more patient than any of the national gods of Egypt.

The God who raised up Pharaoh was far *more powerful* than they dared imagine. Pharaoh's royal crown bore the image of the cobra-goddess Wadjet, the divine protector of his house. Before Moses even brought a single plague on Egypt, he and Aaron first turned their staff into a spitting cobra which devoured the cobra-staffs produced by Pharaoh's court magicians. It was a warning from the Lord that he was more than a match for

---

[6] The Hebrew word *hāzaq*, which is used in these chapters to refer to God *hardening* Pharaoh's heart, is also used in 12:33 to refer to the Egyptians *ratifying* the Hebrews' decision to leave. Romans 1:18–32 explains that God can give us room to choose to disobey while at the same time hardening our hearts in this decision.

[7] Exodus 7:25; 8:23; 9:5, 18; 10:4.

[8] Exodus 7:24; 9:18–19; 10:19, 23.

Wadjet and Egypt's magic.[9] In case we miss this, he takes the two Hebrew words *hāzaq* and *kābad*, which are used in these chapters to refer to Pharaoh *hardening* his heart, and uses them a further ten times in these same chapters to describe himself gaining *glory* by revealing his *strong* hand.[10] Pharaoh might not want to let go of his slaves, but he needed to face facts. He had no power to resist the God who had raised him to his throne.

Moses' shock revelation in these chapters is that the God behind the throne of Egypt was none other than Yahweh, The One Who Really Is. The unseen God of Israel had *"raised you up for this very purpose, that I might display my power in you and that my name might be proclaimed in all the earth."*[11]

So let's not be offended by God's sovereignty in these chapters, any more than the Egyptians were to be offended by his grace and patience. The real surprise of these chapters is not that God allowed Pharaoh to harden his heart ten times, or that he then hardened Pharaoh's heart for him ten times more. The real surprise is that Egypt's idols of wood and stone were not the major players in the story. The invisible God of the Hebrews – the God whose People the Egyptians had despised and enslaved – was in fact the God who controlled Pharaoh's throne. Pharaoh could harden his heart all he liked against the Lord, but he would merely fulfil the invisible God's plan to be seen through his People.

---

[9] It is not clear whether the staff of 7:10–12 was the same staff as 4:2–5, because it is called the staff of *Aaron* rather than of *Moses*. What is clear from the Hebrew word *tannīn* (literally *great monster*) in 7:10 and Ezekiel 29:3 is that this snake was the same huge cobra which symbolized Pharaoh's power on his crown.

[10] *Hāzaq* means *to be strong* in 6:1 (twice); 10:19; 13:3, 9, 14, 16. *Kābad* means *to gain glory* in 14:4, 17, 18.

[11] This is how Paul quotes Exodus 9:16 from the Septuagint in Romans 9:17.

Ten–Nil (7:8–12:51)

I will send the full force of my plagues against you
and against your officials and your people, so you
may know that there is no one like me in all the earth.

(Exodus 9:14)

Spare a thought for Kim Jong-Hun, the one-time coach of the North Korean football team. For a moment his career appeared to be a great success story.

Against all odds, North Korea had reached the 2010 World Cup in South Africa. Their coach had inspired them to play so well that they only lost their first match 2–1 against the five-time champions Brazil. Encouraged, the North Korean leaders threw caution to the wind and lifted their ban on broadcasting live international games. They put their faith in the skill of Kim Jong-Hun to protect them from national embarrassment, but he could only deliver a 7–0 defeat to Portugal and a 3–0 loss to the Ivory Coast. The unfortunate Kim Jong-Hun was summoned back to Pyongyang, exiled from the Party, and sent to work as a forced labourer on one of the government's construction sites. Nobody likes to lose publicly ten–nil. Least of all an insecure dictator.[1]

Perhaps that's why we do not know the name of the Pharaoh who lost ten–nil to Yahweh. The rulers of the Eighteenth Dynasty were just as insecure and media savvy as the leaders of North Korea. The hieroglyphics in their palaces and tombs speak of their great successes and spectacular victories, not of the fifteenth-century-BC equivalent of North Korea's World

---

[1] The London *Daily Telegraph* reported Kim Jong-Hun's fate on 30th July 2010.

Cup campaign. When Pharaoh went head to head publicly with Yahweh as the spokesman for the idols of Egypt, he became the Kim Jong-Hun of ancient history. He was trounced by a humiliating scoreline of ten–nil.

If you don't know much about the gods of ancient Egypt, you may miss the significance of each of these ten plagues. The Lord promised in 12:12 that *"I will bring judgment on the gods of Egypt"*, and Moses tells us in Numbers 33:4 that through these plagues *"the Lord brought judgment on their gods."* There was nothing random about these plagues, because Yahweh used them to take on Egypt's idols one by one to show that he was mightier than all of them put together.

Egypt worshipped Hapy, the god of the River Nile, and sang hymns that *"It is his power that creates everything, and none can live without him."*[2] The Lord exposed Hapy's weakness when the first plague turned the Nile into blood.[3] He turned next to the frog-goddess Heket and demonstrated that he, not Heket, was the true "Lord of the frogs". He directed his third and fourth plagues against the creator-god Amun and the beetle-god Khepri, creating gnats out of the dust as he had in Genesis 2:19 and terrorizing the Egyptians with dense swarms of insects.[4] Although the court magicians were able to replicate (but not reverse) the first two plagues by their magic, they were forced to concede defeat after plagues three and four and to confess to Pharaoh in 8:19 that the God of the Hebrews was behind all these disasters.[5] Scoreline: Yahweh four, gods of Egypt nil.

---

[2] Quoted from *The Hymn to the Nile Flood*, an Egyptian worship song at the time of the Exodus.

[3] The Lord may have chosen to tackle Hapy first because the Nile had taken the lives of the Hebrew babies in 1:22. Similarly, the second plague struck Heket, who was the Egyptian goddess of fertility and midwifery.

[4] The Hebrew simply refers to a fourth plague of *"swarms"*. Although some translations assume they were swarms of flies, Young's Literal Translation takes the view that the insect which swarmed was the *beetle*.

[5] Worshippers of the modern idol Rationalism still struggle to confess this. They argue that the Nile was full of red sediment, so the frogs came on land,

The fifth plague struck Egypt's livestock and exposed the inability of the bull-god Apis, the cow-goddess Hathor and the ram-god Khnum to save them.[6] The sixth plague of boils so completely defeated the magic-god Thoth and the magic- and healing-goddess Isis that the magicians could no longer appear before Pharaoh in 9:11 because they were covered in so many boils. They could only watch as the seventh and eighth plagues defeated their sky-goddess Nut, their storm-god Set, their fertility-god Min, their harvest-god Osiris and their locust-headed harvest-god Senehem. By the time that the ninth plague exposed the weakness of the sun-god Amun-Ra, the Egyptians had a shocking scoreline to consider by torchlight during seventy-two hours of darkness: Yahweh nine, gods of Egypt nil.

The time had come for God's grand finale. *"Israel is my firstborn son"*, he told Moses to warn Pharaoh in 4:22, and Pharaoh's stubborn refusal to let God's firstborn go would mean the death of his own firstborn in the tenth and final plague. As Thutmose IV felt keenly when he commissioned his *Dream Stele*, the crown prince meant everything to Pharaoh and no amount of younger sons could ever offset their father's first love. Right across Egypt, men placed similar hopes in their own firstborn heirs, but watched their god-king Pharaoh, their death-god Abubis and their resurrection-god Osiris all fall before Yahweh. By the time the Passover angel finished his night-time rounds, not a single unrepentant Egyptian's firstborn was left alive. Yahweh ten, the gods of Egypt nil. It was a scoreline which made even Kim Jong-Hun look like a good manager.

Most Western presentations of the Gospel emphasize the problem of guilt and the offer of forgiveness. This is part of the Gospel message but it is not the part which resonated most

---

bringing with them many gnats. This fails to explain how the water in ponds and buckets turned to blood, or why a week passed before the frogs came on land, or how this produced any of the later plagues.

[6] Ironically, the furnace in 9:8 was probably one of those used by the Hebrews in their brick-making.

strongly in ancient Egypt, or which still resonates most loudly in modern-day Africa or South America. In "fear cultures", the biggest question is which of the gods or spirits is able to protect his own. That's why the Lord declares in 8:22–23 that *"I will deal differently with the land of Goshen, where my people live… I will make a distinction between my people and your people."*[7] The Lord was not simply content to prove he was more powerful than Egypt's idols. He was also concerned to reveal to the world that he is God the Saviour, the ultimate protector of his People.

Through this ten–nil victory, the Israelites placed their faith in their invisible God and were able to sing *"Who among the gods is like you, O Yahweh?"* They were so impacted by these plagues that they still used them many centuries later to build their corporate faith that their unseen God would save his People.[8]

In fact, this scoreline was so impressive that many Egyptians abandoned their homeland and their defeated gods to follow Yahweh and his People in their Exodus.[9] News spread to Midian, where Jethro rejoiced that *"Now I know that the Lord is greater than all other gods."*[10]

Such a scoreline should capture our own attention too. It should make us renounce our own idols once and for all, and give ourselves wholeheartedly to the God who wants to be seen through his People. This is the God who trounced the gods of Egypt and who still wants to make himself visible through those who follow him today.

---

[7] See also Exodus 9:3–7, 26; 10:23; 11:7.

[8] Exodus 15:11; 10:1–2.

[9] Moses includes them in the *mixed ethnic rabble* which he describes literally in 12:38. The Lord's agenda was to be seen by the Egyptians as well as the Israelites in 7:5; 8:10; 9:14, 20–21, 29.

[10] Exodus 18:11. The Hebrew verb is a "perfect aspect", meaning *"Now I have known…"* What happened to Israel confirmed to God's priest in Midian that what he had long believed about the Lord was true.

The Next Best Thing to Winning (10:7–11, 24–26)

Then Pharaoh summoned Moses and said, "Go, worship the Lord. Even your women and children may go with you; only leave your flocks and herds behind."

(Exodus 10:24)

Pharaoh was stubborn, but he wasn't stupid. He saw early on that his showdown with Yahweh was very unlikely to go his own way. But if he could not defeat the invisible God of the Hebrews, he hoped at least to be able salvage something. If he could be as wise as the camel in the old Arabian story, he hoped at least to avoid unconditional surrender and to emerge from the battle with the next best thing to winning.

One cold night, according to the story, a camel poked its nose into its master's tent. *"It is so cold outside,"* it pleaded. *"May I just keep my nose in the warmth of your tent?"* The Arab felt sorry for the camel and granted its request, but when he woke after an hour the camel had its whole head in the tent and was shivering just as much as before. *"May I put my neck inside your warm tent as well?"* Once again, the soft-hearted Arab obliged. The next time he awoke, he found the camel's forelegs on either side of his pillow. *"I'm concerned that my body is opening the tent flaps up too wide for you,"* the camel told him. *"May I step inside and close the tent behind me so we both can stay warm?"* An hour later and the one-man tent was increasingly uncomfortable for the Arab and his animal. *"There is not room for both of us in here,"* observed the camel. *"Perhaps you would kindly move outside, since you are so much smaller than I."* The shivering Arab lay awake outside the tent and pondered the lesson of the camel's nose. His small acts of compromise had all seemed very logical, but those short-sighted moments of weakness had left him outside in the cold.

When Pharaoh suspected that Yahweh would win, he tried to cut a deal with Moses to get a camel's nose inside the tent. *"Go, sacrifice to your God here in the land"*, he offered magnanimously in 8:25. He tried a second time in 8:28, *"I will let you go to offer sacrifices to the Lord your God in the desert, but you must not go very far."* Moses refused to cut a deal with the enemy of his People, because anything less than unilateral surrender would mean disobeying the Lord and handing Pharaoh the next best thing to winning. Undeterred, Pharaoh made a third attempt in 10:8–11 by suggesting, *"Have only the men go."* There was even a patriarchal precedent for leaving wives and children behind in Genesis 50:8, but Moses saw the camel's nose at his tent flaps. The Lord had set out to defeat the gods of Egypt one by one, and Moses would not call truce until the Lord had won ten–nil and secured an unconditional surrender.

Pharaoh was getting desperate, so his fourth offer in 10:24 was his most attractive yet. *"Go, worship the Lord. Even your women and children may go with you; only leave your flocks and herds behind."* It must have been very tempting for Moses as he remembered that only several weeks earlier the Hebrews had seemed doomed to die in hopeless servitude. If they forfeited their cows and sheep, they could go free and Moses could go down in history. He would be known as the man who stood up to the superpower nation of Egypt and won. It must have felt a relatively small price to pay for their freedom, but by God's grace Moses saw the trap and warded off Pharaoh's camel's nose.

Moses knew enough about God's plans for Israel to know to refuse the smiling overtures of Pharaoh. When the Enemy brings gifts and asks for a ceasefire, it is the moment to press home victory, not make premature deals to gain peace at any price. The Devil who was at work behind the idols of Egypt never has any real intention of giving up the fight against God's People. He simply hopes to buy time to regroup and plan a fresh attack, and he only calls for compromise when he is on the verge of being routed. Moses insisted that *"Our livestock too must go with us; not a hoof is to be left behind."* Because he stood his ground and refused to compromise, he finally secured Pharaoh's unilateral surrender in 12:31–32: *"Go, worship the Lord as you have requested. Take your flocks and herds, as you have said, and go."* If we resist the Enemy's smooth attempts at seduction, then we will find that he surrenders to the adamant will of God.

Pharaoh's dirty deals were far more dangerous than they seemed. The Hebrew men might have returned from the desert to discover that their wives and children had been slaughtered, or worse. More than that, there might not have been an Exodus at all because the Lord had told Moses to make this initial request as a deliberate provocation to precipitate something far larger. Moses initially requested that Pharaoh give the Hebrews a week's holiday in which to go to the desert of Sinai and offer sacrifices to the Lord, knowing full well that this small request would elicit Pharaoh's stubborn refusal and eventually lead to total freedom.[1] If Moses had failed to remain true to the Lord's instructions, Pharaoh would never have driven the Hebrews out with enough plunder to repay them for their unsalaried years as slaves.[2] It was only because of his unflinching obedience that the Hebrews had enough milk, meat and animal skins to survive for forty long years in the desert. Moses knew that his invisible God would never compromise with Satan, and because he refused to cut any deals of his own he displayed the glory of Yahweh to the world.

If you want to see spiritual ruin in your life, your family

---

[1] Exodus 3:18; 7:16; 8:27; 10:24–26.

[2] Exodus 12:35–36 fulfilled God's promise to Moses in 3:21–22 and to Abraham in Genesis 15:14.

or your church, then let Satan's camel nose inside your tent flaps. Thousands of ruined families and corrupted churches demonstrate that there is no appeasing the monster or sating his bloodlust.[3] As the novelist Ayn Rand puts it: *"In any compromise between food and poison, it is only death that can win. In any compromise between good and evil, it is only evil that can profit."*[4]

If, on the other hand, you want to see Satan's kingdom divided, destroyed and swept away before your powerful God, then follow Moses' lead in these chapters.[5] Make no compromise and do not hand the Devil the next best thing to winning. Send his camel's nose packing when you hear it sniffling round your tent.

---

[3] See how quickly Pharaoh's tone changes when he feels stronger again in 8:8–15; 9:27–35; 10:16–20; and 14:5–6.

[4] Ayn Rand in her novel *Atlas Shrugged* (1957).

[5] Exodus 8:19; 10:7; 14:28.

Lesson One: Passover (11:1–13:16)

The blood will be a sign for you on the houses where you are; and when I see the blood, I will pass over you.

(Exodus 12:13)

The Hebrews and Egyptians had learned the basic lesson: Yahweh was the only true Saviour-God. It was now time for him to spell it out to them in greater detail. How did he save, why did he save and what did it mean to be one of his People? The Lord begins to answer these questions with six detailed lessons across the next six chapters. He does not merely want to be seen through his People as the Saviour-God in general. He also wants to communicate through them the comprehensive plan of his salvation.

That's why Moses covers the tenth plague in such great detail, giving almost as much attention to it as the other nine plagues put together. There is a chapter about judgment, a chapter about forgiveness and a third chapter about how we should respond once we are forgiven. These three chapters contain three startling surprises because he wants to capture our attention with his Gospel.[1] He is the Saviour-God and he has a very specific plan about how people must be saved.

First, God tells the Hebrews that they must be saved at the Passover by shedding the *blood of a lamb*. That was very offensive for anyone brought up in Egypt. The favourite

---

[1] I am not using the word "Gospel" anachronistically. Hebrews 4:2, 6 tells us that *"We also have had the gospel preached to us, just as they did."*

god of the Eighteenth-Dynasty pharaohs was the ram-headed Amun, and they found the sacrifice of a male sheep so offensive that Moses worried in 8:26 that they might stone the Hebrews to death if they did so.

That, of course, was precisely the point. The blood of a sacrificial lamb was deliberately offensive because it dealt with sin, which was equally offensive to God. Yahweh is not just God the Saviour, he is also God the Judge, and the Egyptians were about to discover this to their cost. Their lives would be forfeit for their sin when the Lord passed through their houses that evening. Their only hope was for him to "pass over" their houses by seeing that an innocent sacrifice had already been punished in their place.[2] Blood would be shed in every single house in Egypt – the only question was whose blood it was going to be. God the Saviour does not pass over our sin by ignoring it and pretending it isn't real. He does so by punishing an innocent sacrifice instead of us. The Passover lamb was deliberately counter-cultural, but it shouldn't have been for the descendants of Abraham. Theirs was the God who had saved Isaac on Mount Moriah in Genesis 22 by providing a ram to die instead of him. That same Saviour-God now taught them in Egypt that without the shedding of blood there can be no forgiveness.[3]

The second unusual aspect of the Passover was that God saved the Hebrews *together as a community*. Once again, this was not very Egyptian. They had a catalogue of different gods to choose from, and each family worshipped at its own preferred temple. The Lord cut across this individualism by declaring in 4:22–23 that *"Israel is my firstborn son...you refused to let him go; so I will kill your firstborn son."* The

---

[2] The Hebrew word *pesah*, or *Passover*, simply comes from the verb *to pass over* something.

[3] Leviticus 17:11; Hebrews 9:22. God spared the Hebrews from the other plagues in Exodus 9:3–7, 26; 10:23; 11:7, but he only did so because the Passover was coming.

God who had chosen the younger brothers Abraham, Isaac, Jacob, Joseph and Ephraim as his spiritual firstborns, now chose Israel as a whole to be his spiritual firstborn as one united nation.[4] They must recognize this by sacrificing lambs as family units and by observing the Passover as *"the whole community of Israel"*. Small families and single people must find others with whom to share their salvation. God would not save them in a manner which maintained their isolation because he does not simply want to be seen through various disparate individuals. He would save them together as one Firstborn Nation, so that his invisible Triune nature could be made visible through them. He would save them by one Passover Feast, lead them by one pillar of cloud and fire, make one path for them to cross the Red Sea together, and make one covenant with them through Moses at Mount Sinai. John Wesley was right when he said that *"The Bible knows nothing of solitary religion."*

The third unusual aspect of the Passover was that those who were saved must respond by *abstaining from yeast*. Don't miss how poignant this command must have been to anyone who had been brought up in Egypt. This was the land that had pioneered the use of yeast in baking bread and in brewing beer as the national drink of Egypt. Yeast was as distinctively Egyptian as a hieroglyphic pyramid! Yahweh was teaching the Hebrews that he wanted to do more than simply bring them out of Egypt; he also wanted to bring Egypt out of them.

He commanded each Hebrew family to take a lamb into their home for the four days leading up to the Passover, so that they could understand the tragic price which needed to be paid to atone for their sin. They were to slaughter it, roast it and dip its meat in bitter sauce (12:3–9) as a pointer to the

---

[4] See *Straight to the Heart of Genesis*. God chose Abraham over Haran, Isaac over Ishmael and Jacob over Esau, then blessed Joseph and Ephraim with the double inheritance of a firstborn heir.

fierce judgment which would be borne by another for their redemption. Foreigners were strictly barred from inclusion in the meal unless they converted to following Yahweh (12:43–49), and even the Hebrews were tested for seven days after the meal to see if their profession of faith was real. They ate the meal dressed up to travel (12:11) because salvation is not an end in itself, but the start of a journey of faith in the Saviour-God. If they ate yeast during the Feast of Unleavened Bread, they proved their faith was play-acting (12:15, 19), so they must therefore be cut off from God's People like the Egyptians. God the Saviour saves by faith alone, but the faith by which he saves can never remain alone.

The Hebrews did not yet fully know that the blood which saved them from the tenth plague pointed to the Passover Lamb, Jesus, God's true firstborn Son.[5] They simply obeyed the Lord's command to choose a lamb without blemish, not to break any of its bones,[6] and to smear its blood on the doorposts and lintels of their homes.[7]

We, on the other hand, can see the true Passover Lamb in his glory. We understand more than the Hebrews why blood had to be shed, why we need to be saved in community and why we must therefore turn from sin as the proof of our salvation. As Paul urged the Corinthians many centuries after the Exodus:

> *Don't you know that a little yeast works through the whole batch of dough? Get rid of the old yeast that you may be a new batch without yeast – as you really are. For*

[5] Jesus is not God's firstborn in the sense that he was ever created, but in the sense that he is God's supreme heir (Colossians 1:15–16) through whom God has made us firstborn heirs too.

[6] John makes it clear that Exodus 12:5, 46 were prophetic pictures fulfilled in John 19:4, 33, 36.

[7] The blood on the doorposts and lintels pointed to the vertical and horizontal wood of Jesus' cross. Hebrews 10:29 may explain why they were not told to put blood on the threshold.

Christ, our Passover lamb, has been sacrificed. Therefore let us keep the Festival, not with the old yeast, the yeast of malice and wickedness, but with bread without yeast, the bread of sincerity and truth.[8]

---

[8] 1 Corinthians 5:6–8. Moses talks in 12:39 about the Hebrews avoiding yeast because they were in a hurry, but Paul brings out the far deeper spiritual meaning behind this command.

Lesson Two: Handbrake (13:17–15:21)

> *That day the Lord saved Israel from the hands of the Egyptians, and Israel saw the Egyptians lying dead on the shore.*
>
> (Exodus 14:30)

When I was twenty-two, I was given a company car. So were the other fresh-faced graduates who started work with me. A few weeks earlier we had all been students, and none of us had been able to afford cars as expensive and powerful as these. We said our goodbyes and roared off into the sunset to enjoy the motorway drive home, ready to compare notes on Monday.

When Monday came, Barney wasn't smiling. He had found the journey home more eventful than the rest of us. At the end of a 300-mile drive to his parents' house, he discovered he had left the car's handbrake on all the way. He was too new to driving to register that the car felt sluggish and reluctant to move, so he simply gave the car a bit more gas. He didn't even notice the warning light on his dashboard or the tell-tale smell of burning. It was only when his car broke down that he realized the mistake he had made. Barney was driving a replacement car that Monday morning. Driving with the handbrake on can cause a lot of damage.

That's the second lesson the Saviour-God wants to teach us. It's why he didn't lead Moses and the Israelites on the eastern road to Canaan, but gave the rather strange instruction to *"turn back and...camp by the sea."* This meant going in the opposite direction to the Promised Land and getting dangerously hemmed in against the shore of the Red Sea.[1] It was so counter-intuitive that Moses even needed a direct word from the Lord to help him trust the direction in which the pillar of cloud was guiding him. God led the Israelites to the Red Sea to cement all that had happened through the Passover lamb, and to take the handbrake off their lives before they fell into the same trap as Barney. Paul wrote later in 1 Corinthians 10:2 that the Hebrews *"were all baptized into Moses in the cloud and in the sea"*.

The Israelites' water baptism took off the handbrake on their *past*. For all Pharaoh's panic in 14:5, he had not yet officially let his slaves go. At this stage he had simply agreed to Moses' request to go and offer sacrifices in the desert, and it was only the Red Sea which made their freedom much more permanent. Chapters 11–13 were very clear that God saves through the blood of the Passover lamb and not through water baptism, but chapters 14 and 15 now stress that something happens at baptism that is more than just a symbol. This morning I heard news from a group of Afghan Christians whose conversion to Christ was tolerated by their former imams until they decided last week to get baptized. Suddenly, the death threats have begun because Satan knows that baptism takes off the spiritual handbrake, even if we do not. While we sometimes treat it as nothing more than a symbolic gesture, the Devil fights it tooth and nail because he understands all too clearly what God teaches in these two chapters. Baptism is the moment when God takes off the handbrake and lets new converts power forward, unhindered by their past.

Once again it is Paul who sheds light on what happened here, this time at the start of Romans 6: *"We died to sin; how*

---

[1] Exodus 13:20–14:4. The Hebrew *Yam Sūph* means literally *Sea of Reeds*, so some scholars query whether it was the Red Sea at all. What we do know is it was a saltwater sea, since the Hebrews ran out of drinking water only days after crossing it, and it was a big enough sea to drown both a plague of locusts (10:19) and the Egyptian army. The translators of the Septuagint, living in BC Egypt, identified it as the Red Sea.

can we live in it any longer? Or don't you know that all of us who were baptized into Christ Jesus were baptized into his death...in order that, just as Christ was raised from the dead through the glory of the Father, we too may live a new life." When someone is pushed down beneath the waters of baptism, they proclaim that they have died to their former life as a minion of the great slave-driver Satan. When they come up out the water, they declare to spiritual principalities that they have risen to a new life of serving Christ as their new Master. Were the Israelites saved before they crossed the Red Sea? Undoubtedly. Did they experience greater freedom once they had passed through the waters of baptism and seen their former slave-masters swept away? Of course. We can celebrate like Moses and the Israelites in chapter 15 when we look back on our baptism and say to Satan that in consequence, *"I don't work for you any more!"*[2]

The Israelites' water baptism also took off the handbrake on their *present*. In 14:11–12, they still burn with nostalgia for their pre-Passover days in Egypt, but once they reach the opposite shore of the Red Sea they know for sure that the Lord has closed that chapter in their lives.[3] They celebrate in 15:2 that the Lord *"**has become** my salvation"*, and *"**is** my strength and my song"* in the present. The Lord wants to use baptism in the same way to close the chapter on our own pasts, so that rather than just praising him for what he has saved us *from* in the past, we can also praise him for what he has saved us *for* in the present.

Consequently, the Israelites' water baptism also took off the handbrake on their *future*. Until the Red Sea, they struggled to share Moses' bold faith that the Lord would surely lead them into the Promised Land as he had promised Abraham,[4] but their

---

[2] The Passover lamb saved them, but they only sang the song of the redeemed in 15:13, 16.

[3] They would forget this in 16:3, but only because they first forgot the lesson of these two chapters.

[4] Exodus 5:21; 6:9; 14:11–12.

baptism proved to be a turning point in their confidence for the future.[5] They sing a worship song full of future tenses, that *"In your unfailing love you **will** lead the people you have redeemed. In your strength you **will** guide them to your holy dwelling... You **will** bring them in and plant them on the mountain of your inheritance."*[6] That's what water baptism does for a believer, as we look back across the water which dealt a death knell to Satan's slavery, and rejoice that we now live on the side of all God's promises for our future.

If you can grasp the lesson of the handbrake in these chapters, then you will understand why Moses emphasizes in 14:30 that *"Israel saw the Egyptians lying dead on the shore".* God wants you to go back in your mind regularly to the waters of your baptism to remind yourself that it dealt with your past and launched you into a glorious present and future.

Don't be a Barney. Don't try to drive with the handbrake on. If your Christian life feels sluggish or you still feel enslaved to the past, perhaps the lesson of these two chapters is particularly for you. If you haven't already, then Jesus calls you to *"Repent and be baptized".*[7] If you have, then he tells you to go and feast your eyes on the corpses washed up on the shore.

---

[5] Rightly so, given that 15:8 tells us that the Lord had to blow with his *nostrils* so as not to blow too hard and destroy the Hebrews along with the Egyptians.

[6] In 15:13–18, the Hebrews sing twelve times in only six verses about what God *will* do.

[7] Acts 2:38. Does the order here suggest that infant christening may be a case of Satan's "next best thing to winning"? Acts 16:30–34 indicates that whole households were only baptized when every member believed.

Lesson Three: Wood
(15:22–27)

Then Moses cried out to the Lord, and the Lord showed him a piece of wood. He threw it into the water, and the water became sweet.

(Exodus 15:25)

On 4th July 1942, the German Afrika Korps were beating the British in North Africa. They were so close to Alexandria that the civil servants there were burning their paperwork for fear that it would fall into German hands. As the British battle lines began to crumble, 1,100 crack German soldiers suddenly broke cover with their hands up in surrender. Their puzzled captors could hardly believe this sudden change in fortune, so they questioned them to find out what had caused them to give up at the moment which should have marked their victory.

The German officers explained that they had gone twenty-four hours without any water under the fierce Egyptian desert sun. As they pushed back the British, they had discovered a water pipe and shot holes in it to satisfy their maddening thirst. Their parched throats took time to issue a warning to their brains that the pipe was jetting out salt water instead of the precious drinking water that they craved. Major Peter Rainier, the British engineer who was testing that new section of pipe using seawater at the time, later wrote in an article entitled "A Drink that Made History" that *"The balance of that crucial desert battle was so even that I believe the enemy without the salted torture might have outlasted us; and then defenceless Alexandria would have fallen into their hands."*[1] The disappointment of hopes raised and dashed underneath the cruel Egyptian skies proved too much for the German soldiers, and forced them to surrender.

Moses and the Hebrews needed far more drinking water than 1,100 German soldiers. They numbered 600,000 men, not to mention wives and children, which meant that every single day they needed the equivalent of three Olympic swimming pools of water to survive. Seventy-two hours had passed since they left the salty Red Sea, and now they feared that they would all die of thirst unless they found an oasis. When they suddenly spotted one, they rushed forward with the same mad excitement as the German Afrika Korps. They praised God for his provision until suddenly their faces fell. The water was bitter and undrinkable, and it crushed their fragile spirits. They were ready to learn a third lesson from their Saviour-God.

The Lord had not merely led them on this strange, long route to Canaan in order to avoid the string of Egyptian fortresses to the north.[2] He also did so to teach them that they needed to keep following him in exactly the same way that they had begun. We do not "outgrow" the simple message of God's Passover lamb being sacrificed in our place. We simply learn to respond to it in ever-deeper ways at each new stage along our journey. That's why God heard their bitter cries and ordered Moses to throw a piece of wood into the water.

Have you noticed this recurring theme in Exodus so far? When God the Saviour set out to defeat the gods of Egypt, he ordered Moses to confront Pharaoh holding nothing but a wooden staff, turning it into a snake which defeated the cobra-goddess Wadjet and her royal court magicians. He told Moses and

---

[1] Major Peter W. Rainier published this article in the *Reader's Digest* in January 1944.

[2] The Egyptians built fortresses against the Canaanite Hyksos. God knew the Hebrews were not ready to fight the Egyptians, so he did not test them beyond what they could bear (1 Corinthians 10:13).

Aaron to *"Take your staff and stretch out your hand"* to turn the Nile to blood, to summon frogs and locusts, to turn the dust into gnats, and to bring down burning hail.[3] He told them to smear the Passover blood on the wooden doorframes of their houses, and to part the Red Sea by holding up their staff yet again.[4] There has been more wood in the story of Exodus so far than in an Ikea superstore, so throwing wood into the bitter waters of Marah is not as strange a remedy as it sounds. The third lesson which the Hebrews needed to grasp on the way to Sinai was that all of God's salvation emanates from something made of wood. Our Saviour-God leads us on our spiritual journey by revealing to us new aspects of the cross of Jesus Christ.[5]

Do you see now why Paul told a group of mature Christians in Romans 1:15 that *"I am so eager to preach the gospel also to you"*? He knew that Christian maturity only comes from learning what Jesus' death and resurrection have achieved on so many different levels. That's what Knox Chamblin means when he writes that *"The Spirit does not take his pupils beyond the cross, but ever more deeply into it."*[6] It's why we must not be too quick to judge the Hebrews, even though they had just witnessed the greatest Old Testament miracle only three days earlier and had spent those three days following God's visible presence in the form of a pillar of cloud and fire. The truth is it is all too easy for us to think we can "graduate" beyond the Gospel message. Lesson three in the desert is that we cannot and we mustn't.

I was recently part of a discussion between church leaders over the question of how much we should preach the Gospel

---

[3] Exodus 7:9–12, 17–20; 8:5, 16; 9:23; 10:13. Since 9:24 speaks literally of *"fire flashing in the midst of the hail"*, most literal translations take it to mean not so much *lightning* as *burning hail*.

[4] Exodus 12:22; 14:16.

[5] The Greek word used for Moses' piece of *wood* in the Septuagint of Exodus 15:25 is *xulon*, the same word used for Jesus' *cross* in Acts 5:30; 10:39; 13:29; Galatians 3:13; 1 Peter 2:24.

[6] J. Knox Chamblin, *Paul and the Self: Apostolic Teaching for Personal Wholeness* (1993).

every Sunday. The majority opinion was that this would bore believers and send them home feeling cheated that the message had been aimed at non-Christians instead of them. Now I am aware that many Gospel messages are shallow, formulaic and predictable (I'm sure I have been guilty of that crime myself), but the very premise of the question was utterly misconceived. The Gospel is not an "entry-point message" for unbelievers before they graduate towards a message of Christian maturity. It is how we are saved, how we mature and how we progress on every new stage in our journey!

Do you need to know the Lord by the name *Yahweh-Rophek*, *The Lord Who Heals You*, which he reveals to us here in verse 26? Matthew 8:17 tells you Moses' piece of wood held a promise that Jesus would carry our sicknesses and diseases on the cross. Do you need to know God as *Yahweh-Nissi*, *The Lord My Banner of Victory*, as in Exodus 17:15? Then hold up the cross as Moses held up his staff, because that is where Jesus won his great victory. Do you need to know God as *Yahweh-Yireh*, *The Lord Will Provide*, like Abraham on Mount Moriah with Isaac? Then remember that his provision involved Abraham sacrificing a ram upon his altar.[7]

This lesson is so important that God took the Israelites to the bitter waters of Marah to crush their hearts into surrender like those 1,100 men of the Afrika Korps. They would only truly know him as the Saviour-God he truly is if they surrendered to the Gospel in every single aspect of their lives. God still wants to be seen through us, his People, as we lay hold of the wooden cross of Jesus through which all of his blessings continually flow.

---

[7] Since Calvary was an outcrop of Mount Moriah, Abraham predicted in Genesis 22:14 that *"on the mountain of the Lord it **will be** provided"*. Jesus explains in John 8:56 that Abraham saw a better Ram yet to come.

Lesson Four: Food and Drink (16:1–17:7)

Then the Lord said to Moses, "I will rain down bread from heaven for you. The people are to go out each day and gather enough for that day. In this way I will test them and see whether they will follow my instructions."

(Exodus 16:4)

Ask three theologians why God led Israel on a forty-year journey through the desert, and you will probably get four different answers. There's no shortage of opinions as to what the Lord was doing, but God gives us his own commentary within the Pentateuch itself. Moses told the Hebrews in Deuteronomy 8:3 that *"He humbled you, causing you to hunger and then feeding you with manna...to teach you that man does not live on bread alone but on every word that comes from the mouth of the Lord."* The Saviour-God led his People deep into the desert to teach them what his salvation is like. There was simply no better place to teach them to live on his spiritual food and drink.

Believe it or not, escaping from Egypt was the easy part of God's plan. Surviving in the desert was a far bigger challenge. Within a month of crossing the Red Sea, the Hebrews were so hungry and thirsty that they genuinely thought they were going to die. They fantasized about the food and drink back in Egypt and accused the Lord of luring them into the desert to watch them die.[1] With our fridges full of food, their words

---

[1] In accusing Moses, they were really accusing the Lord who had saved them through the plagues, the Passover and the Red Sea. They lost perspective,

seem faithless and melodramatic, but these were the words of a nation at the end of its resources and which truly believed it was hours away from death. The Lord's fourth lesson about salvation was that we must depend on his Word and his Spirit every day of our lives.

God did not provide manna for the Israelites straight away, but only when they had no other food left to rely on. We often need the Lord to strip us of our own strength before we lift up our eyes and beg for his divine strength instead.[2] When Satan tried to tempt Jesus to turn stones into bread during his forty days and nights in the desert, he quoted this same Deuteronomy verse to reply that God used manna in the desert to teach the Israelites to feed daily on his Word.[3] Moses was about to start writing some of the earliest books of the Bible,[4] so the Lord used their hunger to teach them to devour what he wrote like starving men and women.

God taught them that Scripture is a gift of astonishing grace. Five days a week he provided 4 million litres of manna to feed the 2 million Israelites, and each Friday he doubled it to 8 million litres. Manna came in a form that needed gathering, preparing and baking to remind them that studying God's Word requires discipline. He also gave them a day in every seven when they rested so they would not become too legalistic in this discipline. God does not want us to be like the Pharisees who tried to save themselves through Bible study in John 5:39–40, but to note that *"he who gathered much did not have too much, and he who gathered little did not have too little."* There are weeks when I have the luxury of spending hours reading the Bible, and other weeks when I struggle to snatch a few quick verses in the midst of chaos. I can honestly say that the Lord speaks as much

remembering the food but not the oppression of Egypt.

[2] It was so different from anything they could create themselves that they called it *manna*, meaning *what is it?*

[3] Matthew 4:4.

[4] Exodus 17:14; 24:4; 34:27; Deuteronomy 28:58; 30:10; 31:24–26.

to me through the short times as the long, because he looks at the heart and makes the most of what we gather. Five-minute snacks and five-hour feasts are both equally valid and equally satisfying.

Ultimately every verse of Scripture points to Jesus, the Word of God in human flesh. Jesus taught the true meaning of manna in John 6:48–58 when he told a later generation of Hebrews that *"I am the living bread that came down from heaven... This bread is my flesh, which I will give for the life of the world... Whoever eats my flesh and drinks my blood has eternal life... He who feeds on this bread will live forever."* Perhaps that's why the word "Sabbath" appears in Scripture for the first time here in Exodus 16, as the Lord instructs us to rest in what Jesus has done for us instead of trying to save ourselves. Perhaps it is also why God gave the Hebrews quail in verse 13, but later struck them with a plague in Numbers 11 for demanding quail instead of manna because they complained that bread from heaven was getting boring.

In chapter 17 God also taught the Hebrews to receive the Holy Spirit. When they cried out for water, he pointed to a rock which Paul tells us in 1 Corinthians 10:4 was a picture of Jesus. The Lord told Moses to strike it with his wooden staff as a prophecy that Jesus would be nailed to a cross and would ascend to heaven after his resurrection to receive the promised gift of the Holy Spirit for God's People. When water flowed from the rock to satisfy 2 million people, it was such an amazing miracle that the Jews were still celebrating it 1,500 years later at their Feast of Tabernacles when Jesus gave his great invitation in John 7:37–39: *"On the last and greatest day of the Feast, Jesus stood and said in a loud voice, 'If anyone is thirsty, let him come to **me** and drink. Whoever believes in me, as the Scripture has said, streams of living water will flow from within him.' By this he meant the Spirit, whom those who believed in him were later to receive."*

This of course begs the question, *are we truly thirsty?* Are we as aware as the Israelites in the desert that our resources are insufficient for the life to which the Lord has called us? Strangely, many Christians live their lives as if reading Scripture and being filled with the Spirit were optional extras. Just as strangely, some Christians love to devour the Bible but neglect the Spirit, while others love to soak in the Spirit while neglecting disciplined study of the Bible. God tells us in these chapters that we need food and drink in equal measure. We dare not divorce what the Lord has joined together.

Jack Deere warns that

> *Somewhere along the way, the church has encouraged a silent divorce between the Word and the Spirit. Divorces are painful, both for the children and the parents. One parent usually gets custody of the children, and the other only gets to visit occasionally. It breaks the hearts of the parents, and the children are usually worse off because of the arrangement. Many in the church today are content to live with only one parent. They live with the Word, and the Spirit only has limited visiting rights. He just gets to see and touch the kids once in a while. Some of his kids don't even recognise him any more. Some have become afraid of him. Others in the church live with the Spirit and only allow the Word sporadic visits. The Spirit doesn't want to raise the kids without the Word. He can see how unruly they're becoming, but he won't force them to do what they must choose with their hearts.*[5]

Let's learn to be both chapter-16 and chapter-17 children of God. Let's feed on his Word and drink of his Spirit, as he taught the Israelites in the desert.

---

[5] Jack Deere, *Surprised By the Voice of God* (1996).

Lesson Five: Sabbath (16:21–30)

"Bear in mind that the Lord has given you the Sabbath; that is why on the sixth day he gives you bread for two days."... So the people rested on the seventh day.

(Exodus 16:29–30)

The Hebrews had picked up a bad habit in Egypt. They had learned from their slave-masters to try to impress their God. Pharaoh and his priests devoted vast amounts of money and energy to building idols and temples to curry favour with their gods. Ordinary Egyptians made donations and built their own household shrines to the gods in conviction that their visible gods demanded visible devotion. The Hebrews had assumed that their own God was the same, so they busied themselves to buy his favour.

But the true God is not like the idols of Egypt. He is more glorified by giving than he is by receiving, because he needs nothing from the creatures he has made. He taught this to Moses in chapter 2 when he refused to bless his man-made attempt to save the Israelites from Egypt. He reinforced it at the burning bush when he replied to Moses' question, *"Who am I?"*, by shifting his gaze on to the fact that *"I AM WHO I AM"*. The Lord's fifth lesson for the Israelites in the desert was therefore that salvation is not about working, but resting. God wants to be seen through his People *at rest* in faith that he saves them for free.

Moses first hinted at the Sabbath at the start of Genesis. He told us that God created the world in six days and then rested on the seventh, not because he needed to recover but because *"the Sabbath was made for man"*.[1] Adam's first day of life was to be a day of resting in all the Lord had done without him, so the Hebrew word for *resting* or *stopping work* in Genesis 2:2 is *shābath*, from which we get the English word *Sabbath*.

Moses does not tell us whether the patriarchs and the Israelites in Egypt observed the Sabbath, but they do not appear too surprised here in chapter 16 when the Lord tells them not to gather manna on a Saturday.[2] In any case, the Lord had been emphasizing repeatedly that their salvation was a gift they could neither earn nor repay. In 13:18 they *"went up out of Egypt armed for battle"*, but in 13:17 the Lord diverted their journey because he knew they were not as capable as they pretended. *"The Lord will fight for you; you need only to be still,"* he told them at the Red Sea, and the Egyptians cried out in horror when they realized that *"The Lord is fighting for them against Egypt!"*[3] The Egyptians boast seven times in 15:9 that their salvation is all about *"I"* and *"my"*, but the Hebrews respond in the rest of the chapter with twenty-eight boasts that their hope is entirely in *"you"* and *"your"* salvation.

This is how John Piper summarizes the nature of God's salvation:

> *What is the greatness of our God? What is His uniqueness in the world?... All the other so-called gods make man work for them. Our God will not be put in the position of an employer who must depend on others to make his business go. Instead He magnifies His all-sufficiency by doing the work Himself. **Man** is the dependent partner in this affair. His job is to wait for the Lord.*

---

[1] Mark 2:27. See also Isaiah 40:28; Psalm 121:4; John 5:16–17.

[2] If they did, it would explain why the Lord tells them to *remember* the Sabbath in Exodus 20:8.

[3] Exodus 14:14, 25.

> *What is God looking for in the world? Assistants? No. The gospel is not a help-wanted ad. It is a help-available ad... God is not looking for people to work for Him but people who let Him work mightily in and through them... But isn't there something we can give to God that won't belittle him to the status of beneficiary? Yes. Our anxieties. It's a command: "Cast all your anxieties on him" (1 Peter 5:7). God will gladly receive anything from us that shows our dependence and His all-sufficiency... The only right way to serve God is in a way that reserves for Him all the glory.*[4]

That's why the Lord thwarted the efforts of those who disobeyed him in verses 27–30 by trying to gather manna against his orders on the Sabbath. It's why he intensified his command when the Hebrews reached Sinai by making it one of the Ten Commandments in 20:8–11 and by expanding it in 23:10–12 to include fields and vineyards and olive groves too. It's why he clarified in 35:1–3 that it included lighting fires, and in 34:21 that it even applied at harvest time, the busiest period of the year. It is why he ordered that any Sabbath-breaker be cut off from his People altogether in 31:12–17.[5] Our Saviour-God wants to be seen through his People, through a People who rest by faith in his work and not their own.[6]

Sometimes Christians point out that God does not command us explicitly anywhere in the New Testament to observe the Sabbath day. They are in danger of missing what the Sabbath was all about. To begin with, Jesus taught in Mark 2:27 that *"The Sabbath was made for man,"* and that we are fools not to take

---

[4] John Piper, *Brothers, We Are Not Professionals* (2003).

[5] Note from Exodus 31:14 that being "cut off from God's People" often meant execution rather than exile.

[6] We also see this in Deuteronomy 11:10–12. Egypt was irrigated by man-made foot-pumps, but the Promised Land was watered by God-given mountains and rivers.

rest for the sake of our bodies. The God who created us to spend a third of our lives asleep, and to take frequent rests during the other two-thirds to take on food and water, still warns us not to live our lives as if we were little gods ourselves. Every time we take a break, we proclaim that our real trust is in something other than the effort of our hands.

But even more importantly, the Sabbath principle runs through the whole of the New Testament. It is at the heart of the message that God came down to earth as a man to live a perfect life for us because we cannot, and to die a perfect sacrificial death on our behalf with a cry that *"It is finished!"*, or *"It is done!"*[7] The God who led Israel into the desert and *"gave them my Sabbaths as a sign between us, so they would know that I the Lord made them holy"*[8] still wants us to live out his New Covenant Sabbath. Not by observing meticulous rules which turn the Sabbath into seriously hard work, but by admitting that the sole contribution we make to our salvation is our sin and our helplessness. The Gospel is a promise that Jesus has done the work so we don't have to.

The fifth lesson that God teaches us through Israel's journey to Mount Sinai is therefore the Sabbath principle that *"To the one who does not work, but believes in the one who declares the ungodly righteous, his faith is credited as righteousness."*[9] Take a rest in God's salvation. It's seriously Good News.

---

[7] John 19:30.
[8] Ezekiel 20:12.
[9] Romans 4:5.

Lesson Six: Hands Up (17:8–16)

As long as Moses held up his hands, the Israelites were winning, but whenever he lowered his hands, the Amalekites were winning.

(Exodus 17:11)

Whoever first referred to an easy task as "child's play" clearly didn't have any children of their own. Kids ask the toughest questions and they expect us to have answers. The other day a child asked me, *"Why does God want us to pray? If he is so powerful, then why does he ask for our help?"* It was a very good question, and the answer I gave was rooted in the sixth and final lesson that the Lord taught the Israelites en route to Sinai. God the Saviour asks his People to pray because he wants to be visible through answering their prayers.

That's why God finally let the Hebrews see battle when the Amalekites attacked them at Rephidim. As the descendants of Esau's grandson Amalek, they were Israel's distant relatives and should have respected them as brothers.[1] Instead, although the Hebrews were still miles away from Amalekite territory, they launched an unprovoked surprise attack. The Lord used it to teach Israel what happens when we pray, and how he uses prayer as a way to be seen through his People.

Prayer displays that God is the true *strength* of his People. Although Joshua led the Israelite army into battle, the spotlight

---

[1] Genesis 36:12.

of the story shines on Moses at the top of the hill.[2] Joshua's work in the valley didn't change very much throughout the day, but he found in verse 11 that *as long as Moses held up his hands, the Israelites were winning, but whenever he lowered his hands, the Amalekites were winning.* What mattered was not the strength of Israel's army but the strength of Israel's God, as Moses laid hold of his throne in prayer.[3] Most of us know this deep down, but we never make it quite so visible as when we give ourselves by faith to persevering prayer.

I have a friend who leads a church in north London. Five years ago he gathered only 80 people on a Sunday, but today he gathers over 800. I therefore visited his church with my notepad at the ready so I could learn some lessons to reapply for my own church in south London. It made me realize how much I need to be reminded of the message of Exodus 17. He was attentive to the "Joshua" work of organizing, advertising and welcoming new guests,[4] but so are plenty of plateauing and declining churches down the road. What was different was the "Moses" work, which was evident from a church diary full of calls to pray: prayer breakfasts, prayer nights and whole Sunday services given over to laying hold of God in prayer. I saw the invisible God through his People in north London as they invested their energies in the God who answers prayer.

Prayer also displays that God is the *Saviour* of his People. Moses had not forgotten the lesson he learned at the waters of Marah, and he held up his wooden staff to the Lord as the reason why he expected him to answer his prayer. When God did so, he

---

[2] Some scholars argue that text must be missing here, since Moses mentions Joshua for the first time without any introduction. But remember that Moses anointed Joshua as his successor while he was writing the Pentateuch. He gives Joshua no introduction because his readers didn't need one.

[3] Verse 16 means literally that *"A hand was on the Lord's throne"*. Although some read this to mean the Amalekites sinfully laid a hand on God's throne, it is more likely an encouragement for us to do so in prayer.

[4] Exodus 17 reminds us that "Joshua" work is vital too! It also attributes the victory to Joshua's sword in verse 13.

built an altar which he named *Yahweh-Nissi*, or *The Lord is My Banner [of Victory]*, to testify that his staff had acted as a rallying point for God to make his victory visible. Isaiah picks up on this when he uses the same Hebrew word to prophesy that God's Messiah will be the true and better *Banner* who rallies people from every nation to God's salvation victory. Jesus carried on the theme by talking to the crowds about his death and promising that *"I, when I am lifted up from the earth, will draw all men to myself."*[5] The death and resurrection of Jesus are the basis upon which we are to make requests of God, and he loves to answer such Gospel-focused praying because it demonstrates to the watching world that he alone is God the Saviour.

Prayer also displays that God is the *Sustainer* of his People. Prayer is difficult, really difficult, and in some ways it's meant to be. God makes it difficult enough to force us to rely on the Holy Spirit, because Rephidim was also the place where the rock gushed out water to satisfy Israel's need. Moses sat on a rock while Aaron and Hur held up his hands, and Jesus invites us to rest on him and let him turn our stumbling prayers into mighty intercession.[6] *"The Spirit helps us in our weakness,"* Paul explains. *"We do not know what we ought to pray for, but the Spirit himself intercedes for us... The Spirit intercedes for the saints in accordance with God's will."*[7] God has designed prayer to be difficult so that even this cannot be a work of our own. He helps us to pray so that he is made visible as the only true hero in the story of our salvation.

The Father knows you find prayer difficult, so he sends the Son and the Spirit to prop you up like Aaron and Hur. What's

---

[5] Isaiah 11:10; John 12:32–33.

[6] Moses does not tell us who Hur was, perhaps because he was as well known to his readers as Joshua. He was Moses' key co-leader alongside Aaron until Joshua was fully trained (24:14). The Jewish historian Josephus speculates that he was Miriam's husband and Moses' brother-in-law (*Antiquities of the Jews*, 3.2.4).

[7] Romans 8:26–27, 34.

more, he provides you with human helpers too, who can help you pray when you feel little energy or faith to do so. Martin Luther confessed that *"At home in my own house there is no warmth or vigour in me, but in the church, when the multitude is gathered together, a fire is kindled in my heart and it breaks its way through."*[8] If even Martin Luther needed earthly Aarons and Hurs to help him to pray, then we need them too! So let's gather with others in prayer. God loves to be seen as the Sustainer of his People.

Let's pray because prayer also displays that God is the *Responder* to his People's requests. He answered Moses' prayers at Rephidim so powerfully that Israel's victory carried on for many centuries to come. Because Moses laid hold of God's throne, verse 16 tells us, *"the Lord will be at war against the Amalekites from generation to generation."* Sure enough, we discover in the rest of the Old Testament that this prophecy came true.[9] God wants to be seen through his People – especially through answering their persevering prayer.

Let me end with an example from yesterday. Two weeks ago I preached a similar message to the chapter on "Wood", and called people to come forward if they wanted to be healed through Jesus' sacrifice on the cross. Yesterday, a lady testified that at that very moment she was instantly healed of colitis, an inflammation of the intestines, which had caused her pain for over forty years. She had waited to testify until she could go to the hospital for a colonoscopy, but now the mystified doctor had pronounced her totally cured.

So back to the child's question: *"Why does God want us to pray?"* Because the sixth and final lesson he taught the Israelites on their way to Sinai is that he loves to be seen through his People by helping them to pray, and then giving mighty answers when they do.

---

[8] Quoted by Robert G. Rayburn in *O Come, Let Us Worship* (1980).

[9] Deuteronomy 25:17–19; 1 Samuel 15:18; 30:15–18; 1 Chronicles 4:42–43.

The Management Consultant from Midian (18:1–27)

Moses' father-in-law replied, "What you are doing is not good. You and these people who come to you will only wear yourselves out. The work is too heavy for you; you cannot handle it alone."

(Exodus 18:17–18)

Moses had become a very good leader. Gone was the self-confident palace boy who had tried to free the Hebrews in his own strength by attacking an Egyptian. Forty years of lonely shepherding had seen to that. Gone also was the disillusioned failure who had stood in front of the burning bush and complained, *"Who am I?... What if they do not believe me or listen to me?... Please send someone else."* Moses had managed to lead Israel from slavery to within sight of Mount Sinai.[1] He had become a national hero.

This, however, posed a new problem. How could any of the leaders around Moses compare to the man who had led Israel to victories at the Red Sea, at Marah and at Rephidim? When Moses' father-in-law came to reunite him with his wife and children at their prearranged rendezvous,[2] he found his

---

[1] The Hebrew of 18:5 is ambiguous as to whether Moses was *at* or *near* Mount Sinai. The dramatic description of his arrival at Sinai in 19:1–2 clarifies that he was merely within sight of the mountain.

[2] Exodus 3:12. Since the Hebrew word *shālah*, or *to send*, can sometimes mean *to divorce*, some scholars speculate that Moses divorced Zipporah after 4:20–26. But since the same word is used in verse 27 to describe him

son-in-law struggling with a superhuman workload. The Lord had made him *"like God to Pharaoh"* in 7:1 for his showdown with Egypt's idols, but now Moses was acting too much like God towards Israel. He could not take the Hebrews any further on their journey without Jethro helping him to share leadership with others. As this first section of Exodus draws to a close, the Lord uses plurality of leadership to emphasize in graphic terms that there is only room for one Saviour-God to be seen through his People.

Note the deliberate emphasis at the start of chapter 18. We are told at least nine times in the first eleven verses that the Lord was the one who rescued Israel from Egypt. Linked to this, we are told for the first time that Moses had a second son named Eliezer, meaning *God is a Helper*.[3] The spotlight shines unequivocally on Yahweh, culminating in blood sacrifices being offered on his altar in verse 12.[4] The Lord wants to make it clear that none of his leaders are indispensable. The God who is big enough to save his People is also big enough to keep them.

The truth was that Moses had only been able to succeed in his mission so far by relying on the quality of the leaders around him. He needed Aaron to stand with him before Pharaoh. He needed the leaders of the tribes and clans to mobilize the Hebrews in 12:51 when *"the Lord brought the Israelites out of Egypt by their divisions."* He needed Joshua to lead the Israelites into battle with the Amalekites, plus Aaron and Hur to help him pray on top of the hill. Even here in verse 12, he offers sacrifices with Aaron and *"all the elders of Israel"*. The Lord had rescued Israel thus far through a massive team effort, so that no human

---

sending Jethro away in peace, and the relations between them are very cordial, I find this totally unconvincing. Moses appears to have sent his family back to Jethro out of fear for their safety from Pharaoh.

[3] Until now we have only been told in 2:22 and 4:25 about his first son, Gershom, meaning *Alien*.

[4] Note that Jethro offered these sacrifices as the priest of Midian, modelling for Aaron the priestly role he was about to be given as a leader next to Moses. God's sacrificial Lamb is the only true hero of salvation.

leader would obscure his glory and prevent him from being seen as God the Saviour through his People.

Jethro offered Moses some timely advice that the primary task of a senior leader is to *pray*. He must lead the People by remembering and modelling the six lessons they had learned in the desert en route to Mount Sinai. He must live the Sabbath principle and direct the burden of leadership onto the Lord who invites us to rest while he works. He must devote himself to eating and drinking the spiritual food and drink which the Lord alone can provide. He must lift his hands in prayer to lay hold of God's throne through the messages of blood and wood and the handbrake. Jethro warned, *"You and these people who come to you will only wear yourselves out. The work is too heavy for you; you cannot handle it alone."* On the other hand, if he acted as the People's representative before God, *"you will be able to stand the strain, and all these people will go home satisfied."* The Lord calls senior leaders to remember he is God and they are not, by resting in his presence through prayer.[5]

Jethro reminded Moses that the second task of a senior leader is to *teach*, both by preaching and by modelling how to live. Leaders set the culture and values of those they lead, and in doing so provide a healthy context for other leaders around them to flourish in their own ministries. If Moses helped the Hebrews to think the Lord's way in every area of their lives, God would be seen through them without Moses having to carry the heavy burden of making him visible on his own.

Jethro also encouraged Moses that the third task of a leader is to *multiply* and *release* new leaders all around him. Moses could trust the Lord to provide him with God-fearing, honest men who could each oversee ten Hebrew families, and with others who could oversee these overseers. Some things should not be delegated, but for everything else he must find

---

[5] Moses' tells us in 33:7 that he spent long hours with God in his tent even before he built the Tabernacle.

leaders with calibre to lead ten, fifty, a hundred or a thousand. If he failed to do so, he would place a ceiling on his leadership gifting and do more than Pharaoh ever could to hinder God's plans for his People. He would destroy himself under the strain of a task the Lord had not called him to bear, and destroy God's People by becoming a bottleneck to all he wanted to do through them.

Thankfully, Moses listened to his father-in-law's advice and was able to lead Israel to the next stage on their journey. When Joshua resisted his willingness to multiply leadership in Numbers 11:29, he replied *"Are you jealous for my sake? I wish that all the Lord's people were prophets and that the Lord would put his Spirit on them!"* Sadly, not all Christian leaders are as humble as Moses. Many love to talk in theory about following God the Saviour, but in reality they are so desperate to play the role of co-star that they stand in his way. They fail to raise up new leaders out of fear that the newcomers will somehow diminish their own standing. Consequently, they wear themselves out as Jethro prophesied and reap the tragic reward of anyone who dares obscure the fullness of God's saving glory. This first section of Exodus ends with a call for us to get out of the way and let God be seen as the only Saviour of his People.

Charles Spurgeon, who raised up thousands of church leaders in nineteenth-century London, warned:

> *I tremble for a church whose continuance depends upon the talent and cleverness of one man... May none of us fall into a mean, poverty-stricken dependence on man!... Given a host of men who are steadfast, immoveable, always abounding in the work of the Lord, then the glory of God's grace will be clearly manifested.*[6]

---

[6] Charles Spurgeon in one of his prayer meeting addresses, published in *Only A Prayer Meeting* (2010).

God calls his leaders to let his saving glory shine unimpeded. He calls us not to think too much of ourselves, and to do nothing to prevent him from being seen as God the Saviour through his People.

Exodus 19–40:

God the Indweller

God's Postcode (19:1–40:38)

I am the Lord their God, who brought them out of
Egypt so that I might dwell among them.

(Exodus 29:46)

This is the point at which many readers start to struggle with the book of Exodus. Up until now, it is full of non-stop action: murder, cobras, miracles, plagues, judgment, sacrifice, last-gasp provision, battles and destruction. But there's a reason why the movie *The Prince of Egypt* ends with the arrival of the Hebrews at Mount Sinai.[1] Drama gives way to detail as Moses writes down God's Law, and adventure gives way to architecture as he describes at length God's Tabernacle. Many readers respond by skim reading or even giving up on the rest of the Pentateuch altogether. In doing so, they miss out on what the Exodus is all about, because the second half isn't a digression or anticlimax, but an explanation of why God brought the Israelites out of Egypt.

Most people assume that God rescued Israel because he had compassion on them in their slavery. That was one of his reasons, but it wasn't the main one. Nor was it simply to fulfil his word to the patriarchs that he would give the Promised Land to their descendants.[2] The Lord begins the second section of Exodus at the start of chapter 19 by giving us an explanation

---

[1] *The Prince of Egypt* (Dreamworks Pictures, 1998) tells the story of Exodus 1–18 and took almost $220 million at the box office.

[2] Although important (see Leviticus 26:13; Deuteronomy 6:23), these were secondary reasons.

of his motive: *"You yourselves have seen what I did to Egypt, and how I carried you on eagles' wings and **brought you to myself**."*[3] Israel's ultimate destination was not the land of Canaan, but the Lord himself, as he descended on Mount Sinai and set up his home at the heart of the Israelite nation. He clarifies in 29:45–46 that the reason why he rescued them was to *"dwell among the Israelites and be their God…who brought them out of Egypt **so that I might dwell among them**."* So don't assume for a moment that these chapters about the Law and the Tabernacle cut across the main story. They *are* the main story. The Lord wants to be seen through his People as God the Indweller.

Can you sense how excited Moses is about this as he starts chapter 19 by telling us that in the third month the Israelites finally arrived at the rendezvous God had set for them back in 3:12?[4] The Lord had been with them in Egypt, but it was nothing compared to what he was about to do among them at Mount Sinai. He was about to descend visibly in a dense cloud with thunder and lightning and fire and a trumpet blast. He was about to boom out the Ten Commandments in the hearing of all the Israelites and shape them into his *"holy nation"*, his *"treasured possession"* and a *"kingdom of priests"* who carried his presence to the nations, making him visible to the world.[5] God was about to take up an earthly postcode at the heart of the Hebrew nation. The second half of Exodus couldn't be more exciting.

---

[3] As in Isaiah 40:31, eagles' wings speak of God's great strength. He used his talons on Pharaoh and the Egyptians but carried Israel lovingly on his wings.

[4] Jewish tradition is that Moses received the Ten Commandments at Pentecost, fifty days after the Passover. If this is true, the Hebrews left Egypt on the fifteenth day of the first month (early April) and received the Ten Commandments on the sixth day of the third month (late May).

[5] 19:5–6. The Egyptians had looked down on their Hebrew slaves as valueless workhorses, but God calls them his *treasured possession* here and in Deuteronomy 7:6; 14:2; 26:18. The Hebrew word *segullāh* is used in 1 Chronicles 29:3 and Ecclesiastes 2:8 to refer to the *private treasure collection* of a king, and this theme is picked up in Malachi 3:17; Psalm 135:4; 1 Peter 2:9; Ephesians 1:14; Titus 2:14.

The Law was necessary because when God moves into a neighbourhood everything around him must change. Anyone unauthorized who touched Mount Sinai would die, which is why God's presence was trumpeted by a frighteningly loud fanfare. It gave the Hebrews twenty-twenty vision – *Exodus 20:20* vision – to see God and sense *"the fear of God...to keep you from sinning."*[6] The Law called them to live holy lives and stay spiritually pure, and taught them how to offer blood sacrifices every time they failed so that judgment would fall on another instead of them. The Hebrew word for Law is *Torah*, which means literally *Instruction*, and these chapters instructed them how to make God visible as he dwelt among them. They revealed his holiness when they obeyed his moral instruction, and revealed his mercy when they sinned and repented according to his sacrificial instruction.[7] Either way, the Law was necessary because God the Indweller wants to be seen through his People.

The Tabernacle was also necessary because Mount Sinai was *not* the Hebrew equivalent of the Greek Mount Olympus. Sinai was not a place that God had chosen to be his permanent dwelling place, far away from man. It was simply the place where he had arranged to meet the Hebrews to show them how to build him a more permanent abode. The Tabernacle would be his dwelling place at the heart of Israel's campsite because through it he would be visible as the inhabiter of his People.

Christians who skim read these chapters not only miss the point of the Exodus, they also miss the point of their own salvation. When John 1:14 explains that Jesus *"made his dwelling among us"*, it uses a Greek verb that means literally

---

[6] Proper fear of God is a good thing, as stressed by those who knew him intimately in the Old Testament (Genesis 31:53; Nehemiah 5:15; Job 1:1; 28:28; Proverbs 1:7; Hebrews 11:7; 12:21). Hebrews 12:22–29 warns that the New Covenant means we should now fear God *more*, not less.

[7] Many commentators split the Law into *moral*, *ceremonial* and *sacrificial*, but the Pentateuch does not actually make this division and often lurches back and forth between them.

that he *"tabernacled among us"*. John 14:23 expands on this by recording Jesus' promise that *"If anyone loves me, he will obey my teaching. My Father will love him, and we will come to him and **make our home with him**."* The writers of the New Testament got very excited about these chapters, and so should we, paying particular attention to their warning for us not to *"neglect such a great salvation."*[8]

Because that is precisely what the Hebrews do in this chapter. Although they promise like godly Noah and Moses in verse 8 that *"We will do everything the Lord has said"*,[9] they shrink back in fear when God's presence actually becomes available. They get cold feet over his invitation to climb the mountain with Moses, and when they hear God booming out the Ten Commandments they panic and beg Moses to meet God in their place in 20:18–21. They should have personally enjoyed the glorious intimacy with God which Moses and his seventy elders experienced in chapter 24, but instead they retreated to safer ground.[10]

Therefore since God's plan is still to set up his postcode among his People, and since fear is still the number one reason why Christians shrink back from being filled with his promised Holy Spirit, let's not rush over the second half of Exodus. The Lord inspired Moses to write these chapters for you and for me, because he still wants to be seen through his People as God the Indweller.[11] He calls us to slow down and to study these chapters attentively, so that we can make him visible as he shows us what they say.

---

[8] Hebrews 2:3. The rest of Hebrews explains that these chapters point to a better Tabernacle for us.

[9] Compare this statement with Genesis 6:22; 7:5; Exodus 7:6, 10, 20.

[10] The narrative of Exodus 19:9–25 leads straight into 20:18–21 and then into 24:1–18. Moses clarifies what happened in Deuteronomy 4:9–15; 5:4–5, 23–31; 18:16, as does Hebrews 12:18–20.

[11] Stephen says in Acts 7:38 that Moses received them as *"living words to pass on to us"*.

The Ten Commandments (20:1–17)

And God spoke all these words: "I am the Lord your God, who brought you out of Egypt, out of the land of slavery. You shall have no other gods before me."

(Exodus 20:1–3)

God doesn't want you to try to be like the Greek hero Hercules. He was haunted by crimes committed in a moment of madness, and went to astonishing lengths to try and make atonement for his sin. The Greek gods commanded him to perform Ten Labours as penance, and when he completed them they moved the goalposts by adding two more. Hercules performed the Twelve Labours in an attempt to buy forgiveness and acceptance by the gods. A surprising number of Christians try to copy him.

They assume that the Ten Commandments are the Christian equivalent of Hercules' Labours. If they try hard to obey them, they feel good about themselves, until their consciences move the goalposts and tell them God still wants more. They are right that the Ten Commandments are the pinnacle of God's Law – that's why he wrote them personally on two *"tablets of the Covenant"* and told Moses to place them in a box named the Ark of the Covenant after them[1] – but they are wrong to assume that God gave these commandments as the equivalent of Hercules' Labours. They were actually God's testimony about the Gospel which was to come.

They forget that the Lord chose not to give these tablets to

---

[1] For example, Exodus 31:18; 32:15–16; 34:28–29; Deuteronomy 4:13; 9:9–11; 10:3–4; 1 Kings 8:21.

Moses when he met him for the first time at Sinai in the burning bush. He didn't ask Moses to carry them to Egypt as an escape plan for the Israelites to follow to be saved. He only gave them to Moses after saving the Israelites through the Passover lamb and the parting of the Red Sea. They were not the means by which they could tunnel their way to salvation, but instruction about how they should respond to the salvation they had received. Before he gives any of the Ten Commandments, he clarifies in verse 2 that he is their Saviour-God *already*! Greek mythology had nothing to compare with Israel's God.

God used the Ten Commandments to convince the Hebrews that none of them had any hope of being a spiritual Hercules. Jesus explained that the first four commandments can be summarized as *"Love the Lord your God with all your heart and with all your soul and with all your mind"*. None of us has done that. He summarized the other six commandments as *"Love your neighbour as yourself"*, and told a follow-up story about the Good Samaritan to demonstrate the full scope of that command.[2] Not murdering means not getting angry, not hating anyone and not leaving anyone to die when we can help. Not committing adultery means not lusting, not fantasizing and not putting our own pleasures above commitment to those we should love.[3] God did not give Moses the Ten Commandments to offer Israel terms by which they could be saved, but to convince them that his standards were so far above their reach that their only hope was to lay hold of him as God the Saviour.

The Ten Commandments were given to stop us trying to be heroes, but they were also given to make us cry out to God for a better hero. Jesus warned his hearers, *"Do not think that I have come to abolish the Law or the Prophets; I have not come to abolish them but to fulfil them."*[4] He would be the only man in history ever to truly love the Lord with all his heart and soul and mind

---

[2] Matthew 22:35–40; Luke 10:25–37. See also Mark 10:17–27.

[3] Matthew 5:21–30.

[4] Matthew 5:17–20.

and strength, and the only man in history ever to truly love his neighbour as himself. When Moses' successors arrested him and put him on trial, they would be unable to find a single incident of lawbreaking in his life.[5] They would find him a mightier hero than Hercules, fully obeying the Ten Commandments and the additional instructions which accompanied them at Sinai.

Paul celebrates this in Romans 3:20–31:

> *No one will be declared righteous in God's sight by observing the Law; rather, through the Law we become conscious of sin. But now a righteousness from God, apart from Law, has been made known, to which the Law and the Prophets testify. This righteousness from God comes through faith in Jesus Christ to all who believe… Do we, then, nullify the Law by this faith? Not at all! Rather, we uphold the Law.*

We can be saved through these Ten Commandments, but not by striving like Hercules. We must put our faith in Jesus who performed these labours faultlessly on our behalf.

Nor must we think that the Lord gave these commands to the Hebrews as a necessary step before he could dwell among them. There is still quite a common view among Christians that "the Holy Spirit only fills clean vessels", and that we therefore need to spruce up our act before the Lord will grant us a share in the Day of Pentecost. The rest of the Pentateuch tells us this simply isn't so. In Leviticus 16:16 the Lord refers to *"the Tent of Meeting, which is among them in the midst of their uncleanness"*. In fact, our uncleanness is precisely the reason why God fills us with his Spirit. He promises in Ezekiel 36:27 that *"I will put my Spirit in you and move you to follow my decrees and be careful to keep my laws."*

Stop for a moment and re-read the Ten Commandments

---

5 Mark 14:55.

in the light of that promise in Ezekiel 36. Does anything strike you as unusual about the way they are phrased? Most of the commandments are not commands in the classic sense of the word at all. The Hebrew refers to them literally as the *"Ten Words"* rather than as the *"Ten Commandments"* because what God actually says to the Israelites in Hebrew is *"You **shall have** no other gods"*, *"You **shall not** misuse the name of the Lord"*, *"You **shall not** murder"*, *"You **shall not** commit adultery"*, and so on. These are not just ten warnings not to try to act like Hercules or that we need a heavenly hero to labour on our behalf. They are also ten promises that God will make us holy from the inside out by filling us with his Spirit: *"The fruit of the Spirit is love, joy, peace, patience, kindness, goodness, faithfulness, gentleness and self-control. Against such things there is no Law."*[6]

My apple tree does not strain to yield a bumper crop of apples. It simply lets its God-given sap produce fruit in accordance with the kind of tree it is. In the same way, God warns us not to labour away like Hercules, but to put our faith in Jesus the Hero and to let him work his holiness in our hearts from the inside out through his Spirit. God the Saviour wants to be seen through his People as we stop playing at Hercules and let his Son and his Spirit take centre-stage instead. Only then can the Ten Commandments truly be fulfilled, as God the Saviour and God the Indweller fulfil the Gospel preached at Sinai.

---

[6] Galatians 5:22–23.

The Law of Sinai
(21:1–23:33)

You are to be my holy people.

(Exodus 22:31)

In the TV Series *The West Wing*, President Bartlet baits a religious talk-show host who has quoted the Law of Sinai as the basis for modern policy. He turns on her and tries to humiliate her in front of a crowded White House reception:

> *I wanted to ask you a couple of questions while I had you here. I'm interested in selling my youngest daughter into slavery as sanctioned in Exodus 21:7. She's a Georgetown sophomore, speaks fluent Italian, and always clears the table when it is her turn. What would a good price for her be?*
>
> *While thinking about that, can I ask another? My Chief of Staff, Leo McGarry, insists on working on the Sabbath. Exodus 35:2 clearly says he should be put to death. Am I morally obligated to kill him myself or is it okay to call the police?*
>
> *Here's one that's really important 'cause we've got a lot of sports fans in this town. Touching the skin of a dead pig makes us unclean – Leviticus 11:7. If they promise to wear gloves, can the Washington Redskins still play football? Can Notre Dame? Can West Point? Does the whole town really have to be together to stone my brother, John, for planting different crops side by side? Can I burn my mother in a small family gathering*

for wearing garments made from two different threads?
Think about those questions, would you?[1]

The talk-show host squirms silently in her seat, hoping that such awkward questions will simply go away. As God follows up the Ten Commandments with three long chapters of specific and sometimes bewildering legal detail, we have to think carefully about what they mean for us today. Paul tells us in 2 Timothy 3:16 that *"All Scripture is God-breathed and is useful for teaching, rebuking, correcting and training in righteousness,"* but that doesn't mean all Scripture is equally easy to understand or apply. As something of an introduction to the many chapters of legal detail in the Pentateuch, let me give just three reasons why we should be grateful that God inspired Exodus 21–23.

These chapters are still very important today because they show us *what the invisible God is like*. Moses calls these three chapters the "Book of the Covenant" in 24:7 because they seek to unpack the Ten Commandments in more detail. The Israelites promised in 19:8 that *"We will do everything the Lord has said"*, so he spelt out his character in more detail so they would enter into his covenant at Sinai with their eyes wide open. He revealed himself as the champion of the oppressed, who will not stand by and allow people to be murdered, maimed or manhandled without intervening as the defender of the weak (21:2–25).[2] He will punish those who injure others through their disregard for health and safety (21:26–36), and will do the same to anyone who lines their pockets through dishonest means (22:1–15, 21–27). If someone sins sexually (22:16–19)[3] or takes the life of

---

[1] *The West Wing*, Season 2, Episode 3: "The Midterms".

[2] Don't assume that the Lord is condoning ancient slavery in 21:2–11. He begins the Book of the Covenant with rules safeguarding and freeing slaves, and goes on to order the execution of slave-traders in 21:16.

[3] Ancient Hebrews would not marry a girl who was not a virgin, so the Lord commanded any man who seduced a virgin either to marry her or to pay her such a hefty sum that she could still attract a husband.

an unborn baby (21:22–25),[4] they will also feel his wrath. The Israelites must not enter into the covenant of Sinai lightly. Their God was far too holy to accommodate their sorcery, idolatry, blasphemy, injustice, selfishness or lying.

The chapters are also very important because they show us *what God's People must be like*. The Book of the Covenant is a three-chapter explanation of what God means when he says in 22:31 that *"You are to be my holy people"*. Although President Bartlet laughs at the detail God used to express his holiness through a group of Bronze Age, desert-dwelling nomads, he misses the overarching point behind these ancient commands: *"I am Who I Am...therefore be holy, because I am holy."*[5] Although Paul tells us in Colossians 2:14–17 that the detail is superseded, he quotes these ancient principles in his letters in order to apply them to God's New Covenant People.[6] He draws out what the Law reveals about how God wants to be visible through his People, just as Jesus warned his followers that their righteousness must exceed that of the teachers of the Law, who observed the detail of Sinai but forgot its principles.

If this sounds difficult, you have grasped the third reason why these chapters are so important. They also show us *how to be the People God calls us to be*. It is not through the finger-wagging moralism of the talk-show host, but through grasping the message about God the Indweller. The detailed Law raises the bar of holiness so high that we are forced to run to the Spirit every day of our lives for the help only he can give. He cripples us in order to reveal himself seven times in the Law as *Yahweh M'Qaddesh*, meaning *The Lord Who Sanctifies You*,[7] because he

---

[4] The *"serious injury"* referred to in verse 22 includes the baby as well as the mother.

[5] Leviticus 11:45, but echoed throughout the Pentateuch.

[6] For example, in 1 Corinthians 9:8–10 and 1 Timothy 5:18 Paul uses a verse about oxen from Deuteronomy 25:4 to teach a timeless principle about Christian fairness and generosity.

[7] Exodus 31:13; Leviticus 20:8; 21:8, 15; 22:9, 16, 32. Seven is the biblical number of perfection.

is not just the forgiver of sin but also the one who frees us from sin's residual power. The God who made humans in his image in Genesis 1:26–28 restores his image in his People so they can reflect him to the world. Paul points the Corinthians to Mount Sinai when he tells them excitedly that *"We, who with unveiled faces all reflect the Lord's glory, are being transformed into his likeness with ever-increasing glory, which comes from the Lord, who is the Spirit."*[8]

That's why the Lord peppers these chapters with references to his Messiah, just in case we become as confused and as cynical about the Law as President Bartlet. Jesus would pledge better obedience to the Father than any Hebrew slave in 21:5–6, when he told him *"My ears you have pierced... I desire to do your will, O my God; your law is within my heart."*[9] He would be sold for the price of a slave in 21:32, because he is the true *"Lord of the Sabbath"* in 23:10–12, who works our salvation so we can rest in what he has done.[10] He is the one who appears in 23:20–33 as the Angel of the Lord to protect and lead God's People into victory and blessing and health and fruitfulness.

So let's not treat these three chapters like President Bartlet, as a boring and irrelevant embarrassment. They are a detailed description of the character of God, the character he wants to be seen through his People as they surrender to his Spirit. Will we skim read, squirm and stay silent like the superficial talk-show host, or will we celebrate their message because we see what lies beneath the surface? These chapters end on a high with the Angel of the Lord, because they are even more worth shouting about for Christians today than they were when the Lord dictated them to Moses at Mount Sinai.

---

[8] 2 Corinthians 3:18.

[9] Psalm 40:6–8, which Hebrews 10 tells us is a prophecy about what the Messiah would say. It also tells us that, through Jesus, God's laws are now written on our hearts so we can live by their principles.

[10] Matthew 26:14–16; 27:1–10; Luke 6:5.

How to Experience God
(24:1–18)

*God did not raise his hand against these leaders of
the Israelites; they saw God, and they ate and drank.*

(Exodus 24:11)

In part two of Exodus, the Lord reveals himself as God the
Indweller. He tells us how to experience him and how to let him
live inside us. That makes chapter 24 the pivotal bridge between
the promises made in chapters 19–23 and the construction of
the Tabernacle in chapters 25–40. This is the chapter where
Moses and his fellow leaders see the invisible God. It is the point
where God gives us seven steps to do the same.

First we must *recognize how holy God is*. Perhaps that's
why Aaron's sons Nadab and Abihu are singled out by name
among the seventy-five who climbed the mountain.[1] They saw
God and ate and drank with him on Mount Sinai, but they failed
to develop the "Exodus 20:20 vision" through which fear of God
keeps us from sinning. When they downplayed God's holiness
later on in Leviticus 10, they were struck down dead. God
warns us that one of the greatest reasons we do not experience
him more is that we haven't learned to steward what we have
experienced of him already. It is God's mercy which prevents us
from experiencing him any more than we do, and it is his grace
which invites us to fear his holiness so we can see him more.

Even though Moses tells us in verse 11 that *"they saw*

---

[1] Moses, Aaron, Nadab, Abihu, Joshua and seventy elders. Did Miriam
rebel in Numbers 12 because she resented this list being entirely male? God
warned her to let him do the choosing.

God", he helps us fear the Lord by barely describing him at all. Instead he describes the glory of the pavement he stood on, just as Ezekiel 1:28 talks not about God himself but about *"the appearance of the likeness of the glory of the Lord"*. This is the same God who would tell Moses in 33:20 that *"No one may see me and live."* The Lord warns us in this chapter that the first step to experiencing him is to recognize his holiness and to approach with reverent awe.

Second, we must *fix our eyes on Jesus' cross*. As is usually the case in the Pentateuch, the seventy-five only approach the Lord after slaughtering blood sacrifices at his altar. They were permitted inside the mountain limits set in chapter 19 because they put their faith in the power of God's blood sacrifice to render them holy enough to approach him.[2] Many Christians experience far less of God than he intends because they convince themselves like the Israelites in 20:19 that they are too unworthy to come near. The Lord urges us to learn the lesson of Hebrews 10:19–22: *"Since we have confidence to enter the Most Holy Place by the blood of Jesus…let us draw near to God with a sincere heart in full assurance of faith."*

Third, we must *pursue God's agenda and not our own*. Although half of the sacrificial blood was poured out on the altar for forgiveness, Moses took the other half in bowls and sprinkled it on the Israelites in response to their commitment in verse 7 that *"We will do everything the Lord has said; we will obey."* Since Moses was entering God's presence on their behalf – as demonstrated by the twelve stone pillars he erected round the altar – to experience him they needed to surrender to his agenda. *"Without holiness no one will see the Lord"*, Scripture warns. We must submit to his desire to be seen through his holy People.[3]

---

[2] God had already warned in 19:13 that no one could approach him without a dead ram's horn being blown.

[3] Hebrews 12:14. This principle is also found in Psalm 51:10–11 and John 14:21–23.

GOD THE INDWELLER

Fourth, we must *pursue God for his own sake and not for what we can get out of him*. Those who merely seek God's hand will never truly see his face, but he delights to be seen by those who simply love him for who he is. He invited the seventy-five to join him on the mountain so that they could eat and drink and enjoy each other's company in verse 11. They ate the meat of their sacrifices and fellowshipped with the Lord, just as we do today when we eat the manna of his Word and feed on the body and blood of his sacrificed Son. The same God who ordained the Passover Feast and its New Covenant equivalent of eating bread and drinking wine, now invites us through the Gospel to seek his presence for its own sake. *Come dine with me* is the invitation of our God.

Fifth, we must *get rid of distraction*. Moses got up early in verse 4 to start seeking God's face before the pressures of the day began. Although he fell into the trap of thinking his work was indispensable in 18:15, he had since learned Jethro's lesson well. He delegated everything to Aaron and Hur in 24:14 so he was free to spend forty undistracted days and nights with the Lord at the top of Mount Sinai. He even tells us later in Deuteronomy 9:9 that he was so determined to be free from distraction that he fasted from food and drink entirely during that time. Paul Yonggi Cho founded the largest church in the world on this principle in Seoul, South Korea: *"Treasure would not be treasure if it were easily accessible... I learned many years ago that it takes effort to get the treasures that God desires to give me... It takes discipline and effort to live your life at the doorpost of the Lord."*[4]

Sixth, we must *be patient and not despise small beginnings*. Note in verse 16 that it was only after Moses had waited for the Lord for six days within the cloud that the Lord finally spoke to him on day seven after 150 hours of waiting! The truth is most of us get tired and restless after ten minutes. *"We don't wait*

---

[4] Paul Yonggi Cho, *Prayer: Key to Revival* (1984).

well. We're into microwaving. God, on the other hand, is usually into marinating," observes one church leader.[5] Moses knew how to marinate patiently in God's presence and he taught his fellow leaders to do the same when he led them partway up the mountain. This whetted the appetite of Aaron and Joshua, who refused to be satisfied with only going partway. Because they copied the patient persistence of Moses, they later had their own times of experiencing God as Moses had on Mount Sinai.[6]

Seventh, *be expectant that God wants you to experience him*. The epilogue to this chapter comes in 34:29–35, when Moses comes down from Mount Sinai with his face glowing so brightly with God's reflected glory that the rank-and-file Israelites beg him to wear a veil. They simply cannot bear to see God's splendour in the face of a person who has truly experienced him. God the Indweller wants to be seen through his People, and he calls us to take these seven steps into his presence. Moses climbed the mountain to meet with God, and in doing so pulled the trigger for God to come down the mountain with him and start living among the Israelites. In the same way, the Lord calls us to step into his presence with a promise that as we do so he will come and live inside us too.

That's why Paul told the Corinthians that what happened on Mount Sinai was simply a foretaste of something better which has come to us. Because Jesus is the fulfilment of Moses' Law and Moses' Tabernacle, *"what was glorious has no glory now in comparison with the surpassing glory"* of the New Covenant.[7] So let's pursue this greater glory with the same passion as Moses. God wants us to experience him and open the door to him coming to live among his People.

---

[5] Dutch Sheets, *Intercessory Prayer* (1996).

[6] Exodus 28:30; Joshua 7:6, 10. Although Joshua went further up the mountain than any of the others, it is clear from 32:17 that he did not go to the summit with Moses and hear all that God said to him.

[7] 2 Corinthians 3:10.

The Tabernacle (25:1–31:18 & 35:1–39:43)

*Have them make a sanctuary for me, and I will
dwell among them. Make this tabernacle and all its
furnishings exactly like the pattern I will show you.*

(Exodus 25:8–9)

Tomorrow morning I am going camping. I don't really want to.
I'm going because I'm speaking at a Christian summer festival,
but if I could avoid the whole camping experience then I would.
Why does anyone choose to spend their holiday in a tent in rainy
Britain when they have a comfortable bed, a hot shower and
dry clothes at home? It seems primitive, retrograde and in my
view best avoided, which is why this section of the Pentateuch
really captures my attention. A quarter of Exodus describes in
painstaking detail God's surprising decision to live in a tent on
the Israelite campsite.

Could anything speak more loudly about *the humility of
God's presence*? The same God who defeated Pharaoh, a ruler
whose name was Egyptian for *Great House*, condescended to
make his dwelling place in a lowly desert tent. The main Hebrew
word used for the Tabernacle is *ōhel*, simply meaning *tent*, but it
is also called his *mishkān*, meaning a *dwelling place* even as basic
as a shepherd's hut or a lion's den. The book of Exodus goes
out of its way to express that the glorious, transcendent God
the Saviour is also the intimate, immanent God the Indweller.
It surprised Solomon so much that even when he upgraded the
Tabernacle to a gold-encrusted stone Temple, he still exclaimed,
"Will God really dwell on earth? The heavens, even the highest

heaven, cannot contain you. How much less this temple I have built!"[1] If you are puzzled by the level of detail Moses records in these chapters about the Tabernacle, you need to rediscover this sense of breathless amazement. The mighty, invisible God of the Hebrews is humble enough to dwell in a tent among his People.

The New Testament tells us that this was just a taster for an even greater act of divine humility yet to come. God would not merely descend in a cloud to live inside a tent. He would humble himself still further, *taking the very nature of a servant, being made in human likeness.*"[2] John 1:14 and 2:21 tell us that Jesus' flesh-and-blood body was God's true Temple through which he *"tabernacled"* on earth, and Hebrews 10:19–22 adds that it was the breaking of his tabernacle-body which has gained us access to God's presence today.[3] The Tabernacle was such a picture of what the risen Jesus wants to do in each of our lives today that Paul asks us *"Don't you know that you yourselves are God's temple and that God's Spirit lives in you?"*[4] These long chapters about the design of God's tent could not be more exciting.

The Tabernacle was also an emphatic reminder of *the holiness of God's presence.* The third Hebrew word which is used in these chapters to describe the tent is *miqdāsh,* meaning *holy place* or *sanctuary.* The Lord would dwell between the cherubim which were on the lid of the Ark of the Covenant in the inner room of the tent, in a curtained-off area known as the Most

---

[1] 1 Kings 8:27. Exodus 33:7–11 literally tells us Moses *used to take* a makeshift Tent of Meeting outside the camp to meet with God. The Tabernacle itself was therefore an upgrade at the heart of the Hebrew camp.

[2] Philippians 2:7.

[3] This is why Exodus is at pains to point out that Moses obeyed the Lord's design entirely. See 25:9, 40; 26:30; 27:8; 31:11; 39:1, 5, 7, 26, 31, 42–43; 40:16, 19, 21, 23, 25, 27, 29, 32.

[4] 1 Corinthians 3:16. He repeats this in 2 Corinthians 6:16, quoting Leviticus 26:11–12 about the Tabernacle.

Holy Place.[5] This could only be accessed by passing through the outer room known as the Holy Place, which in turn could only be accessed by entering the Tabernacle courtyard through its one door and going past the huge bronze altar and basin which stood in the way. God dwelt humbly among the Hebrews, but this didn't mean that they could stagger unprepared into his presence. God was not just any old neighbour, as Nadab and Abihu would discover to their cost. The Tabernacle was an earthly copy of God's holy dwelling place in heaven, so he gave Moses a detailed blueprint which begins with the Ark and then works its way outside.[6] God wants to dwell among us, but he wants us to grasp how very different from us he is.

Linked to this, the Tabernacle spoke of *the glory of God's presence*. A tent was a humble dwelling place, but it was the best tent money could buy. These chapters begin with seven verses which invite Israel to hand over the gold, silver and other precious materials they had plundered from the Egyptians. Even though the Hebrews were living hand-to-mouth in the desert, they gave so willingly that Moses had to order them to stop in 35:4–36:7.[7] The Lord's Tabernacle was worth more than the rest of the Israelites' tents put together, and required such unprecedented skill in its builders that these chapters mention spiritual gifts for the first time in the Bible, as God fills Bezalel and Oholiab with his Holy Spirit to make them equal to the task. Every time the Israelites looked at God's portable palace made of precious metals, fine yarn, expensive wood and sparkling gems, they were reminded of the glory of their magnificent Saviour-God. The Lord is so majestically otherworldly that he can be humble even as he demonstrates his glory.

---

[5] Exodus 25:22; 30:6, 36. The Hebrew phrase is literally *the Holy of Holies*, but this is simply the normal Hebrew way of saying *the Most Holy Place* (as in 29:37 or 30:10, 29, 36).

[6] Hebrews 8:5. Moses' description moves inside-out, not outside-in.

[7] Exodus 38:21–31 tells us that they gave a tonne of gold, 3½ tonnes of silver and 2½ tonnes of bronze.

Together, these three things reinforce *the centrality of God's presence.* When the Lord told Moses at the burning bush in 3:12 that *"I will be with you"*, Moses failed to value the promise as he should. After he had seen the blueprint for the Tabernacle, however, he insisted in 33:15–16 that *"If your Presence does not go with us, do not send us up from here... What else will distinguish me and your people from all the other people on the face of the earth?"* If you find these chapters about the Tabernacle overly long and excessively detailed, you need to slow down and enjoy the same journey which took Moses from Sinai to Egypt and back again. The Lord gives us such detail because he wants us to grasp that the purpose of salvation is his coming to dwell inside us. *"I am the Lord their God, who brought them out of Egypt **so that I might dwell among them**,"* he tells us in 29:46. He brings this up to date for us as Christians in Galatians 3:13, where Paul tells us that *"He redeemed us **in order that...we might receive the promise of the Spirit.**"*

The Lord wants us to grasp through these chapters that the message of God the Indweller is not just a tag-on to that of God the Saviour. Let's not be like the Israelites when they shrank back from God's presence initially at Mount Sinai. Let's be like them in these chapters where they hold nothing back, and give all they have because they value the promise of God's presence so highly. If you are a Christian, God wants to fill you with the Holy Spirit today: *"Repent and be baptized, every one of you, in the name of Jesus Christ for the forgiveness of your sins. And you will receive the gift of the Holy Spirit."*[8]

---

[8] Acts 2:38.

The Men Who Came Close
(28:1–30:38)

Anoint Aaron and his sons and consecrate them so
they may serve me as priests.

(Exodus 30:30)

One of my heroes is Ethan Hunt from *Mission: Impossible*. Tom Cruise's character breaks into maximum security buildings, knowing that one wrong move will cost him his life, because he knows that his nation needs him to fetch an object that lies inside. I love watching Ethan Hunt make his way past each security barrier, so I also like reading about Aaron and his sons. God's presence in the Tabernacle was cordoned off as securely as any building in the *Mission: Impossible* movies, and setting one foot out of line would prove just as deadly. So let's take a look at Aaron and his sons, the Ethan Hunts of the Pentateuch.

First they needed to enter the Tabernacle courtyard, twenty-five metres wide and fifty metres long. There was no peering over the 2½-metre-high walls, but finding the single entrance and squeezing past the curtain that covered it was the least of their problems. The white linen walls proclaimed that only the righteous could enter, and that no one was pure and spotless enough to make the grade.[1] The only reason they could enter at all was that the linen was held to the posts with hooks made out of the silver taken from the Israelites as redemption money in 30:11–16 and 38:25–28. It spoke of the day when God's Messiah would be sold for silver coins and shed his blood

---

[1] Revelation 19:8.

as God's pure and spotless sacrifice for sin. Our righteousness still hangs on his work alone.[2]

Next, Aaron and his sons had to cross the courtyard to reach the Tabernacle itself. As they did so, the bronze bases and silver hooks were replaced with silver bases and gold hooks to warn them that they were getting ever closer to the dangerous presence of God. They must stop first at the bronze altar of blood sacrifice, two and half metres square and one and a half metres high. Since a grate halfway inside the altar allowed ash to keep on burning deep inside the hollow altar as well on the top, they were reminded that they needed God's blood sacrifice to cleanse them inwardly as well as outwardly. Once they had offered a sacrifice, they could move to the bronze laver, a massive basin made out of bronze mirrors. They saw their faces as they washed and drew faith that God had cleansed them.[3] They were now ready to approach the Tabernacle itself.

Here the access grew even more restricted, as Aaron and his sons stepped inside a tent that was barred to every Israelite but themselves. The walls were made of wood covered by gold, then linen curtains, then goat-hair curtains, then two coverings of ram skins dyed red and further leather skins on top.[4] The wooden crossbar and gold hooks were so secure that there was no way of breaking and entering without using the door. The Ethan Hunts of the Pentateuch would have to take their lives in their hands and push back the thick curtain.

Even the priests could only ever enter the Holy Place, the anteroom to God's inner chamber, by special invitation. Only the

---

[2] Matthew 26:14–16; 27:1–10.

[3] Unusually, Scripture does not give us the dimensions of this laver, perhaps to emphasize that God's sanctifying grace is unlimited. Ephesians 5:25–27 links the laver to Jesus' cross, God's Spirit and his Word.

[4] The New Testament does not unpack what these signified in detail, but many readers assume that they are further pictures of the blood Jesus shed on a wooden cross to make us righteous.

on-duty priest was permitted to enter,[5] and he needed to be wearing the elaborate clothes which the Lord commanded in chapter 28. He spoke a password in the form of a golden plaque upon his turban, which declared that he was *"Holy to the Lord"*, and his clothes were designed to speak yet again of the sacrificial death of the coming Messiah. His pristine white garments had been sprinkled with sacrificial blood at his consecration in chapter 29, because even the best human whites are not white enough without being washed in Jesus' blood. As the priest's eyes slowly adjusted to the light shed in the Holy Place by the seven-branched Golden Lampstand known as the *menorah*, he saw the twelve loaves of showbread laid out permanently on the Golden Table, and he offered incense which burned non-stop on the Golden Altar because God's People's prayers must never cease.[6] As he did so, the bells on the hem of his robe announced his presence and prevented him from being struck down for intruding into a room so full of pictures of God's Spirit and his People.[7]

Only the high priest could go any further, and even he could only do so on one day of the year, the Day of Atonement. When he entered the Most Holy Place, he felt more scared than Ethan Hunt, giving rise to the (almost certainly untrue) legend that he attached a rope to his ankle so his brothers could pull out his corpse if he dropped dead from the sheer weight of seeing God's glory. He even wore special underpants in 28:42–43 for fear of exposing his nakedness and courting sudden death.[8]

Like Ethan Hunt, Aaron braved the journey because he knew it was a matter of life or death for his nation. Before

---

[5] Aaron's family later grew so large that King David organized them into twenty-four divisions. Each division took turns to serve and drew lots to see which individual would act as priest (1 Chronicles 24:1–19; Luke 1:5–9).

[6] Exodus 30:7–8. Hebrews 9:1–12 tells us that this altar was later moved into the Most Holy Place, but this was not what the Lord stipulated here in Exodus.

[7] Exodus 28:34–35; Revelation 4:5.

[8] Exodus 20:26 led to 28:42–43.

Sinai, the Lord had simply allowed each family head to act as priest to his own household,[9] but when he called Israel to be a whole nation of priests who made him visible to the world, it meant they needed a high priest of their own to approach God on their behalf. Aaron bore the names of the twelve tribes on two onyx stones on his shoulders, and the name of each tribe on the twelve precious gems on his breastplate.[10] The Lord dwelt inside the Most Holy Place – at five metres wide and five metres deep, it was less than half the size of its anteroom – in between the cherubim angels on the "atonement lid" of the Ark of the Covenant. That made it the most precious twenty-five square metres in the world, because the Ark was the throne of Israel's King within his palace,[11] and held more power than any object in the *Mission: Impossible* movies. Since there was no light in the room because God's presence was enough, Aaron risked everything to enter and sprinkle sacrificial blood on the lid of the Ark to make atonement once a year by the light of God's own glory.

Praise God, he does not call us to be Ethan Hunts today, risking everything to venture into his presence. The book of Hebrews devotes 131 of its 303 verses to explaining that Jesus is our great Ethan Hunt, who has performed God's *Mission: Impossible* for us. God's presence is no longer contained in the quiet, dark, curtained-off inaccessibility of the Most Holy Place. He has torn apart the Tabernacle curtain and has created a new Most Holy Place in each of his believers through the Holy Spirit.[12]

So let's not neglect what Aaron and his sons prized so highly, and treat the message of God the Indweller as peripheral to salvation. Let's lay hold of Jesus, the true Ethan Hunt, and ask God to fill us with his Spirit.

---

[9] Exodus 19:22.

[10] Exodus 19:5; 28:6–30. *Urim* means *Lights* and begins with the first letter of the Hebrew alphabet. *Thummim* means *Perfections* and begins with the last. They were a form of sacred dice for obtaining guidance from God.

[11] Exodus 25:22; Numbers 7:89; 1 Chronicles 13:6; Isaiah 37:16.

[12] Mark 15:37–38; Hebrews 9:7–10:23.

God is Not a Statue
(32:1–35)

When Aaron saw this, he built an altar in front of the calf and announced, "Tomorrow there will be a festival to the Lord."

(Exodus 32:5)

Most people assume that the story about the Golden Calf is a warning for us not to break the First Commandment: *"You shall have no other gods before me."* But it isn't, at least not primarily. It is first and foremost a warning not to break the Second Commandment: *"You shall not make yourself an idol in the form of anything in heaven above or on the earth beneath or in the waters below."* This *idol* or *image* – the Hebrew word is the same[1] – is a terrible reminder of the subtlety of sin. The sobering reality of Exodus 32 is that the Israelites genuinely thought they were worshipping an image of Yahweh as they danced around a Golden Calf at the foot of Mount Sinai.

Israel did not cope well with the prolonged absence of their figurehead Moses. They were so used to the idols of their slave-masters in Egypt than even the ten–nil defeat of those animal-headed gods had not taught them to worship the unseen God alone. They worked out their faith in the Lord by looking at his gifted leader, Moses, and when their human hero disappeared they reverted to the worship rituals of Egypt. Even as they ate the manna their invisible God provided, they urged Aaron to *"Come, make us gods who will go before us. As for this fellow*

---

[1] The Greek word *eidōlon*, the root of our word *idol*, also comes from the verb *to see* and means a *visible image*.

Moses who brought us up out of Egypt, we don't know what has happened to him."

Aaron thought quickly, but he came to the wrong conclusion. They were trying to persuade him to help them break the First Commandment, so he tried to work a compromise that would keep them worshipping Yahweh. He made them a Golden Calf which looked like one of Egypt's idols, but announced that it was actually what the Lord had looked like all along.[2] He built an altar of blood sacrifice in front of the idol and proclaimed that *"Tomorrow there will be a festival to the Lord"*. They would look at the image and worship God for his oneness, his majesty, his strength and his promise to atone for sin through the sacrifice of bulls and lambs. Sure, it had required a little compromise to achieve this greater goal, but the Gospel needed to keep up to date if it was to connect with the culture of these 2 million Hebrews. Aaron tried to stop them from breaking the First Commandment by helping them to break the Second.

It is easy to judge Aaron harshly in this chapter. Moses had entrusted leadership in his absence to Aaron and Hur, but Aaron buckles very quickly to the crowd without appearing to involve Hur at all.[3] He tries to blame the people and to argue that the calf simply "came out of the fire" in verses 22–24, but the Lord lays the blame very firmly at his door in verse 35. Yet *"do not judge, or you too will be judged,"* because we can all be as guilty as Aaron of such compromise.[4] We can all treat visible things as a substitute for worshipping the invisible God. Depending on our Christian persuasion, we can look to human leaders, to icons and crucifixes, or even to Scripture itself as a substitute for the Lord.[5] Even if

---

[2] Although the Hebrew word *elōhīm* can mean either *God* or *gods*, the verbs in verses 1, 4, 8 and 23 are plural, clarifying that the Hebrews wanted to choose other gods and that Aaron hoped to win them back to Yahweh.

[3] Jewish tradition (probably unfounded) is that Hur was lynched, scaring Aaron into giving in so easily.

[4] Matthew 7:1.

[5] Any Protestant who thinks idolatry is exclusively a Catholic problem should read the chapter "Confessions of a Bible Deist" in Jack Deere's *Surprised By*

we manage to resist the draw to external idolatry, Ezekiel 14:3 warns about people who *"set up idols **in their hearts.**"* Which one of us has never carved out an image of the Lord as we would prefer him to be? To satisfy ourselves or our public, we can chisel off his holiness, his anger, his fiery judgment or his statement that there is no salvation outside his Son. Exodus 32 is not just Aaron's story, but our own.

Making an image of the invisible God *conceals his true nature, rather than revealing it.* The Golden Calf expressed something of the Lord's strength and vigour, but it obscured his holiness, his love and compassion, his patience, his grace, his wisdom and much more. An image of God is therefore not his likeness, but his *unlikeness.* The Lord carried Israel in 19:4, but the Golden Calf would need to be carried by them. The Lord had enabled them to plunder the Egyptians' gold in 12:36, but the Golden Calf would rob them of that same gold. The Lord had made their bitter water sweet in 15:25, but the Golden Calf would make their precious drinking water bitter in 32:20.[6] It doesn't matter how sincere we are about our visible aids to worship, they can all detract from the invisible God who wants to be seen through his idol-hating People. John Calvin observes that *"A true image of God is not to be found in all the world; and hence... His glory is defiled, and His truth corrupted by the lie, whenever He is set before our eyes in a visible form."*[7]

Making an image of the invisible God therefore actually *stops him from being seen through his People.* The Israelites had worshipped the Lord only a few weeks earlier at the Red Sea by singing, *"Who among the gods is like you, O Lord?"*[8]

---

the Voice of God (1996).

[6] Moses wanted their sin to turn their stomachs as it had the Lord's, but Deuteronomy 9:21 tells us that this water came from a stream flowing from Mount Sinai. Even God's judgment was mixed with covenant grace.

[7] John Calvin in his sixteenth-century commentary on Exodus 20:4–6.

[8] Exodus 15:11. Acts 7:40–42 tells us that image-making very quickly leads to out-and-out apostasy.

When they worshipped the Golden Calf, they answered their own question by comparing him favourably with the Egyptian bull-god Apis or one of the Canaanite idols. They worshipped a deformed image, and they found in verse 7 that very quickly their lifestyle became corrupted too. We become like what we worship,[9] so idolatry leads inexorably to immorality. They were soon *"running wild"* in sexual sin and became *"a laughing-stock to their enemies."*[10] The ones who had been called to make the invisible God visible to the nations were actually doing his reputation more harm than good. No wonder the Lord almost destroys the Israelites in this chapter, since their breaking his Second Commandment was a refusal to let him be seen through them properly at all.[11] He strikes them with a plague, despite having formerly protected them from the Ten Plagues in Egypt, because breaking the Second Commandment was every bit as serious as breaking the First.

By God's grace, he will listen to the desperate prayers of Moses, but for now let's stand back and consider the terrible message of this chapter. The Lord wants to be seen through his People as they worship him for the God he really is. If we chisel off his edges and try to repackage him as a God of our own making, we prevent ourselves and those around us from knowing God the Saviour or God the Indweller. This chapter calls us to burn and grind our man-made images to powder, so that the invisible God can be seen in all his glory through his People.

---

[9] Psalm 115:8; Romans 1:21–32. Sexual immorality was part and parcel of worshipping the Canaanite idols.

[10] The word *tsāhaq* in verse 6 simply means *to play*, but it is the same word that Moses used in Genesis 26:8 for Isaac fondling his wife. The word for *"running wild"* in verse 25 literally means *loose* (see Numbers 5:18). It is *perā'ōh*, deliberately similar to *pare'ōh*, meaning *Pharaoh*, as a hint that they were acting just like the Egyptians.

[11] Moses breaks the two tablets in verse 19 as a prophetic sign that in breaking the Second Commandment they had effectively broken the whole covenant.

Answer Back (32:11–14 & 33:12–17)

Then the Lord relented and did not bring on his people the disaster he had threatened.

(Exodus 32:14)

Some people will do anything to get famous. On 15th October 2009, the parents of six-year-old Falcon Heene made a frantic 911 call to Colorado State Police to report that their son was aboard a giant home-made helium balloon which had become untethered from its moorings at their house and was currently flying away at altitudes of over 7,000 feet. CNN cut away from coverage of President Obama addressing survivors of Hurricane Katrina, and for several hours the 2-million-dollar rescue operation dominated the news channels. Finally, the balloon landed, only for the Coastguard to discover the boy was not inside at all. When interviewed later that day on live TV, Falcon Heene admitted that *"We did this for the show."*[1] His parents were jailed for their high-profile hoax out of an insecure desire to become famous.

A day's coverage on CNN was nothing compared to the mouth-watering opportunity which the Lord offered Moses. The Hebrews' sin with the Golden Calf meant that he was not going to make his covenant with them at all, but would create a new nation out of Moses and his two sons through whom he would fulfil all his promises to Abraham. It was the chance of a lifetime to become a great patriarch, but Moses refused to chase fame at the expense of God's purposes for Israel. Numbers 12:3 tells us

---

[1] This was on CNN's *Larry King Live* on the evening of 15th October 2009.

that *"Moses was a very humble man, more humble than anyone else on the face of the whole earth,"* and his reaction to God's offer was the absolute opposite of Falcon Heene's family.[2] He stood his ground and answered back, which was precisely what God wanted him to do.[3]

Moses reminded the Lord of his *great purposes* for Israel. They are *"your people"*, he insists in 32:11 in response to the Lord's shocking statement in verse 7 that they are *"your people, whom you brought up out of Egypt"*. No, Moses insists, it wasn't me who brought them out of Egypt. It was you, so make sure you remember why you did it. You chose Israel because you want to be seen through your People, so show yourself by continuing to be God the Saviour even when they trample on your salvation.

Next, Moses reminded the Lord of his *great history* with Israel. They are *"your people, whom you brought out of Egypt with great power and a mighty hand"*. They were only at Mount Sinai at all because the Lord had appeared out of a burning bush on this very mountain, and had sent Moses to order Pharaoh to let his Hebrew slaves go in the name of their unseen God. The Lord turned Moses' staff into a snake, inflicted ten plagues on the Egyptians, drowned Pharaoh's army in the Red Sea, led the Hebrews with a pillar of cloud and fire, and provided them with manna each day and with water from the rock. It was therefore unthinkable that Israel's history should now end with 2 million corpses scattered around Sinai.

As a result of this, Moses continued in 32:12, the Lord's *great name* was now thoroughly intertwined with Israel's. If news filtered back to Egypt that the God who had defeated their idols ten–nil had then abandoned his People in the desert, any glory he had earned through the Exodus would be swallowed

---

[2] This comment must have been inserted by a later editor, like Genesis 14:14; 36:31; Exodus 1:11; 12:37; 16:35; Numbers 14:45.

[3] Moses' courage is all the more impressive in the light of having seen God's power and holiness first-hand. A priest would die even if he failed to wash correctly (30:20), but Moses loves Israel enough to answer back.

up by even greater shame. People would assume he was not strong enough to defeat the gods of Canaan and conquer the Promised Land. The Lord could not start afresh by making a new nation out of Moses' descendants. He had revealed himself as the Saviour-God of Israel. If he turned his back on them, Egypt would assume he was actually God the Traitor.

Besides, the Lord could not abandon Israel because of his *great promises* to the patriarchs. He had promised Abraham, Isaac and Jacob that he would make their descendants as numerous as the stars in the sky and would lead them to possess the Promised Land. He had even inspired Jacob to prophesy this over each of his twelve sons in Genesis 49. There simply was no option for him to wipe out every tribe except for one small family from Levi. Moses therefore drew courage to answer God back very firmly in 32:32: *"Please forgive their sin – but if not, then blot me out of the book that you have written."*[4] This was brinkmanship of the highest order, but Moses would genuinely rather die than become famous at the expense of the grumbling, rebellious Israelites God had called him to lead. He loved them and was willing to lay down his own life for them, and as he did so he triggered the wave of grace which he was looking for.

The Lord was very pleased that Moses refused his offer. He was delighted that Moses dared to answer him back in prayer. He loved the fact that he had not tried to argue that Israel deserved his mercy through any merit of their own, and he loved the fact he had laid down his life as an unsuspecting pointer to the Messiah who was to come. Now the Lord could do what he had wanted all along and forgive them. He always can when his People answer back and let him be seen through their prayers.

The Levites followed suit and slaughtered 3,000 of the worst offenders, providing a vivid picture of repentance which

---

[4] The idea of a *book* in which God writes the names of those he has chosen to save is also found in Malachi 3:16 and Revelation 17:8; 20:12–15.

draws the Lord's blessing, not rebuke.[5] The massacre sobers up the Israelites, and they come weeping and repenting in chapter 33 to receive the forgiveness Moses won them when he dared to answer back.[6] The Lord still loves it today when any of his People dare to stand up for the lost and plead for them in Jesus' name.

Perhaps Paul drew encouragement from this passage of Scripture when he wrote that *"I could wish that I myself were cursed and cut off from Christ for the sake of my brothers, those of my own race, the people of Israel."*[7] Ever wondered how Paul opened nation after nation to the Gospel, and planted church after church across the Roman Empire? He learned to plead with God like Moses, spurred on by the shocking truth of Exodus 32:14 that God *"relented"*, or literally *"changed his mind"*, in response to Moses' prayers.

There's more. Moses didn't just answer God back with a reminder to be seen as God the Saviour. He pressed on in 33:12–17 and reminded him to be seen as God the Indweller too. Did the Lord say in 33:3 that the promise of the Tabernacle was permanently on hold? Would his promise to place his postcode at the heart of Israel be a casualty of the Israelites' sin? Once again, Moses treated God's words as a willing invitation to answer him back in prayer. He demands of God in verse 16, *"How will anyone know that you are pleased with me and with your people unless you go with us? What else will distinguish me and your people from all the other people on the face of the earth?"* If God's plan was to be seen through his People, then his presence was non-

---

[5] Up until now, the Lord has not identified the tribe of Levi to serve at the Tabernacle, other than Aaron's small family within it. In fact, the only prophecy over Levi has been the negative one in Genesis 49:5–7. Now the Lord evidently sees in the Levites a zeal for his holiness which he can use (Luke 14:26).

[6] Since the Day of Pentecost celebrated the Lawgiving at Mount Sinai, the 3,000 who repented and were baptized in Acts 2:41 may be a gracious counterbalance to the 3,000 who were massacred here.

[7] Romans 9:3–4.

negotiable, for without it we are nothing. Again, the Lord was delighted by Moses' courageous faith and by this proof that he prized God's visibility as he should.

Moses rescued the Israelites from disaster, when fame and fortune beckoned, and the question God poses us is *will we do the same?* Will you look at the crowds of unsaved men and women in your town or city, and fall to your knees to plead with the Lord until he saves them? Will you look at the crowds of Christians who are unaware of his promises to fill them with his Spirit and pray until God fills them as he desires? The Lord is still as eager to save and to fill with his Spirit as he was in the days of Moses and of Paul. He is simply looking for people who will answer him back in prayer and remind him of his great purposes, his great history, his great name and his great promises.

Surprise, Surprise, Surprise (33:18–34:14)

Do not worship any other god, for the Lord, whose name is Jealous, is a jealous God.

(Exodus 34:14)

Exodus is full of surprises. If you were taken aback by Moses' boldness in prayer, you are going to love the verses which follow. They contain three surprises that shed light on the lessons we are meant to draw from what happened with the Golden Calf, and they are also a test of whether we have truly understood the message of Exodus. So brace yourself for three surprises, because God wants to make sure that you understand Exodus before he takes you into the final three books of the Pentateuch.

The first surprise is what Moses says at the end of his prayer for idolatrous Israel: *"Now show me your glory."* Take a step back for a moment. Israel's sin had been to demand a visible aid for their worship, so Moses' prayer is just about the last thing we might have expected him to say. The Lord prompted him to make this request, however, so that he could clarify what happened with the Golden Calf.

The problem was *not* that the Israelites wanted the Lord to be visible. God has spent the entire book of Exodus making himself visible through the Plagues, the Passover, the Red Sea, the six lessons in the desert, the Lawgiving and now through the Tabernacle too! The issue was that false images obscure what he is really like and make his People less like him, whereas a true glimpse of his glory transforms his People into those who make him seen.[1] Even as the Israelites excreted their powdered Golden Calf outside the camp where it belonged, the Lord was renewing his plan to be seen *by* his People and therefore to be seen *through* his People. He would reveal his true glory so powerfully to Moses that the Israelites would beg him to wear a veil at the end of chapter 34 to shield their hurting eyes from God's reflected glory.[2]

The second surprise is the Lord's response to Moses, when he tells him that he will cover him with his hand in the cleft of a rock because *"my face must not be seen."* Moses would only see his back after he had passed him by, because *"You cannot see my face, for no one may see me and live."* This is very surprising since we were told only a few verses earlier in 33:11 that *"The Lord would speak to Moses face to face, as a man speaks with his friend."* We were also told in 24:11 that Moses and the seventy-four other leaders *"saw God"*. So what is the Lord trying to clarify for us now?

He is telling us that what Moses saw at Mount Sinai is nothing compared to what we can see today. *"The Law was given through Moses; grace and truth came through Jesus Christ,"* John explains in his gospel. *"No-one has ever seen God, but God the One and Only, who is at the Father's side, has made him known."*[3] The Lord is warning us that nothing Moses saw can compare with what we can see right now in Jesus, who *"is the image of the invisible God... For God was pleased to have all his fullness dwell in him."*[4]

John progresses this thought further in one of his letters: *"No one has ever seen God, but if we love one another, **God lives**"*

---

[1] 1 John 3:2 tells us that seeing God as he really is always results in people becoming more like him.

[2] There is a play on words in the Hebrew of Exodus 34:29–35 since the word *qāran*, or *to be radiant*, means literally *to have horns*. The Israelites sinfully tried to make God visible through a horned Golden Calf, but the Lord made himself truly visible by "horning" one of his People.

[3] John 1:17–18.

[4] Colossians 1:15, 19.

in us...because he has given us of his Spirit."[5] Jesus didn't just make God visible for thirty-three years in Galilee and Judea. He ascended to heaven as the victorious King of kings and poured out the Holy Spirit so God the Indweller can be permanently visible through his People. *"It is for your good that I am going away. Unless I go away, the Counsellor will not come to you; but if I go, I will send him to you... In a little while **you will see me no more, and then after a little while you will see me**."*[6] Far from letting us hanker back to the days of the Exodus, or letting the Hebrews assume that the covenant at Sinai was his final word, the Lord surprises us this second time in order to teach us that Moses' beaming face was just a foretaste of something better. He does not want us to envy the bright face of Moses, because the New Covenant is *"more glorious"* and *"what was glorious has no glory now in comparison with the surpassing glory."*[7]

This leads to the third surprise, which is the name the Lord gives himself as he reveals himself to Moses in chapter 34. There was no surprise in 33:19 that he is *good, merciful* and *compassionate*. Nor is there any surprise in 34:6 that he is *compassionate, gracious, slow to anger, abounding in love and faithfulness, maintaining love to thousands* and *forgiving*. The surprise comes at the end of verse 14, when he tells us that *"The Lord, whose name is Jealous, is a jealous God."* The Hebrew word *qānā'*, meaning *to be jealous*, has been used so far in the Pentateuch to describe the wicked Philistines, frustrated Rachel and Joseph's murderous brothers, so it isn't a word we would have naturally associated with Yahweh.[8] Once again, he wants to clarify what happened with the Golden Calf.

When the Lord boomed out his Second Commandment in

[5] 1 John 4:12–13.

[6] John 16:7, 16. The context of verse 16 is Pentecost, not his Second Coming.

[7] 2 Corinthians 3:7–18.

[8] Genesis 26:14; 30:1; 37:11. Yet if we try to chisel away this aspect of God's character, we break the Second Commandment ourselves.

20:5, he did so with the statement that *"I, the Lord your God, am a jealous God."* He repeats the same words in the aftermath of Israel breaking that commandment, to reinforce that he burns with a jealous love for his People which far outstrips the love of any human husband for his wife. He was not angry with them because he hates them, but because he is lovingly committed to his covenant with his Bride. It was this love which refused to sweep their sin under the carpet, forcing them to drink their powdered idol as a direct parallel to the test for an adulterous wife in Numbers 5:11–31. The Lord who *"does not leave the guilty unpunished"* in verse 6 forgave them by making a way in verse 7 to be *"slow to anger...forgiving wickedness, rebellion and sin"*. We now know, looking back, that this way was the death of Jesus, the loving sacrifice of a jealous Bridegroom who is determined to save his Bride. Paul's command, *"Husbands, love your wives, just as Christ loved the church and gave himself up for her"*, clarifies what the Lord is saying through this third surprise.[9] The Lord had sacrificed his Son in order to forgive his adulterous People, and he would come to dwell among them as the Jealous God who saves.

So let's make sure that these surprises stop us looking back on Exodus as more exciting days than today. Through Jesus, God is more visible to us than to Moses and the Israelites, and he dwells in us through his Spirit far more closely than the Tabernacle builders dared to dream. The events of the Exodus were only the beginning of a far greater plan which culminated in Jesus Christ. Through Jesus, we can enjoy the fullness of the God who still wants to be seen through his People.

---

[9] Ephesians 5:25. This is why Moses' sacrifice in Exodus 32:32 secured the atonement he sought in 32:30.

Moving Day (40:1–38)

Then the cloud covered the Tent of Meeting, and the glory of the Lord filled the tabernacle.

(Exodus 40:34)

Question: What do *Dr. Strangelove*, *Butch Cassidy and the Sundance Kid*, *The Sixth Sense* and *The Usual Suspects* all have in common? Answer: They have all been voted "the best movie ending of all time". If the topic is just movies, then my vote goes to *The Usual Suspects*, but not if it also includes book endings as well. In that case, I'd be voting for the end of the book of Exodus every time, because it outclasses the very best of Kevin Spacey and Keyser Söze.

Technically, Moses didn't end the book of Exodus with chapter 40. In fact, he didn't end the book of Exodus at all. He wrote one long book, which was probably only divided into five distinct volumes by the translators of the Septuagint. Nevertheless, there is a shift in tone at the start of the book of Leviticus which makes this chapter the perfect ending for the story which has gone before. As the curtain falls on this part of Moses' drama, let's take a few moments to appreciate why.

First, the final verses of Exodus are the perfect conclusion to the book's introduction. In Exodus 1 the Hebrews felt abandoned and alone, hanging on to God's promise to the patriarchs that *"I will be with you and will bless you"*.[1] In the midst of slavery and infanticide, the Hebrews felt as though God had abandoned them as his People, but the message of Exodus is that he never will. He answered their prayers and delivered them from slavery so

---

[1] Genesis 21:22; 26:3, 24; 28:15; 31:3; 48:21.

that he could fulfil his promises to the patriarchs through them. *"I am the Lord their God, who brought them out of Egypt* **so that I might dwell among them**," he declared in 29:46, and these final verses express this with a loud crescendo as God at last does as he promised and descends on the finished Tabernacle. The same God who appeared centuries earlier to Abraham in the midst of *"thick and dreadful darkness"* using *"a smoking brazier with a blazing torch"* comes to dwell in Moses' Tabernacle in a thick cloud which blazes with the brilliance of his glory.[2] It is the ultimate conclusion to Exodus' message about God the Saviour and God the Indweller.

Second, the end of Exodus is the perfect conclusion to the crisis that dominated chapters 32–34. In the wake of Israel's sin with the Golden Calf, the Lord informed them that his plan to live among them was permanently on hold. The Tabernacle, so painstakingly described in chapters 25–31, would not in fact be necessary after all. *"I will not go with you, because you are a stiff-necked people and I might destroy you on the way."*[3] That's why chapters 35–39 are not an unnecessary repetition of what was already recorded in chapters 25–31. They are a grateful celebration that the Lord atoned for Israel's sin and renewed his plan to live among them. Because Moses answered back to God, the promise of the Tabernacle had been put back on the table. Fifteen times in chapters 39 and 40 alone, Moses emphasizes that they built the Tabernacle *"just as the Lord had commanded."*[4] He is full of excitement that God the Saviour and Indweller was coming to take up residence at the heart of the Israelite camp. These last verses of Exodus are a magnificent finale to the promise of the book that God will be seen through his People.

Third, the final verses of Exodus form the perfect cliff-hanger ending to whet our appetites for Leviticus. The third

---

[2] Genesis 15:12, 17.

[3] Exodus 33:1–3.

[4] Exodus 39:1, 5, 7, 26, 31, 42, 43; 40:16, 19, 21, 23, 25, 27, 29, 32.

book of the Pentateuch is perhaps the least read book of the Bible, because most people struggle to understand its theme. Like any good writer, therefore, the Lord ends Exodus with such high drama that the reader wants to carry on into Leviticus straight away. After so many long chapters about God the Indweller, the Lord finally does what he promised he would do. He exceeds even Moses' high expectations and begins the next theme in his drama.

We can tell from 39:43 that Moses was very impressed by what Bezalel, Oholiab and their team of skilful workers had managed to produce. The Tabernacle was a magnificent work of art and was perfectly in line with the blueprint the Lord had revealed to Moses on the mountain, yet even this Tabernacle proved very insufficient to house God's glory when he came. There is no room for Moses to enter in verse 35, and he is forced to wait outside until he is finally able to enter at the end of Leviticus 9. This ending reminds us that God is far greater than we realize, no matter what revelations we may have seen. God the Saviour delivered Israel because he wanted to reveal himself to them as God the Indweller, but the knock-on effect of part two of the drama is that the plot thickens further and launches another theme. When God the Indweller arrives on a campsite, everything around him must change. The dramatic end to Exodus therefore tells us that the Lord is God the Holy One, which will form the theme of the whole book of Leviticus. With God's presence on the inside of the Tabernacle and Moses waiting, confused, outside the door, the Lord hopes to capture our attention to prevent us from skim reading the vital message of Leviticus which is just about to begin.

For these three reasons, this final chapter is the perfect ending to the book of Exodus. It challenges us to respond to its message of God the Saviour and God the Indweller, and it encourages us to carry on reading to discover the message of God the Holy One too. Have you responded to Jesus, the true

Passover Lamb, and dealt ruthlessly with the "yeast" of your old life? Have you applied the six lessons which God taught us on the desert road from Egypt to Mount Sinai? Have you responded to the Lord as he really is in all his glory, instead of trying to chisel him into a god of your own making? Have you asked him to dwell inside you through the Holy Spirit in the New Covenant fulfilment of what happens in Exodus 40?

If you have, then you have grasped the first two reasons why the ending to Exodus beats *The Usual Suspects* hands down. You need to let this finale build your excitement for Leviticus so that its under-charted waters can lead you further into God. He still wants to be seen through his People, as their Saviour, their Indweller and their Holy One today.

So let's stand next to Moses on the outside of the Tabernacle and let's wait in expectation for what Leviticus has to say.

Leviticus:

God the Holy One

There Will Be Blood (1:1–7:38)

*The Lord called to Moses and spoke to him from the
Tent of Meeting.*

(Leviticus 1:1)

Nobody was more surprised by the ending of Exodus than
Moses himself. We can look back and see that it formed the
perfect ending, but at the time it must have felt like a terribly
confusing anticlimax. God the Saviour had brought the Israelites
to Mount Sinai as he had promised, and had commissioned a
Tabernacle to make himself visible as God the Indweller. Yet
on the day when Moses dedicated the completed Tabernacle,
neither Moses nor the priests could enter inside because it
was too full of the Lord's glory. Leviticus therefore begins with
a statement which Moses had not expected. Instead of God
speaking to him face to face as before in Moses' makeshift Tent
of Meeting in Exodus 33:7–11, we read that *"The Lord called
to Moses and spoke to him **from** the Tent of Meeting."* Moses
was shut outside the tent, longing to go in. Make sure you don't
miss the confusion in his tone as he begins the third book of
the Pentateuch.

Many modern-day readers find Leviticus so confusing
that they give up on reading it altogether. Others persevere
but whizz through its twenty-seven chapters in search of the
easier narrative which begins again in Numbers. Although we
will move faster through Leviticus than the other books of
Moses, I want to encourage you that this book deserves your
fullest attention. It is quoted at least sixteen times in the New

Testament, which is twice as often as all the history books from Joshua to 2 Chronicles put together. What's more, 90 per cent of the book is a quotation of God's direct speech to his People. That's a bigger percentage than any other book in the Bible, and a warning that these chapters have some vital things to say. We must take Paul seriously when he tells us that *"all Scripture is God-breathed and is useful for teaching, rebuking, correcting and training in righteousness, so that the man of God may be thoroughly equipped for every good work."*[1] The book of Leviticus builds on the message of Exodus by explaining that the Lord is also God the Holy One. He wants to be seen through the holiness of his People, and he expects us to study these pages very carefully.

The Lord had become a permanent resident on Israel's campsite, and that meant the neighbourhood could never be the same again. Moses wrote the book of Leviticus in four weeks at the Tabernacle at Mount Sinai,[2] and he intends his detailed stipulations to reinforce to his readers that God the Holy One is not like us. If Moses had to receive the first nine chapters by listening to the Lord calling out to him from inside the Tent of Meeting, only finally being allowed to step inside in 9:23, we must all accept that we need to change in response to this revelation of the Lord as God the Indweller.

That's why the first seven chapters of Leviticus emphasize that blood must be shed on God's altar whenever sinful humans want to fellowship with God.[3] *"I am Yahweh your God; consecrate yourselves and be holy, because I am holy,"* he will

---

[1] 2 Timothy 3:16–17.

[2] Exodus 40:17 tells us that Leviticus began on the first day of the first month, and Numbers 1:1 tells us that it ended on the first day of the second month. Although many English translations refer to God speaking these things to Moses *on* Mount Sinai in Leviticus 7:38, 25:1, 26:46 and 27:34, Moses tells us in 1:1 that we are to translate the Hebrew preposition *b'* in those verses as *by* Mount Sinai – that is at the Tabernacle.

[3] In fact, he told the Hebrews never to come into his presence empty-handed in Exodus 23:15 and 34:20.

warn us in 11:44. He begins his invitation to experience him as God the Holy One by listing five different types of sacrifice which are necessary to do so.

First there are three different types of "thank-you" offering, which express our gratitude that we can even come into God's presence at all. The *burnt offering* in chapter 1 was the voluntary blood sacrifice of an unblemished bull or ram or bird. It atoned for unintentional sin and was completely burnt up on the altar as *"an aroma pleasing to the Lord"*.[4] The *grain offering* in chapter 2 was the only bloodless sacrifice listed, but it was usually offered alongside a blood sacrifice as a grateful promise of devotion for what he had done.[5] The *fellowship offering* in chapter 3 was a voluntary peace offering to celebrate the fact that the Lord has welcomed us as his friends. Instead of burning the meat of the unblemished sacrifice, the worshipper ate it in the Lord's presence along with the priests as a kind of "dinner with God".[6]

Next the Lord lists the two different types of "sorry" offering, which were the reason why the "thank-you" offerings were possible at all. The *sin offering* in 4:1–5:13 was mandatory to atone for specific, unintentional sin. It involved confession of sin and ceremonial cleansing through the blood of a bull or goat or lamb or pigeon, depending on how much the worshipper could afford. Anything not eaten or burnt at the Tabernacle

---

[4] Further guidelines for the burnt offering are also found in 6:8–13, 8:18–21 and 16:24. The Lord adds in Numbers 15:1–12 that it must always be offered with flour mixed with oil and a drink offering of wine – all pictures of the body and blood of Jesus, applied through the Holy Spirit. These sacrifices must be *"without defect"* on the outside and their inner parts must be washed, to speak of Jesus' perfection inside and out.

[5] Further guidelines for the grain offering are in 6:14–23. It was never offered with *yeast* or *honey*, since these spoke of corruption and fleshly works. God wants our devotion out of gratitude, not out of a misguided attempt to pay him back for his sacrifice through works of our own.

[6] Further guidelines for the fellowship offering are in 7:11–34 and 19:5–8. Like the burnt offering, Numbers 15:1–12 tells us that it was always offered with flour mixed with oil and a drink offering of wine.

was taken outside the camp to be burnt as a sign that the worshipper's sin had been taken away. It pointed to the true and better Lamb of God, who would suffer *"outside the city gate to make the people holy through his own blood"*.[7] The *guilt offering* in 5:14–6:7 was also a mandatory blood sacrifice to atone for unintentional sin, but it particularly dealt with wrong committed against neighbours and involved making restitution and offering compensation to those wronged.[8] Forgiveness from God did not instantly solve the relational damage that sin causes, so God helped the Israelites to be reconciled to one another, because he did not just want to be seen through holy persons, but through the unity of his holy People.[9]

Most modern readers find these seven chapters laborious, and that's exactly how God wants us to find them. This book is called "Leviticus", meaning *"things relating to the Levites"*, because the tribe of Levi demonstrated such passion for God's holiness in the aftermath of the Golden Calf in Exodus 32:25–29. Before then, the Lord had only commissioned Aaron's family, but he was so delighted with the Levites' passion for his holiness that he singled them out as his own special tribe from 38:21 onwards. He wants you to study these chapters until they give you a similar passion for his holiness too.

The Levites had learned that blood needed to be shed and that repentance was necessary before entering the presence of God. Let's take time to learn with them that the Lord is passionate about raising up holy men and women who reflect his glory. These sacrifices are fulfilled in Jesus Christ, but the

---

[7] Hebrews 13:11–13. Further guidelines for the sin offering are in 6:24–30; 8:14–17; 10:17; 16:3–22.

[8] Further guidelines for the guilt offering are in 7:1–7. Although there is no blood sacrifice in these seven chapters for *intentional* sin, the Lord extends hope to those who sin intentionally in 19:20–22.

[9] Those who truly understand the Gospel offer even more than 20 per cent restitution. See Zacchaeus in Luke 19:8–9.

underlying message has not gone away. God the Holy One still wants to be seen through his People.[10]

---

[10] Leviticus 4:13 should stir us to make the Lord visible to our neighbours and to unreached people groups. Ignorance of the Gospel does not mean they are innocent. Their only hope is to see God through us.

Burnt Up on Entry
(8:1–10:20)

*Aaron's sons Nadab and Abihu took their censers,
put fire in them and added incense; and they offered
unauthorized fire before the Lord, contrary to his
command. So fire came out from the presence of the
Lord and consumed them, and they died before the
Lord.*

(Leviticus 10:1–2)

A little thing can make a massive difference. On 16th January 2003, a small piece of foam insulation broke off the wing of the Space Shuttle Columbia as it launched into space, and punched a tiny nine-inch hole in the layer of thermal protection that surrounded its left wing. Mission Control were not too concerned, and gave the go-ahead two weeks later on 1st February for the shuttle to commence its re-entry. That would mean temperatures of over 1,500°C, but a fully shielded Columbia had re-entered the earth's atmosphere successfully twenty-seven times before. Like Nadab and Abihu in Leviticus 10, they underestimated the importance of an intact thermal shield. There was a series of bright flashes, then smoke in the clear Texas sky. The Space Shuttle Columbia had been destroyed with no survivors.

Nadab and Abihu were more privileged than any astronaut. They had been chosen by God, along with their father and two younger brothers, to enter the Tabernacle on behalf of their nation. They underestimated the fiery holiness of God's presence and how much they needed the Gospel shield he had provided. As a result, they were burnt up on entry.

It wasn't as if the Lord hadn't warned them it would happen. In chapter 8 they obeyed the commands of Exodus 29 perfectly. They were ordained as priests exactly as God had directed, with special robes, ceremonial washing, blood sacrifices, sprinkling with blood and anointing with oil.[1] 8:35 tells us all this was necessary *"so you will not die"*, and so was waiting for seven days in sober meditation at the entrance to the Tabernacle. On the eighth day they offered sin offerings, burnt offerings, grain offerings and fellowship offerings, and were warned yet again to obey God completely, *"so that the glory of the Lord may appear to you."*[2] As they watched their father, one-time maker of the Golden Calf, sacrificing a bull calf in verse 2, they should have marvelled at the depth of God's grace towards their family. Instead, they took it as a reason to treat his holiness lightly.

Finally, after nine long chapters, Moses and Aaron stepped into the Tabernacle. Would they see God and be permitted to live? The Hebrews cheered when they saw them emerge unscathed to bless them. Moses excitedly describes the moment when: *"The glory of the Lord appeared to all the people. Fire came out from the presence of the Lord and consumed the burnt offering and the fat portions on the altar. And when all the people saw it, they shouted for joy and fell face down."*

Now it was Nadab and Abihu's turn. They had seen the Lord on Mount Sinai back in Exodus 24:9–11. They had just watched fire shoot out thirty metres from the Tabernacle to the altar. They had heard the Lord's command in 6:9–13 not to let this God-given fire go out because man-made fire could

---

[1] Not only does Leviticus 8 strongly echo Exodus 29, but Moses also emphasizes twelve times that they obeyed the Lord's commands meticulously (verses 4, 5, 9, 13, 17, 21, 29, 31, 34, 35 (twice), 36).

[2] Leviticus 9:6. Moses emphasizes six more times in chapter 9 that they must obey the Lord to the letter (verses 5, 6, 7, 10, 16, 21).

never produce the holiness necessary to approach God.[3] Yet tragically, they let the Lord's grace in the past cause them to trifle with his holiness in the present. In contrast to eighteen statements in chapters 8 and 9 that they completely obeyed God, Moses tells us with horror at the start of chapter 10 that *"Nadab and Abihu took their censers, put fire in them and added incense; and they offered **unauthorized fire** before the Lord, **contrary to his command**. So fire came out from the presence of the Lord and consumed them, and they died before the Lord."* Nadab and Abihu had neglected God's Gospel shield, and as a result they were burnt up on entry.

Some readers struggle with stories like this one. Just yesterday, someone complained to me that the God of the Old Testament comes across as far too angry. Their assumption was that God had mellowed with age in the New Testament, yet the Lord says *"I am Yahweh, I change not. **Because of this**, you sons of Jacob are not destroyed."*[4] Hebrews 12:29 quotes from Deuteronomy 4:24 to insist that even under the New Covenant, *"the Lord your God is a consuming fire, a jealous God"*.

Leviticus warns us not to forget that God is holy and humans are not. If even a shuttle entering the earth's atmosphere encounters heat of 1,500°C, is this fiery tragedy really so out of place for two people sauntering into the Lord's holy atmosphere? We make a mistake if we assume that he has turned down the heat of his holiness, and if we ignore the sacrificial blood which was given as a thermal shield in this passage. Nadab and Abihu were to take the blood which spoke of Jesus' better blood to come. They were to mix it with some of the fire that had burst out from the Lord's presence between the cherubim on the lid of the Ark of the Covenant, as a picture of what Peter described in Acts 4:12 when he preached that *"Salvation is found in no one else, for there is no other name under heaven **given** to men*

---

[3] This is also why they were banned from using man-made tools on God's altar in Exodus 20:25.

[4] Malachi 3:6 (Green's Literal Translation).

by which we must be saved."[5] Like many Christians, Nadab and Abihu treated the message of the first nine chapters of Leviticus as if it were irrelevant. Their cindered remains are proof that it is not.

Mission Control in Houston learned that neglecting a puncture not much bigger than a baseball in the Space Shuttle Columbia's thermal shield was fatal. The Israelites learned that neglecting the Gospel shield is fatal too. Aaron and his two surviving sons, Eleazar and Ithamar, took Moses' words to heart in verse 3 that *"Among those who approach me I will show myself holy; in the sight of all the people I will be honoured."* They renewed their commitment to meticulous obedience,[6] and reprised these ancient pictures of *"Jesus, who rescues us from the coming wrath".*[7]

So let's learn from this passage that God's holiness has not changed, and that God the Indweller is still God the Holy One who burns with anger against sin. Let's praise him for the shield of atonement which he gives us in Jesus' blood through the Gospel. Let's remember that he wants to be seen through us grasping what he means when he warns us that *"in the sight of all the people I will be honoured".*

But most of all, let's praise the Lord that we can be a forgiven Aaron instead of a charred, complacent Nadab or Abihu. If we embrace the thermal shield of the Gospel then, through Jesus, we are saved from being burnt up on entry.

---

[5] Leviticus 16:12 tells us that the fire on the golden altar of incense had to be taken from the bronze altar of blood sacrifice. This is also why sacrifices could only ever be offered at the Tabernacle's bronze altar in 17:1–9.

[6] Moses stressed total obedience eighteen times in chapters 8 and 9, and he does so five times more in 10:7, 11, 13, 15, 18–20. Since Nadab and Abihu died childless (Numbers 3:4), every priest was a child of Eleazar or Ithamar.

[7] 1 Thessalonians 1:10.

The Boundary Breaker
(11:1–15:33 & 18:1–20:27)

I am the Lord who brought you up out of Egypt to be
your God; therefore be holy, because I am holy.

(Leviticus 11:45)

My mother-in-law was in her front garden when it happened. A 1,400-pound intruder broke into her house. A cow had squeezed through a hole in the fence between its field and her garden, stopped briefly to graze on the contents of her flowerbeds and entered her living room through the open patio doors. It was bleeding heavily from the barbed-wire fence and was disorientated by the feel of deep-pile carpet under its hooves. It went on the rampage, smearing blood on the carpets, the curtains and the upholstery. My mother-in-law and her insurance agent were about to discover that when fences are broken and boundaries disregarded, it tends to result in great damage and loss. That's also the message of the long middle section of Leviticus.

Most modern readers find these eight chapters boring, perhaps the least exciting verses in the Bible. Let's stop for a moment, therefore, to consider the fact that each one of them begins with the words *"The Lord said to Moses"*. Skipping over these verses can prove as short-sighted as my mother-in-law leaving her patio doors open. In these chapters God the Holy One sets up fences and boundaries to make his holiness visible to the nations. *"I am the Lord who brought you up out of Egypt to be your God,"* he reminds Israel in 11:45. *"Therefore be holy, because I am holy."*

First the Lord builds fences between the "field" and the "garden" to safeguard the purity of the Hebrew nation. Together with their sister words, Leviticus uses *tāhōr* and *tāmē'* – Hebrew for *clean* and *unclean* – 146 and 76 times. God told Aaron and his two surviving sons in 10:10 that *"You must distinguish... between the unclean and the clean, and you must teach the Israelites."* These middle chapters are the detail of what "clean" and "unclean" meant in practice.

The Lord builds a fence using meat in chapter 11, by forbidding the Israelites from eating animals such as those which rolled in the mud or fed on carrion. He builds more fences using their bodies in chapters 12–15, by telling them that periods, childbirth, discharges, skin disease and ejaculating semen all made them ceremonially unclean.[1] Since the Hebrew word for *skin disease* was also used for *mildew*, he builds more fences using their clothes and houses – any visible object which could demonstrate the holiness of their God.[2] They must shine as God's pure "garden" surrounded by dirty Gentile "fields". The Lord still places the same calling on his People: *"Among you there must not be even a hint of sexual immorality, or any kind of impurity, or of greed, because these are improper for God's holy people."*[3]

But the Lord has not finished. He has three categories, not two. He is purer than even the very purest things in creation. So together with its sister words, he uses the word *qōdesh* 121 times in Leviticus, meaning *holy* or *in a league of its own*. The other half of his command to Aaron and his sons in 10:10 is *"You must distinguish between the holy and the common"*. A garden is much

---

[1] By commanding in 15:18 that worshippers abstain from sex on any day that they came to the Tabernacle, the Lord also broke the link between sexual sin and worship which dominated Canaanite religion.

[2] Jesus clarifies in Matthew 15:1–20 and Mark 7:1–23 that some of these fences were just for BC Israel. What matters under the New Covenant is the outward expression of a pure and holy heart.

[3] Ephesians 5:3.

tidier and cleaner than a field, but a living room is something of a different order altogether. Therefore the Israelites must demonstrate through their everyday lifestyle that, when it came to approaching Yahweh, clean simply wasn't good enough. Seven times in these eight chapters, the Lord instructs the Israelites to *"Be holy, because I am holy."*[4]

The Devil hates the message of these chapters and is only too pleased if we assume they are not for us. He has been boundary breaking from the very beginning and is every bit as destructive as my mother-in-law's cow.[5] He lusts to break through the fence between the "field" and the "garden" in order to pollute the purity of God's People. He does so in chapters 18–20 using fence-cutters such as sexual sin, dishonouring parents, perverted religion, occultism, injustice, deceit and much, much more. Furthermore, nineteen times in Leviticus the Lord uses the word *hālal*, meaning *to profane*, as a warning that the Devil wants to make it past the "garden" to get his hooves on the "living room" carpet. Satan wants to stop the Lord being visible by muddying our holiness so that the nations reject a false image of God on the assumption that some of the filth on our upholstery is an accurate reflection of what he is really like.[6] These eight chapters are far from boring; they describe the battlefield on which God's People fight to make his holiness visible to all.

They also point forwards to a day when the Lord would respond to Satan's rampage by sending a boundary breaker of his own. He would send Jesus the Messiah to rebuild the sagging fence which separates the clean and the unclean, because he is the *"one who is holy, blameless, pure, set apart from sinners"*.[7] Jesus would also reset the boundary between the clean and

---

[4] Leviticus 11:44, 45; 19:2; 20:7, 26; 21:6 (twice). See also 1 Peter 1:14–16.

[5] The command of Deuteronomy 19:14 and 27:17 was about holiness as well as theft.

[6] This is why God treats these sins so seriously, punishing some of them with banishment or death.

[7] Hebrews 7:26.

the holy, rebuking those who hailed him as nothing more than a good human teacher with the question: *"Why do you call me good? No one is [truly] good – except God alone."*[8]

Then, having restored the boundaries between the "field", the "garden" and the "living room", he would go on a boundary-breaking counter-attack of his own. That's why these eight chapters are divided by chapters 16 and 17, which prophesy that through Jesus' death and resurrection filth would not conquer any more. When Jesus touched lepers, infection worked the other way around. Instead of becoming unclean, he ordered them to *"Be clean!"* and sent them running to the priests to announce these chapters had been fulfilled.[9] As he died on the cross, crying out that his work was finished, God tore from top to bottom the thick curtain which fenced off the Most Holy Place, as a proclamation that this message must not be ignored.[10]

So don't imagine that these chapters are not meant for you today. They warn us against Satan the boundary breaker and declare that, in Jesus, God's holiness breaks boundaries the other way. They speak of Jesus who *"loved the church and gave himself up for her to make her holy, cleansing her…without stain or wrinkle or any other blemish, but holy and blameless."*[11] Now God calls us, like the Israelites, to make his holiness visible to the world so that they can come near too. If we are holy because he is holy, no boundary can stand in his way.

---

[8] Mark 10:18.

[9] Luke 5:12–14; 17:12–19. Jesus sent lepers to the priests as a testimony to them that the Temple types had been fulfilled.

[10] Mark 15:38; Hebrews 10:19–22.

[11] Ephesians 5:25–27.

Two Goats (16:1–17:16)

Then he is to take the two goats and present them before the Lord at the entrance to the Tent of Meeting.

(Leviticus 16:7)

Chapters 16 and 17 are the glorious centrepiece of God's teaching in chapters 10–20 about the unclean, the clean and the holy. Moses could have saved these instructions about *Yom Kippur*, the Day of Atonement, for when he mentions it later alongside the other Hebrew feasts in chapter 23. He deliberately inserts them here to describe how God the Holy One can legitimately act as a reverse boundary breaker, and to clarify the full scope of what his boundary breaking means. Jesus would perform the work of two goats, not just one, through his death and resurrection, and Moses wants to make sure that the Israelites see a rounded Gospel picture. The Messiah would not only cleanse God's People from the *guilt* of sin, but also from its *shame*.

Many Christians talk a lot about Jesus as God's sin offering, but are in danger of forgetting there was a second goat at Yom Kippur. They concentrate on the guilt Adam incurred when he ate the forbidden fruit, but talk little about the shame which caused him to hide in the bushes when he did. They focus on Noah's guilt when he got drunk and passed out naked after the Flood, but ignore the shame which that sin also brought on his family when his youngest son called his brothers to come and have a laugh at naked Dad.[1] The Lord inserts these two chapters in the middle of Leviticus 11–20 because a half-gospel simply isn't all the Good News we need to hear.

Take, for example, the Christian young woman who wept as she described the night she had given her virginity to her boyfriend. Although it happened many years before, she cried tormented tears as she offloaded her story. She had been wracked by a sense of guilt but knew she could be forgiven. What had crippled her and driven her from God was the surprise arrival of guilt's evil twin brother, shame. *"I went into the bathroom and vomited all night,"* she sobbed. *"I knew I couldn't go back to church or tell any of my Christian friends. I've spent years away from God in the spiritual wilderness, paralysed by a suffocating blanket of shame."* The half-gospel she had heard drove her away from Jesus when she needed him most. She didn't know he was also the second goat at Yom Kippur, and that when he paid the price for sin's guilt he also bore away its shame.

For 364 days of the year, Aaron and the high priests of Israel were kept at arm's length in the Holy Place, the outer room of the Tabernacle. Only on one day in September, the Day of Atonement, were they permitted to push back the final curtain and step into the Most Holy Place. They knew better than to go the way of Nadab and Abihu by barging into the room where the Lord sat enthroned between the cherubim on the lid of the Ark of the Covenant.[2] Even on the Day of Atonement, they first filled it with smoking incense to avoid a fatal glance in God's direction, and they sprinkled the blood of a bull and the first goat on the lid of the Ark, known as the "atonement cover" for this reason. Having dealt with Israel's guilt through the blood of the first goat as a sin offering, the high priest emerged trembling

---

[1] Genesis 3:7–9; 9:20–27.

[2] Exodus 25:22; Numbers 7:89; 2 Samuel 6:2; Psalm 99:1.

from the Most Holy Place to declare to Israel that their sin had been atoned for.[3]

But the high priest's work was not over. There was a second goat too. He then laid his hands on the second goat's head and confessed over it the wickedness of those who had been forgiven but still felt ashamed. Only after one of his assistants had taken the second goat out into the wilderness, to wander as a pitiful reject until it died, could he then take off his clothes as a sign that he had fully preached the Gospel. Only then could the Lord tell the People in 16:30 that they were clean from all their sins. The message of Yom Kippur was more than the statement in 17:11 that *"the life of a creature is in the blood, and I have given it to you to make atonement for yourselves on the altar"*. It was also the promise that the Messiah would not be crucified in the courtyard of the Temple to deal with guilt in fulfilment of the first goat alone. He would be crucified outside the city walls in fulfilment of the second goat which bore away the People's shame.

Read the gospel accounts of Jesus' execution in this light, and you will find them jam-packed with detail which show he dealt with all our shame. His closest friends rejected him, the priests spat on him, the Roman soldiers stripped him, the Jewish nation rejected him and the crowds preferred a detested murderer to him. When the priests punched and slapped him in the face, they unwittingly laid their hands on him in fulfilment of the second goat in Leviticus 16. When they forced him to carry his cross outside the city gates to Calvary they fulfilled verse 22, which commanded that *"The goat will carry on itself all their sins to a solitary place"*. He went out so pitifully that the women of Jerusalem wept for him, and when he was crucified like the vilest of criminals, even one of his fellow victims cursed and jeered him as he died. The New Testament links this to the

---

[3] Moses emphasizes the priests' sense of fear at entering God's presence by returning to the repeated theme of chapters 8–10 in 16:34. Yet again, *"it was done, as the Lord commanded Moses."*

picture of the scapegoat in Leviticus 16, when it tells us that he *"suffered outside the city gate to make the people holy through his own blood. Let us, then, go to him outside the camp, bearing the disgrace he bore."*[4]

Can you see now why the Lord places his description of the Day of Atonement at the heart of eight chapters about the unclean, the clean and the holy? He does not want Christians to spend years in the spiritual wilderness because they have only heard half the Gospel of Jesus Christ. He wants to warn us not to run away from him into the wilderness, because he has already gone into the wilderness for us! If the girl who was wracked by the shame of her past sexual sin could find faith to return home when she heard about the second goat, then God can do more than forgive your own guilt too. He can also deliver you from a residual sense of shame.

What is more, if you have been the innocent victim of another person's sin, God wants to use these two chapters to cleanse the pollution of your past. Jesus did not merely bear the world's guilt like the first goat so those who sinned against you can be forgiven. He also bore the world's shame like the second goat as the ultimate innocent Victim. The holy God has made a way to cleanse you from the heavy sense of shame which so many innocent victims feel.[5] Through the second goat which died a lonely and isolated death in the wilderness, he wants to call you out of your own wilderness and bring the hurting victim home.

---

[4] Hebrews 13:12–13. Matthew 27:32 and John 19:17 also tell us that Jesus was led *out*. The Hebrew word *'azaz'el* meant literally the *going-away-goat*, conveyed in English by *scapegoat* which is short for *escape-goat*.

[5] He also gives specific assurance to rape victims in Deuteronomy 22:26 that they are innocent of sin.

Yahweh M'Qaddesh (21:1–22:33)

I must be acknowledged as holy by the Israelites. I am the Lord, who makes you holy and who brought you out of Egypt to be your God. I am the Lord.

(Leviticus 22:32–33)

Exodus is the story of God coming to live with his People. Leviticus, in contrast, is the story of God teaching his People how to live with him. To do that they needed to learn how to be holy, so God teaches the priests in chapters 21 and 22. Unless they understood that he was *Yahweh M'Qaddesh*, they were in danger of teaching Israel to act like Simon Curtis.

When Simon Curtis appeared on the British TV quiz show *Mastermind*, he looked a very promising contestant. He had recently won a quarter of a million pounds on another TV quiz show, *Who Wants to Be a Millionaire?* When he took his place in the famous black leather armchair and announced that his specialist subject was "the films of Jim Carrey", no one expected the two minutes of utter humiliation which followed. He passed on twelve questions, gave the wrong answer to four more and only scored one correct answer on his "specialist subject". It was the lowest first-round score in the thirty-four-year history of *Mastermind* and the following morning's papers ran the headline *Dumb, Dumber, Dumbest*. Simon Curtis admitted he had vastly overestimated his knowledge of Jim Carrey, and joked that his next quiz show should be *The Weakest Link*.[1]

---

[1] *"Dumb, Dumber, Dumbest"* ran in the British newspaper *The Independent* on 19th October 2006.

The Israelites must not misunderstand the message of Leviticus, as if God were calling them to make holiness their specialist subject. When God told them in 18:5 to *"Keep my decrees and laws, for the man who obeys them will live by them"*, they must not think that he was telling them to work hard at holiness in order to make him visible. They must carry on reading to the key verse in 19:18 and grasp that no one could ever *"Love your neighbour as yourself"* by sheer willpower alone.[2] The message of Leviticus was that they needed to be holy, but that holiness was the Lord's specialist subject, not their own.

Having just read the whole of chapters 11–20, hopefully you have already got the message. Almost 350 verses of detailed legislation were intended to convince the Israelites that God's holiness lay far beyond their fallen reach. He did not justify them through blood sacrifice, *declaring* them legally righteous, in order to send them away with a call to self-improvement. He promised to sanctify them through those same blood sacrifices too, *making* them righteous in day-to-day experience. God the Holy One is so determined to be seen through his holy People that he tells us six times in chapters 20–22 that his name is *Yahweh M'Qaddesh*, which means *The Lord Who Sanctifies.*[3] We must not try to pretend that holiness can ever be our own specialist subject. Our only hope is to be transformed by faith in *The Lord Who Makes Us Holy*.

Here's the temptation which every believer faces, and which prompted the Lord to state this name six times in these two chapters: even after we have responded to the Gospel and been justified through Jesus as the fulfilment of chapters 1–7, been protected from God's righteous anger through Jesus as the

---

[2] The New Testament treats this as a half-summary of the whole Law in Matthew 22:39; Mark 12:31; Luke 10:27; Galatians 5:14; Romans 13:9 and James 2:8.

[3] Leviticus 20:8; 21:8, 15; 22:9, 16, 32. Since seven is the biblical number of perfection, the Lord also revealed himself by this name on an additional occasion in Exodus 31:13.

fulfilment of chapters 8–10, and been delivered from sin's guilt and shame through Jesus as the fulfilment of chapters 16–17, we still find that our spiritual pride tries to persuade us that it is time to show that we're deserving of his sacrifice. We reason that *"God has poured out so much grace on my life that I must try to make it up to him. I'll make a list of resolutions which makes Leviticus 10–20 look easy. I'm going to get holy and I'm going to make God visible. After all the grace he's given me, it's the least I can do in return."* We fall into the same trap as the Galatian Christians who were so like Simon Curtis that Paul challenged them, *"Are you so foolish? After beginning with the Spirit, are you now trying to attain your goal by human effort?"*[4]

The fact is, human resolutions are simply not strong enough to make us holy. They may result in a few short-lived signs of progress, but Paul warns that eventually, *"Do not handle! Do not taste! Do not touch!...are all destined to perish with use, because they are based on human commands and teachings. Such regulations indeed have an appearance of wisdom, with their self-imposed worship, their false humility and their harsh treatment of the body, but they lack any value in restraining sensual indulgence."*[5] That's why six times in Leviticus 21 and 22 God tells the priests, who were called to teach Israel how to be holy, that his name is *Yahweh M'Qaddesh* and that their name is not. God the Holy One wants to be seen through his holy People, so he personally commits to making them holy. He tells them to stay at the altar where they were justified by grace through faith, and to receive more grace just like it in order to be sanctified through faith as well.

This Passover generation already knew that blood brought not just forgiveness, but also *freedom*. They could laugh at the claim of their old Egyptian masters that they needed to work for them any more. Jesus warned spiritual Simon Curtises

---

[4] Galatians 3:3.

[5] Colossians 2:21–23. This was as much an issue in Colosse as Galatia.

that *"Everyone who sins is a slave to sin"*, but promised that *"If the Son sets you free, you will be free indeed"*. That's why Paul encourages us that *"The grace of God that brings salvation… teaches us to say 'No' to ungodliness and worldly passions, and to live self-controlled, upright and godly lives in this present age."*[6] Holy living is unattainable for any fallen human being but it was well within the reach of the holy Son of God, as he rejected the man-made rules of the Pharisees yet fulfilled to the letter every true command in the Pentateuch.[7]

Here's how it works: we come to the cross of Jesus, admitting our sin and our powerlessness to break free from its clutches. We confess by faith that we have died and been raised to new life with Jesus, and that therefore our old self has been dealt a fatal blow. We then ask the Lord to apply this truth to our lives through his Holy Spirit by coming and dwelling inside us in resurrection power. We stop acting like Simon Curtis and pretending that holiness can become our specialist subject, and we call on *Yahweh M'Qaddesh* to make us holy as he has promised.[8]

When we do so, the Lord rephrases the command of 18:5. No longer does it read for us, *"Keep my decrees and laws, for the man who obeys them will live by them."* Instead, through the Gospel which God unpacked for the priests in Leviticus 21 and 22, it becomes *"You will be able to keep my decrees and laws, for the Man who has obeyed them will set you free to live by them."*[9]

---

[6] John 8:34–36; Titus 2:11–12.

[7] Matthew 5:17. Jesus perfectly obeyed Moses' Law in Matthew 8:4; 17:24–27; 18:16 and 26:59–60, yet those who accused him of lawbreaking in Mark 14:63 broke the command of Leviticus 21:10 even as they did so!

[8] Colossians 2:20–3:10; Romans 6:2–14.

[9] This summarizes Paul's teaching when he quotes Leviticus 18:5 in Romans 10:1–10 and Galatians 3:10–14.

Mementoes (23:1–44)

Speak to the Israelites and say to them: "These are my appointed feasts, the appointed feasts of the Lord, which you are to proclaim as sacred assemblies."

(Leviticus 23:2)

In the movie *Memento*, Guy Pearce's character is worried he will forget. He is suffering from amnesia caused by an attack on his family in which his wife died, and he is determined not to let it stop him finding her killer. He writes notes, takes Polaroid photos and tattoos messages for himself all over his body in a desperate attempt to overcome his amnesia. He must never forget the death of his beloved, or any of the clues which help make sense of why she died.[1]

The Lord was under no illusions about the Israelites. He knew that they suffered from spiritual amnesia too. How could he ensure they would not forget the Gospel which he shared with them again and again throughout the Pentateuch? He decided to do so by giving them the feasts that he lists for us here in Leviticus 23.

He gave them the *Sabbath* in verse 3, as already emphasized in Exodus 16 and in the Fourth Commandment in Exodus 20. He told the Israelites to down their tools in order to rest and gather together for worship on the last day of every week. It would be a weekly reminder to live by faith in God's finished work instead of trusting in the work of their own hands. One day the Messiah

---

[1] *Memento* (Summit Entertainment, 2000).

would fulfil the Law of Moses and shout *"It is finished!"* from the cross as a victory cry when he died.[2] Until then, in case a weekly Sabbath was not enough to overcome their spiritual amnesia, he also scheduled several special midweek Sabbaths throughout the year,[3] and commanded that any Sabbath-breaker must be banished or put to death.

He gave them the *Passover* and its follow-up *Feast of Unleavened Bread* as a perfect annual opportunity for them to teach the Gospel to their children. It was a reminder that it didn't matter how strong or weak a person's faith was in God's blood sacrifice, just so long as they went into a house marked by lamb's blood on its vertical and horizontal wooden doorframe. If a person claimed to believe but failed to put blood on their door, they proved that their confession of faith was nothing more than empty words. If they were plagued by doubt but put the lamb's blood on their doorframe, they were saved because the power is in the blood of the Lamb, not in the size of the sinner's faith. God then called them to abstain from yeast for a week as a token that their outward profession of faith was matched by inward consecration and repentance. The Israelites did not yet know that their high priests would sacrifice the Messiah fifteen centuries later on the fourteenth day of the first month, as commanded in verse 5.[4] They simply laid hold of God's memento as he revealed it for now.

On the Sunday after Passover, the priests were to wave an offering of Israel's early crops as another prophetic picture of events which were yet to come. This was the Sunday when Jesus would be *"raised from the dead, the first-fruits of those who have fallen asleep".*[5] Seven weeks later in verses 15–21, they were to follow this up by remembering the *Feast of Weeks*, which was

---

[2] John 19:30.

[3] See verses 7, 8, 21, 24, 27–32, 35–36.

[4] John 18:28; 19:14.

[5] 1 Corinthians 15:20–23. It is in this sense that the feast is called *'ōlām*, or *everlasting*, in verse 14.

known as *Pentecost* in Greek and which celebrated the fact that God is the Lord of the harvest. It was the anniversary of the day when Israel arrived at Mount Sinai in Exodus 19:1, and it looked forward to a greater Day of Pentecost. Seven weeks after Jesus' resurrection, he would fill the Church with his Holy Spirit and enable them to live holier lives than those described at Sinai. Pentecost would launch a spiritual harvest which continues until the Lord comes again.[6] The Israelites would remember this Second Coming every September at their *Feast of Trumpets* in verses 23–25, as they gathered to worship in anticipation of the Final Trumpet when Jesus returns.[7]

A week later, still in September, the high priest was to make his annual entry into the Most Holy Place on the *Day of Atonement*. As we saw in chapter 16, this served as a memento to Israel that the Lamb of God would not only atone for sin's guilt but also bear away its shame. The very fact that such access to the Most Holy Place was an annual event served as a further reminder that a better covenant was to come. When the priests slaughtered lambs in the Tabernacle courtyard, they pointed to a better High Priest who would sacrifice his own unblemished body as a better sacrifice which grants access to his presence for all of God's People 365 days a year. These Polaroid pictures which God gave them as mementoes of his salvation were deliberately smudged and imperfect to speak of better things to come.[8]

This list therefore culminates in the *Feast of Tabernacles* five days after the Day of Atonement, during which the Israelites lived for a week in makeshift booths. They spent seven days remembering the forty years their ancestors had spent in the desert, and they pondered the lessons recorded in the Pentateuch. They sacrificed large numbers of animals on each of the days as a reminder that the Lord is God the Saviour, and

[6] Ezekiel 36:26–27; Ephesians 1:13–14; 2 Corinthians 1:21–22; 5:5.

[7] Matthew 24:31; 1 Thessalonians 4:16–18; 1 Corinthians 15:51–52.

[8] Hebrews 9:7–12.

they poured water on the altar as a reminder that he is also God the Indweller who provided water from the rock at Rephidim as a promise that he would one day pour out the Holy Spirit on all his People. The Feast of Tabernacles pointed to the fact that Jesus would be born in September 5 BC,[9] that the Holy Spirit would "tabernacle" in him, that he would be the true Rock in the desert who pours out the Holy Spirit into our hearts and that this would turn us into little "tabernacles" who continue his pilgrim mission.[10]

God gave these mementoes as Gospel clues to the Israelites like the ones which Guy Pearce clutches in the movie, both for their sake and for our sake looking back. The Lord warns us not to display the same spiritual amnesia. We must lay hold of these mementoes – along with the New Covenant mementoes of bread and wine, of water baptism and of being filled with the Holy Spirit – and not let go of the Gospel message.

For the Gospel is too precious and God's People are too inclined to forget it. That's why God gave the Israelites feasts to serve as mementoes of salvation, to remind them that God wants to be seen by saving and sanctifying his People.

---

[9] Putting together 1 Chronicles 24:7–18; Luke 1:5, 26 and Luke 3:1, 23, we can tell that the angel appeared to Zechariah in July 6 BC and to Mary in January 5 BC, which means that Jesus was probably born in September 5 BC. We celebrate Christmas in December out of tradition, not as a true anniversary.

[10] Numbers 29:12–40; John 1:14; 1 Corinthians 10:4. Jesus explained the meaning of this festival when he celebrated it in September 29 AD in John 7:2, 37–39.

The Name (24:10–23)

*Then Moses spoke to the Israelites, and they took the
blasphemer outside the camp and stoned him. The
Israelites did as the Lord commanded Moses.*

(Leviticus 24:23)

Ninety per cent of Leviticus is a quotation of God's direct speech
to his People. That's more than any other book in the Bible, and
it means Leviticus takes the form of a 27-chapter-long sermon.
Like any good preacher, God therefore ends his sermon with
some practical application. He uses a rare moment of narrative
here in chapter 24 to remind us how much he prizes being
seen as holy through his People. He is God the Holy One, and he
will not swerve in his desire to create a People who reflect his
holiness to the world.

An Israelite woman from the tribe of Dan had forgotten
God's holiness when she married an Egyptian. Perhaps she
was forced to marry her slave-master in the days before the
Exodus but, whatever the circumstances, her half-Israelite-
half-Egyptian son had made the right choice when he saw the
Lord defeat the gods of Egypt ten–nil. He had sided with the
Hebrews and followed them across the Red Sea to the foot of
Mount Sinai. Moses stresses the irony of what happened to
him next when he tells us that this son of *Shelomith* (meaning
Peaceful) and grandson of *Dibri* (meaning *Wordy* or *Eloquent*)
became embroiled in a fight and committed the unspeakable.
He blasphemed the holy Name of Yahweh, and was put into

custody until Moses and the elders of Israel could hear from the Lord how they were to punish him.

The Hebrew word for blaspheming is *nādaq*, which means literally *to puncture* or *pierce* an object from one side to the other.[1] The word for cursing is *qālal*, which means to *belittle* or *lightly esteem* something important. There is a link here to the example of my mother-in-law's cow, as the man punctured the boundaries between the unclean, the clean and the holy. Most Jews today still see the name "Yahweh" as so holy that they even refuse to say the word out loud, but this man dragged it out of the Most Holy Place, through the mud of the garden, and into the filth of the farmyard. His rash curse revealed the true state of his heart, and that he didn't know God the Holy One at all.[2]

Some people find this passage quite offensive, as the Lord commands that the son of the Danite woman be stoned to death without mercy. They complain that his reaction seems excessively brutal. As if to answer their question, the Lord also fills these verses with a series of commands that restrict the use of capital punishment. Unlike Egypt or Canaan, there would be no Hebrew executions for robbery or for bodily harm. They must honour the *lex talionis* which Jesus quoted from here in Matthew 5:38 as God's command that each punishment must be proportionate to the crime.[3] The Lord inserts this command here in order to tell us defiling his Name is tantamount to murder.[4] Since the nations would only come to salvation if God's People made him visible, any crime that made him appear

---

[1] The same word is used in 2 Kings 12:9 to refer to boring a hole in the lid of a box.

[2] Like Pharaoh and the blasphemous builders of Babel, the Lord deliberately omits to tell us the man's name.

[3] The Lord did not need to insert this aside here unless he were emphasizing the seriousness of blasphemy. He had already given this command in Exodus 21:23–25 and would give it again in Deuteronomy 19:21.

[4] "Murder" included kidnapping somebody into slavery (Exodus 21:16), but even someone who caused death through criminal negligence had a chance buy back his life (Exodus 21:28–30).

unholy was punishable by death as the spiritual slaughter of unsuspecting unbelievers.[5]

The Lord therefore uses this incident to begin four chapters of application at the end of Leviticus, which are relevant in every nation or culture. For the Hebrews, it meant literally executing anyone who dared drag God's holy Name through the "garden" and the "field", and it meant doing so in verse 16 as one united community so that the nations could form their view of Yahweh's character from the holy reaction of the majority, not the evil action of the few. It meant stoning the blasphemer as an expression of such horror over sin that they dared not even touch the offender's cursed flesh in his execution. Thankfully, Jesus wrote his own commentary on Leviticus 20:10 when he forgave and restored an adulterous woman in John 8, telling Christians to apply these things spiritually instead of physically. For us, the application is to put church members out of fellowship if they refuse to repent of sins that make the Lord appear unholy. It also means not grieving over churches that Jesus closes down because their compromised doctrine and practice have long since made his Name an object of derision in their communities.[6]

With this in mind, the stoning of the Danite woman's son is meant to stir us to take seriously our calling to let God be seen as holy through his People. It should encourage us to consider carefully what he taught the priests and the rank-and-file Israelites when he stained their bodies with blood in Leviticus 8 and 14.

First, they were to have blood smeared on their right *earlobe* as a pledge that they would only listen to what was pure

---

[5] Such crimes included cursing parents (Leviticus 20:9), despising priests (Deuteronomy 17:12), entering the Tabernacle uninvited (Numbers 3:10), Sabbath-breaking (Exodus 31:15), prophesying falsely (Deuteronomy 18:20), sorcery (Leviticus 20:27; Deuteronomy 18:9–14) and sexual sin (Leviticus 20; Deuteronomy 22:13–27).

[6] 1 Corinthians 5; Revelation 2:5; Romans 2:23–26.

and only speak pure words themselves. Next, they were to have blood smeared on their right *thumb* as a promise that they would refrain from doing evil. Finally, they were to have blood smeared on their right *big toe* as a pledge to go as Yahweh's messengers to proclaim his character to those who did not yet know him. The Hebrew word *qōdesh* carries the double meaning of *holy* in the sense of *set apart **from*** sin and *set apart **for*** obedience, which is why Jesus could say *"I sanctify myself"* as he lived a life of perfect speech, perfect deeds and perfect obedience to the mission the Father gave him.[7] Although the Israelite priests would prove so backslidden that they actually executed him on a trumped-up charge of blasphemy, there was nothing which demonstrated the absolute holiness of God more clearly than when his Son was pierced and punctured on the cross to save his People.[8]

So as we study God's application at the end of his sermon in Leviticus, he wants us to step up and take our place as part of his Holy Nation by heeding the words of Hebrews 10:28–31:

> *Anyone who rejected the Law of Moses died without mercy on the testimony of two or three witnesses. How much more severely do you think a man deserves to be punished who has trampled the Son of God under foot, who has treated as an unholy thing the blood of the covenant that sanctified him, and who has insulted the Spirit of grace?*

God wants you to gaze on the bloodied corpse of the blasphemous son of the Danite woman, and to grasp the great importance of reflecting his holiness to the world. Then he wants you to gaze on the crucified body of the one falsely accused of blasphemy for your sake, so that God can be seen through your holiness today.

---

[7] John 17:19. See this fulfilment of *ear*, *thumb* and *toe* in the Messianic Psalm 40:6–10.

[8] John 19:34, 37. See Matthew 26:63–66 and the deliberate irony of John 10:36.

Jubilee (25:1–55)

Do not take advantage of each other, but fear your God. I am the Lord your God.

(Leviticus 25:17)

In June 1963, at the height of the Cold War, President John F. Kennedy spoke to a crowd of 120,000 defiant West Berliners and drew their attention to the empty promises of Communism. *"Democracy is not perfect,"* he admitted, *"but we have never had to put a wall up to keep our people in, to prevent them from leaving us... The wall is the most obvious and vivid demonstration of the failures of the Communist system, for all the world to see."*

President Kennedy's argument was simple. It was the same one which God uses at the end of Leviticus. It doesn't matter how fervently a preacher or philosopher makes promises, his message is only as believable as the happiness of the people who live under it. The ideals of Communism might convince the rulers of East Germany, but the Berlin Wall betrayed the lie behind its fine-sounding rhetoric. Although it promised a utopia of freedom, it kept a third of Berliners walled inside an urban prison.

The Lord applied his sermon to individuals in chapter 24, and now he does so corporately in chapter 25. He does not merely want to be seen as holy through isolated persons, but through his united People living out his character together. That's why he deliberately failed to mention the Year of Jubilee in chapter 23 when he listed the other great Hebrew festivals, so that he could dedicate a chapter to it here as the corporate application of Leviticus to the Israelite nation as a whole. The world would assess the true character of Israel's God by watching his People obey his command in 19:18 to *"Love your neighbour as yourself"*. Paul tells us in Romans 13:9 that all the many different rules in Leviticus and the rest of the Law *"are summed up in this one rule"*. It is the verse in the Pentateuch which is quoted the most often in the New Testament and it is the verse which forms the basis for the Year of Jubilee.[1]

The Israelites were to demonstrate the holiness of God by carrying a very different attitude towards the *land*. They must not act as landowners but as *tenants* and *stewards* on behalf of the one who had revealed himself to Abraham *"the Possessor of Heaven and Earth"*.[2] The Lord commanded them in verses 1–7 to let their fields and vineyards lie fallow as a Sabbath every seventh year so that the very poorest could find food.[3] He told them that whatever grew of its own accord would be food for *you (plural)*, meaning that migrants, foreigners and servants could benefit from the land as much that year as the farmer himself. Israel would not need the ancient equivalent of the Berlin Wall to hem in its discontented citizens. Instead, they would receive a steady stream of foreign visitors who had heard about the God whose holiness was seen in the loving generosity of his People.

In verses 8–34, the Lord takes this principle of land ownership one step further. A ram's horn must be sounded on the Day of Atonement in every seventh Sabbath year, to signify the fiftieth Year of Jubilee in which debts were forgiven and

---

[1] Leviticus 19:18 is quoted in Matthew 5:43; 19:19; 22:39; Mark 12:31; Luke 10:27; Galatians 5:14; Romans 13:9; James 2:8. Jesus taught that the entire Old Testament hung on this and one other verse.

[2] The Hebrew word *qānāh* in Genesis 14:19 means either *to possess* or *to create*. This truth made Abraham turn down great riches in 14:22 in case they obscured his Possessor-God's glory.

[3] Letting fields lie fallow periodically avoids raping the soil and results in greater harvests in the long term, but the Hebrews largely didn't know that. They simply had to obey the Lord with the faith of verses 20–22.

land was returned to its original owner.[4] This protected the rights of anyone poor enough to have been forced to sell their land, while the rights of the purchaser were protected by him paying less for land as the Year of Jubilee approached and by him having the chance to make a permanent acquisition if he bought a house inside a walled city. The answer to poverty was not oppressing the rich, but telling each Israelite that they must *"not take advantage of one another, but fear your God"*. When the Hebrews displayed the faith of verses 20–22, they enjoyed provision from God as promised in those verses, and they displayed to the world all around them that their Gospel message was more than just a utopian ideal.

In verses 35–55, the Israelites were also to demonstrate the holiness of God by carrying a very different attitude towards *people*. Because they feared their holy God, they would not act like sharks who oppressed the poor by charging interest on loans or by forcing the hungry to pay inflated prices for their food. Since the land of Canaan would only become Israel's through God's grace, they must reflect a similar gracious generosity towards one another. When they freed their slaves as an act of undeserved mercy during the Year of Jubilee, they proclaimed to the watching nations that they worshipped the Saviour-God who had freed their forefathers from slavery in Egypt.[5] They gave a national demonstration that the Gospel message was true, the spiritual opposite of a walled-in East Berlin.

Centuries later, the prophet Isaiah would explain that this Year of Jubilee was a picture of something even greater. The word *Jubilee* comes from the Hebrew word for *ram's horn*, so Isaiah follows up his song about the sacrificial Lamb of God in

---

[4] Since the Hebrews counted inclusively, the "fiftieth year" probably refers to the seventh Sabbath, even though we would term it the "forty-ninth year". The land was not left fallow for two years running.

[5] The Lord actually upgraded this command for Hebrew slaves in Exodus 21:2–6 and Deuteronomy 15:12–18, calling for Jubilee to come early for Hebrew slaves by freeing them in every seventh year.

chapter 53 with the proclamation of a better Jubilee at the start of chapter 61.[6] God will have his *"day of vengeance"* on those who reject his holy Name, but until then he offers all nations a share in his spiritual *"year of favour"* through Jesus' death and resurrection. That's why Jesus read those words from Isaiah at the start of his ministry in Luke 4:16–21, declaring that *"The Spirit of the Lord is on me, because he has anointed me… to proclaim the year of the Lord's favour… Today this scripture is fulfilled in your hearing."*

So God's second application at the end of Leviticus is for his People to showcase his holy character to the unbelieving world through the way in which they love the poor and needy. This will look different for Christians today from how it did for ancient Israel, but it must be more visible, not less visible, this side of the cross.[7] We must not be like the Israelites who consistently failed to observe the Year of Jubilee as commanded. We must demonstrate without a doubt that the Kingdom of Heaven means happiness and peace.

When President Kennedy finished his speech, Mayor Willy Brandt of West Berlin addressed the millions trapped under Communist rule in the east of the city: *"They would much rather be with us, freely gathered here. We tell them we will not give up. Berlin is as true to those behind barbed wire as to fellow countrymen in the West and friends in the whole world."* Brandt argued that West Berlin was a tiny enclave of freedom inside the borders of the Soviet Empire which exposed its lie for all to see. He urged its citizens to live in such a way that East Berliners would one day sledgehammer down the Wall.

The Lord issues a similar message to his People through the Year of Jubilee in Leviticus 25. God the Holy One wants to be seen through his People, as they corporately demonstrate the beauty of his holy Name.

---

[6] Isaiah 61:1 deliberately uses the same Hebrew phrase for *proclaiming freedom* as is used in Leviticus 25:10.

[7] See Acts 2:44–45; 4:32–37; 2 Corinthians 8:1–5; 9:10–15.

Plan "A" and Plan "B"
(26:1–27:34)

If you follow my decrees and are careful to obey my commands…five of you will chase a hundred, and a hundred of you will chase ten thousand.

(Leviticus 26:3, 8)

The Battle of Thermopylae was one of the most famous contests in history. With just a few thousand Greek reinforcements, King Leonidas and his 300 Spartans resisted a vastly superior invading Persian army for three long summer days in 480 BC. In the end, even Leonidas could not overcome odds of over sixty to one, but the courageous manner in which he and his men tried captured the world's enduring attention. From the Greek poet Simonides to the Hollywood movie *300*, the story of Thermopylae still echoes throughout history.[1]

This came as no surprise to the Lord. He knew that victories against overwhelming odds always make the world sit up and listen. He had already ended the book of Leviticus with a series of promises which put Thermopylae in the shade. Just so long as the Israelites obeyed the Law and reflected their holy God to the nations, he would grant them such success against the odds that the nations around them would fall down in worship. He would make himself visible through each unlikely victory, and convince the world that no idol could save like Israel's God.

In the first few verses of chapter 26, he promises to be

---

[1] Although Herodotus claims that the Persians had an army of 2.6 million men, most modern historians assume that the Persians had 300,000 soldiers against a Greek force of 5,000.

visible through Israel's burgeoning economy. They would sow wheat and barley, just like every other nation, but would gather such a bumper harvest that the fertility gods of their neighbours would be put to shame. It would take them four months from March to July to harvest and thresh all their wheat and barley, by which time the grape harvest would have begun. It would take them another four months from July to October to harvest their vineyards, only finishing just in time to sow seed for the next year. The remaining months of the year could be spent in relaxation, trying to eat their way through their never-ending supplies of food, until finally they had to clear out last year's harvest to make room for another bumper crop the following year. In a world where drought and famine were more common and far more dangerous than a sudden crash on Wall Street, such economic success against all odds would become the talking-point of the world. The nations would turn from their idols and come to worship Israel's God, exclaiming *"Praise be to the Lord your God, who has delighted in you!"*[2]

The Lord would also make himself visible by giving Israel greater military victories than Leonidas' wildest dreams. When he and his Spartans succumbed to odds of sixty to one, the poet Simonides placed an epitaph on their tomb which read: *"Go tell the Spartans, you who pass by, that here, obedient to their laws, we lie."* In contrast, the Israelites would routinely rout armies twenty times bigger than their own, and when they rallied together as one united force they would overcome odds of a hundred to one. Joshua, Deborah, Gideon, Samson, David and Jehoshaphat – any Israelite leader who obeyed God's Law and reflected him faithfully – would find a far better epitaph than the Spartans: *"I promise you, Israelites, obedient to my Law, that I will give you victories, great harvests and much, much more!"* To surpass the Spartans at Thermopylae, all that Israel had to do

---

[2] This is what the Queen of Sheba said in 1 Kings 10:1–10 when she saw Leviticus 26 fulfilled under Solomon.

was obey the Law of Moses and co-operate with God's desire to be seen through his holy People.

Sadly, he knew they would refuse to co-operate. They would ignore the fences which he built in Leviticus to demonstrate his holiness. They would reject his Plan "A" to be seen through blessing his holy People, and would provoke him to unleash his Plan "B" to be seen through disciplining his disobedient People. Although he longed to make them *"a people holy to the Lord your God"* so that he could *"set you in praise, fame and honour high above all the nations he has made"*, he would not sit back and let them misrepresent him to the world.[3] He would strike them with such against-all-odds judgment that the nations would take him seriously, even if Israel did not.

While the other Middle Eastern nations enjoyed economic prosperity, everything the Israelites invested in would fail. They would barely recover the barley and wheat seed they sowed, and their orchards and vineyards would bear no fruit at all. What little harvest they gathered would be snatched by foreign raiders before they even had a chance to eat it. Wild animals and invading armies would force them to abandon their fields and vineyards altogether, and when they fled to the cities they would die in urban plagues. They would suffer defeat in battle despite vastly outnumbering their enemy, and would be taken into exile far away from the Promised Land their sin had so defiled. The Lord would make Israel the world's most tragic news story, in order to reveal himself as holy through a People who refused to co-operate with his Plan "A".

Thankfully, chapter 26 does not end with God's tragic Plan "B". His true desire is to be seen by blessing his obedient People, not by cursing them in their rebellion, so he ends chapter 26 with a wonderful promise. Any time that Israel repented and returned to his Law, he would stop working his Plan "B" and restore them to Plan "A". He would still treat them as the Israelites *"whom I*

---

[3] Deuteronomy 26:19.

brought out of Egypt in the sight of the nations to be their God", and would still make himself visible through blessing instead of judgment.[4] He would be seen again through his People as God the Saviour, Indweller and Holy One, whenever the Israelites returned to wholehearted obedience to his Law.

Perhaps that's why Leviticus ends with chapter 27, an appendix that talks about blood sacrifice and redemption. God's Plan "B" could only be restored to Plan "A" at the cost of the life of his spotlessly obedient Messiah. He would be God's true *firstborn*,[5] sold for shekels of silver and sacrificed by Israel's priests,[6] and as he tasted the bitter pain of God's Plan "B", he would pave a way for those who deserve Plan "B" to be restored to God's glorious Plan "A".

Therefore this halfway point between Exodus and Deuteronomy marks a good time for each of us to kneel and pray to God.[7] Tell him that you have had enough of his Plan "B", mixing righteousness with worldliness and reaping its deadly against-all-odds reward. Tell him that through Jesus you want to be forgiven and restored to Plan "A". Tell him that you know he is the holy God who wants to be seen through his holy People, and that you have grasped the message of Leviticus. Tell him that through Jesus you surrender your life to him afresh today.

---

[4] Note the way in which these punishments ascend gradually in seriousness, demonstrating God's desire to punish the Israelites no more than was necessary to draw them to repentance.

[5] Colossians 1:15, 18; Hebrews 1:6; 12:23; Revelation 1:5. Since Jesus is the eternal Son of God, he is not the firstborn because of temporal birth but because of his superiority over the brothers he has saved.

[6] Matthew 27:1–10.

[7] Do not be fooled that these words no longer have relevance to Christians living under the New Covenant. Paul quotes from 26:12 in 2 Corinthians 6:16 and applies it directly to the Church.

Numbers:

God the
Faithful One

11 × 1,250 (1:1–10:36)

*On the twentieth day of the second month of
the second year, the cloud lifted from above the
tabernacle of the Testimony. Then the Israelites set
out from the Desert of Sinai and travelled from place
to place.*

(Numbers 10:11–12)

If you don't find the book of Numbers surprising, consider for
a moment the length of time it covers. Leviticus records what
happened in four weeks at Mount Sinai, and Deuteronomy
records what happened in two weeks on the plains of Moab.
Numbers should have covered a similar period of time, because
it took only eleven days to travel by foot from Mount Sinai to the
border of the Promised Land.[1] In fact, Numbers covers thirty-
eight and a half years – 1,250 times longer than was necessary.
This makes it the tragic act of the Pentateuch.

God wanted to be seen through his People. Having already
defeated the Egyptian gods ten–nil, he wanted to give Israel a
similar scoreline against the Canaanite gods as well. The gods
of the Hyksos, once so feared in Egypt, would prove unable to
protect their wicked worshippers when the Israelites invaded
to conquer the Promised Land. The Lord would be seen as God
the Indweller when he led his People against them,[2] as God
the Saviour when he defeated them and as God the Holy One
when he judged their sin. He had been patient with them for six

---

[1] Deuteronomy 1:2.

[2] Although God dwelt at the centre of Israel's camp in chapter 2, he marched
at the front of the nation in 10:14–28 whenever they advanced.

long centuries since Abraham, but now their sin had reached full measure and he would be seen by his judging them through his People.[3]

In preparation for this victory, the first ten chapters of Numbers celebrate that Yahweh is God the Faithful One. In chapters 1–4 he tells Moses to hold a census, which reveals that Israel's numbers have actually increased during their year in the uninhabitable desert: 600,000 Israelite men crossed the Red Sea a year earlier, but now there are over 600,000 men in the twenty-to-sixty age bracket alone, not even including the 22,000 Levites counted separately.[4]

The Lord continues to emphasize his faithfulness in chapters 5–10. He fulfils his promise to be seen through them as God the Indweller by telling them in 5:4 and 7:89 that *"I dwell among them...between the cherubim above the atonement cover on the Ark of the Testimony"*. He stresses this by telling them to camp as a nation in a particular way around his Tabernacle, and he underlines the fact that he is God the Holy One by telling Moses and the priests to camp like guards at the doorway to the Tabernacle courtyard, while the Levites camp like guards on its other three sides too. He orders unclean people to leave the camp in chapter 5, but purifies the twelve tribes in chapter 7 through their blood sacrifices and lets them each approach him in turn. Chapters 8 and 9 continue to celebrate Yahweh as God the Faithful One, as the Levites are consecrated and the Passover Feast is observed. And yet, if we read carefully we notice several warning signs that the Israelites are about to prove themselves anything but faithful in return.

First, Moses refers to Reuben in 1:20 as *"the firstborn son"* of Jacob. That's unusual because Reuben had been born first but

---

[3] Over six centuries had passed since the Lord predicted the annihilation of the Canaanites in Genesis 15:16. The Lord was gracious and gave them plenty of time in which to repent (Genesis 19:1–14).

[4] Compare Numbers 1 with Exodus 12:37. This meant that Israel's total population was now well over 2 million.

then lost his birthright through disobedience. It was obedient Joseph who had made God visible in Egypt and became Jacob's spiritual firstborn, the father of Ephraim and Manasseh.[5] Put this together with the fact that the Lord proclaimed in Exodus 4:22 that *"Israel is my firstborn son"*, and it acts as a hint that Israel must not take God's faithfulness for granted. To underline this further, Moses reminds us in 3:2–4 that Nadab and Abihu were Aaron's two eldest sons, but that they both died childless for forgetting God is holy. Even as he installs the Levites as helpers to the priests at the Tabernacle, Moses issues another warning when he tells them not to enter the Tabernacle unless they want to die.[6] Moses is preparing us for the tragedy of Numbers, when Israel refused God's Plan "A" and reaped his terrible Plan "B".

That's also why chapter 6 lies at the heart of these first ten chapters, as a call to consecration and to blessing. Anyone, regardless of tribe, age or gender, could choose to become a Nazirite for a special period of consecration to Yahweh. The Hebrew word *nāzīr* simply means *consecrated* or *set apart*, and a Nazirite avoided touching grapes, alcohol, razors and corpses as an outward sign of separation from the sin which was increasingly prevalent in their nation. Later, the Lord would call Samson, Samuel and John the Baptist to revive the backslidden Israelite nation by becoming Nazirites for life,[7] but for now he uses it to call each man and woman to choose to remain faithful to him, even if their fellow Israelites were not. He wants to be visible through his People through the blessing of 6:22–27

---

[5] Genesis 35:22; 49:3–4, 22–26; 1 Chronicles 5:1–2.

[6] Numbers 3:10, 38; 4:15, 19, 20. Despite the name, Numbers actually contains more detail about the role of the Levites than Leviticus. The priests were one of the Levite families, and the other Levites became God's special tribe as a substitute for the firstborn Israelites who had been spared at the first Passover.

[7] Judges 13:7; 16:17; 1 Samuel 1:11; Luke 1:15–16. Samson despised his calling as a Nazirite by eating from a dead body in Judges 14:8–9, taking part in a *drinking-feast* in 14:10 and having his hair cut in 16:19–20.

instead of through the judgment of 5:11–31.[8] Since the Lord is God the Faithful One, his People must also be faithful, so that he can be visible through Plan "A" and not Plan "B".

Tragically, because Israel made the wrong choice, only two individuals counted in the census of chapter 1 would make the census of chapter 26.[9] The rest would die during thirty-eight and a half years of needless wandering, while the Lord *"endured their conduct"* in *"that vast and dreadful desert".*[10]

So let's learn from Numbers to choose obedience and blessing instead of rebellion and loss. Let's follow Jesus the Messiah, who spent forty days in the desert at the start of his ministry as a deliberate mirror to the tragedy of Numbers.[11] He chose God's Plan "A" all the way in the desert, and through his death and resurrection he promises to help us do the same.

For our own story does not have to be like that of the Israelites in Numbers. Paul warns that *"God was not pleased with most of them; their bodies were scattered over the desert. Now these things occurred as examples to keep us from setting our hearts on evil things as they did."* Then he promises that our lives can be different: *"God is faithful; he will not let you be tempted beyond what you can bear... Follow my example, as I follow the example of Christ."*[12]

---

[8] The blessing in 6:24–26 is beautifully crafted in Hebrew, since the three verses contain 3, 5 and 7 words, and 15, 20 and 25 letters respectively. What is more, if we take out the three occurrences of the word "Yahweh", we are left with twelve words – one for each tribe of Israel with Yahweh in their midst!

[9] The translators of the Septuagint called this book Numbers because of the censuses in chapters 1 and 26. The Hebrew name was more descriptive: *In the Desert*.

[10] Acts 13:18; Deuteronomy 1:19.

[11] Matthew 2:23 even takes the name of Jesus' home town of *Nazareth* and uses it to argue that Jesus fulfilled Numbers 6:1–21 and Judges 13:5 by being the ultimate *Nazirite*.

[12] 1 Corinthians 10:5–6; 10:13; 11:1.

Cloud Chasers (9:15–23)

Whenever the cloud lifted from above the Tent, the Israelites set out; wherever the cloud settled, the Israelites encamped.

(Numbers 9:17)

When Matthew tells us that Jesus spent forty days in the desert to walk perfectly where Israel failed, he chooses his introductory words very carefully: *"Jesus was led by the Spirit into the desert."*[1] One of the great themes of Numbers is that the Lord wants to be seen through his People as God the Faithful One by guiding their steps through the presence of his Holy Spirit. That's why Moses rejoices in Deuteronomy 8:2 that *"The Lord your God led you all the way in the desert."* It is also why Numbers is still so relevant to us today.

The Lord wants to use the pillar of cloud and fire to reassure us that *he is eager to guide us*. Although he could shrink the cloud of his presence to be small enough to fit on the lid of the Ark of the Covenant,[2] he normally chose to make the cloud massive, an unmissable pillar above his Tabernacle to be seen by all. Sometimes the cloud would stay in the same place for months at a time because he wanted his People to dig in and serve him faithfully in one place for a season. At other times, the cloud would quickly move on because he wanted his People to chase him day by day. Either way, he made his guidance obvious to Israel, from the first night of their journey in Exodus 13:21

---

[1] Matthew 4:1.

[2] Leviticus 16:2.

to the day on which they entered the Promised Land. Even in their darkest nights, God made it clear to Israel which path they should take by turning the pillar of cloud into a pillar of fire, so that a thousand years later the Israelites could still celebrate that *"Because of your great compassion you did not abandon them in the desert. By day the pillar of cloud did not cease to guide them on their path, nor the pillar of fire by night to shine on the way they were to take. You gave your good Spirit to instruct them."*[3] The Lord gives you his Spirit in order to guide you, no matter how dark your situation may feel.

The Lord wants to use the pillar of cloud and fire to teach you that *he guides out of relationship*. He didn't give the Israelites a map so they could cross the desert without him, but forced them to rely on his Holy Spirit's leading every day. In the same way, Jesus refused to give his followers a religious roadmap, but simply told them in John 14:6 that *"I am the Way"*.[4] God wants to teach us that the Christian life is as much about enjoying the journey with him as it is about arriving at our destination. Sometimes God keeps us waiting and sometimes he forces us to run to keep up with him, because he wants to teach us to watch like the Israelites and be ready to follow quickly. We must not even make the same mistake as the Israelites in 14:40–45 and treat yesterday's guidance as a blueprint for today.

The eighteenth-century theologian William Law warns that Scripture can even become a substitute for genuine relationship with God unless we read it with an ear to what his Spirit says through it today:

> *Without the present illumination of the Holy Spirit, the Word of God must remain a dead letter to every man... It is just as essential for the Holy Spirit to reveal the truth of Scripture to the reader today as it was necessary for him to inspire the writers thereof in their day... Therefore, to*

---

[3] Nehemiah 9:19–20.

[4] God the Father also stresses his desire to guide us through relationship in Deuteronomy 1:31.

say that because we now have all the writings of Scripture complete we no longer need the miraculous inspiration of the Spirit among men as in former days, is a degree of blindness as great as any that can be charged upon the Scribes and Pharisees. Nor can we possibly escape their same errors; for in denying the present inspiration of the Holy Spirit, we have made Scripture the province of the letter-learned scribe.[5]

God teaches us through the pillar of cloud and fire that he wants to be seen through a People who walk by his Spirit every day.

The Lord also wants to teach us that *common sense is no substitute for the Holy Spirit's guidance.* Sometimes he led the Israelites in a very strange direction. Instead of leading them due east towards the Promised Land when they left Egypt in Exodus 13:17, he trapped them against the shore of the Red Sea because his plan to destroy the Egyptian army was far too clever to be discerned by common sense without the Holy Spirit.[6] On another occasion in Numbers 21, he told them to stay in a snake-infested valley so he could teach them more about the Gospel. God uses the arrival of Moses' brother-in-law Hobab to teach us that common sense plays an important role in guidance, since Moses tells him in 10:29–32 that *"You know where we should camp in the desert, and you can be our eyes."* But he also teaches us that we need the Holy Spirit to enlighten our common sense, because Moses tells Hobab that *"If you come with us, we will share with you whatever good things the Lord gives us."*[7]

---

[5] William Law, *An Humble, Earnest and Affectionate Address to the Clergy* (1761). Andrew Murray updated Law's language and reprinted it in under the new title *The Power of the Spirit* (1896).

[6] The Holy Spirit overcomes adverse circumstance. The pillar shielded the Israelites from the Egyptian army in Exodus 14:19–24 so that they had time to cross the Red Sea to freedom.

[7] Judges 1:16 and 1 Samuel 15:6 tell us that Hobab accepted Moses' invitation. He submitted his skills as a scout to the Holy Spirit and was rewarded with a share in God's blessing on his People.

The Lord also wants to teach us that *individualism can prevent us from hearing the Holy Spirit's guidance.* He guided the Israelites corporately through the pillar because we can sense his will together in a way we never can apart.[8] When the apostles based their guidance in Acts 15:28 on the fact *"it seemed good to the Holy Spirit and to us"*, they were simply following the practice of the Israelites before them. Even when the pillar moved, the Israelites didn't move on until Moses sounded a trumpet in 10:1–13 as the elders' interpretation of what they saw together.[9] God places each of us in a local church for a reason. He loves to guide his People as they sense his Spirit as a team.

Chapter 10 therefore marks an important moment in the Pentateuch, when the Lord guides Israel to break camp after over a year of living at Sinai, spanning fifty-nine chapters since they arrived there in Exodus 19. The Lord guides them to move on through his pillar of cloud and fire in order to teach us how to follow his Spirit's guidance every day. If we stay close to his Holy Spirit and listen to his voice in our hearts through Bible-reading, common sense and sharing life with one another, we can experience God the Faithful One as our daily guide. We can sing like the Israelites in their early days following the pillar of cloud and fire: *"In your unfailing love you will lead the people you have redeemed. In your strength you will guide them to your holy dwelling."*[10]

---

[8] Proverbs 11:14 and 15:22 help us submit to Proverbs 3:5–6 and 14:12.
[9] The priests also took a lead in guiding the People using the Urim and Thummim (Exodus 28:30).
[10] Exodus 15:13.

Food, Force and Fame
(11:1–12:16)

Now the people complained about their hardships in the hearing of the Lord, and when he heard them his anger was aroused.

(Numbers 11:1)

Two million Israelites in the desert. That's the equivalent of seven Icelands, two and a half Cypruses or the entire population of New Mexico. Feeding 2 million mouths in a bleak and arid desert was a daily logistical nightmare for Moses. God fed them every morning with fresh manna from heaven, but Jesus had no manna when he followed in their footsteps in Matthew 4. *"After fasting forty days and forty nights, he was hungry,"* Matthew tells us with deliberate understatement. Yet while the Israelites began complaining against the Lord within a few miles of Sinai, Jesus passed the test where Israel failed throughout the book of Numbers.

First, the Devil tempted Jesus with *food*, just as he had tempted the Israelites in Numbers 11. They had enjoyed the taste of manna during their easy months at Sinai, but as soon as God started leading them forwards their gratitude turned to grumbling.[1] God fired a warning shot across their bows by setting fire to the outskirts of their camp at Taberah, which means *Burning*, but it didn't stop them from grumbling yet

---

[1] The Israelites were happy to follow the Lord when it meant going nowhere in Numbers 1:19, 54; 2:34; 3:51; 4:37, 45, 49; 5:4. They started grumbling as soon as he told them to stop talking and start moving.

again.[2] They started fantasizing about the good old days in Egypt when they used to eat free meat and vegetables, forgetting that the reason why their food used to be free was that their cruel slave-owners wanted to be able to keep them working! God gave them manna to teach them to feast daily on his Word and on the true Bread of Heaven who would be crushed to save the world,[3] but they found manna boring and their eyes began to rove for something else to satisfy their hunger. No wonder Moses tells us in verse 10 that *"The Lord became exceedingly angry"*. They would call that place Kibroth Hattaavah, which means *Graves of Craving*, because God struck them with a plague for their rebellion in verse 33.

Jesus was hungrier than any of the Israelites in Numbers 11 when the Devil came to tempt him at the end of forty days in the desert, but he had been devouring Numbers and Moses' commentary on its meaning in Deuteronomy 1–8. When the Devil tried to persuade him to turn stones into bread, he found those chapters were exactly what he needed to reply. *"Man does not live on bread alone, but on every word that comes from the mouth of God,"* he quoted from Deuteronomy 8:3. Unlike the Israelites, Jesus was completely satisfied with the Word of God. He walked a path of perfect obedience where 2 million Hebrews had failed.

Second, the Devil tempted Jesus to try to *force* God's hand, just as he had tempted the Israelites in the second half of Numbers 11. They wailed so loudly for meat that even the normally patient Moses began to wish himself dead in verse 15. They resisted God's plan to be seen through his People

---

[2] The *'aspesūph*, or *mixed-race rabble*, who stirred the Israelites to grumble included some of the foreigners who joined them in Exodus 12:38. The Hebrews were so easily led astray that they could not even remain faithful to Yahweh when they were in the vast majority.

[3] In John 6:48–58, Jesus links the breaking of his body on the cross to the fact that God provided manna in a form that needed to be crushed in a mortar.

and began to demand that he fall into line with their own agenda instead. *"We were better off in Egypt!... Why did we ever leave?"* The Lord gave them large numbers of quail, as he had in Exodus 16, but this time he taught them what happens to those who try to manipulate God.[4] He gave them so many millions of quail, piled a metre high and stretching sixteen miles in each direction, that the Israelites began to loathe quail meat even more than manna, and the desert sun contaminated the meat before they ate it. Psalm 106:15 tells us literally that *"in the desert they put God to the test, so he gave them what they asked for but sent a wasting disease into their souls."*

Jesus had more reason than the Israelites to try to force his Father's hand at the end of forty days in the desert. He was aged thirty and had spent his whole life in obscurity, ignored by the world as he waited to be launched into ministry. When he was baptized in the River Jordan, the heavens opened and the Father hailed him as his Son, which must have made him assume that his moment had finally come. However, instead of catapulting him into a dazzling preaching tour full of miracles and publicity, the Father sent him straight away to even greater obscurity in the desert. Jesus submitted and drew strength from these chapters, which prepared him to resist the Devil's temptation to force the Father to reveal him publicly as the fulfilment of Psalm 91. Instead he simply quoted from Deuteronomy 6:16: *"Do not put the Lord your God to the test."*

Third, the Devil tempted Jesus to clutch at personal *fame* instead of submitting humbly to the Father's plan. He had tempted Miriam and Aaron in the same way in Numbers 12.

---

[4] 11:23 means literally *"Has the arm of the Lord grown shorter?"*, so the Lord was telling Moses that he was about to repeat the miracle of Exodus 16:12–13. This time he would do so out of judgment instead of blessing.

Moses' wife Zipporah was a Cushanite, a Midianite foreigner,[5] and her family was increasing its influence over Moses. Her brother Hobab had just become Moses' trusted guide, and Israel's grumbling in chapter 11 had prompted Moses to fully implement her father's advice at Sinai a year earlier in Exodus 18.[6] This evidently annoyed Aaron and Miriam, who did not share their brother's humility. Moses begged the Lord in 11:14–15 not to make him a one-man ministry team, and he laughed at Joshua's concern for his fame by praying for Pentecost to come fifteen centuries early: *"I wish that all the Lord's people were prophets and that the Lord would put his Spirit on them!"* In contrast, Aaron and Miriam nursed their hurt pride and complained that Moses and his in-laws were crowding out their own gifting as God's priest and prophetess.

We are told by an editorial insertion in 12:3 that Moses was more humble than anyone else on the face of the earth. When the Devil tempted Jesus at the end of his forty days in the desert, he proved that he was even humbler still. He didn't show even a trace of the clutching ambition which struck down Miriam with leprosy and stopped God's People from advancing.[7] Jesus quoted back to the Devil from Deuteronomy 6:13: *"Worship the Lord your God, and serve him only."* This is the Saviour who

---

[5] Some scholars argue from 12:1 that Moses must have divorced his wife Zipporah and taken a new wife from *Cush*, or Upper Egypt, especially since the Hebrew word for *sent away* in Exodus 18:2 can also mean *divorced*. However, another name for Midian was *Cushan* (Habakkuk 3:7) and this refers to Zipporah his *Cush[an]ite* wife. Jethro and Hobab would not have helped Moses if he had divorced Zipporah!

[6] 11:14 is meant to echo Exodus 18:18. Moses had appointed leaders as Jethro suggested, but organization was only half the battle. Now the Lord turns those *appointed* leaders into *anointed* leaders.

[7] Numbers 12:15 reminds us that nothing slows down the advance of God's Kingdom as much as selfish ambition on the part of church leaders. Since Miriam is mentioned first and her name means *Rebellion* in Hebrew, she appears to have been the main instigator and is punished more severely than Aaron. The Lord addresses her *outside* the Tabernacle as a poignant reminder that she was not like Moses or Aaron.

"did not consider equality with God something to be grasped" in Philippians 2:6, and who gladly humbled himself to wash his disciples' feet like a slave before dying a shameful death for them. He calls us to follow in his footsteps too.

Jesus won his duel with the Devil in the desert, walking perfectly where Israel failed, in order to lead God's People into a true and better Promised Land. He comes beside you today as you face those same temptations, and he promises to help you to resist at every turn. *"For we do not have a high priest who is unable to sympathise with our weaknesses, but we have one who has been tempted in every way, just as we are – yet was without sin."*[8]

---

[8] Hebrews 4:15.

Blind Unbelief (13:1–14:45)

How long will these people treat me with contempt?
How long will they refuse to believe in me, in spite
of all the miraculous signs I have performed among
them?

(Numbers 14:11)

GOD THE FAITHFUL ONE

"Faith is the great cop-out, the great excuse to evade the need to think and evaluate evidence. Faith is belief in spite of, even perhaps because of, the lack of evidence." Those are the words of Richard Dawkins, Britain's leading atheist, and there are plenty of people who believe that he is right.[1] He despises faith as *"blind trust in the absence of evidence, even in the teeth of evidence"*, which is why it is important that we read Numbers 13 and 14 slowly enough to notice that the Lord fundamentally disagrees with this false definition of faith.

These two chapters are the turning point in Moses' drama, the reason why Numbers spans thirty-eight and a half years instead of only a few days, and why only two of the men counted in the census of chapter 1 would ever live to enter the Promised Land. This was the moment when the Hebrews were called to trust in God the Faithful One, and the reason they failed to do so was precisely the opposite of Richard Dawkins' theory. God did not tell them to squeeze their eyes shut and take a blind leap of faith to invade the Promised Land. He suggested they send spies to make a forty-day tour of the land because feasting our eyes on facts is the best way to build faith.

---

[1] Richard Dawkins said this in a lecture at the Edinburgh International Science Festival in 1992.

The Lord had promised the Israelites that he would give them a land *"flowing with milk and honey, the most beautiful of all lands"*, so the twelve spies would report back to Israel whether what the Lord had told them was true.[2] He wanted to open their eyes to see what he can see, because facts lead to faith in God as surely as ignorance leads to unbelief. When all twelve spies bore united testimony that *"It does flow with milk and honey! Here is its fruit!"*, the samples of fruit should have bolstered Israel's faith. Sadly, however, ten of the spies closed their eyes to the facts and told a very different story to that of Joshua and Caleb.[3]

First, they argued that the Canaanites were invincible giants who lived in giant-sized fortresses which could not be taken. Some of them were Anakites, the descendants of the mighty Nephilim of old, and they must view the normal-sized Hebrews as nothing more than grasshoppers under their feet. Note how this argument ignores the fact the Nephilim were all wiped out in Noah's Flood,[4] and the fact the Lord had already helped the Edomites, Moabites and Ammonites to defeat the giant-sized cousins of the Anakites.[5] It also ignores the proof they found on their tour in 13:22, that these Canaanites were linked to the Hyksos who had once ruled Egypt from their capital at Zoan. If God had drowned the Egyptian army that had driven out the Hyksos, and had done so without the Hebrews sustaining a single casualty, then those Canaanites were not to be feared. In fact, far from seeing them as grasshoppers,

---

[2] Exodus 3:8, 17; Ezekiel 20:6. The Hebrew word for *searching* in Ezekiel 20:6 and Numbers 13:2 is the same. Faith comes when we open our eyes.

[3] The twelve spies listed in 13:4–15 were not the tribal chiefs listed in 1:5–15. The spies did a round trip of 500 miles in 40 days, so the chiefs sent younger deputies to spy out the land for them.

[4] Genesis 7:21.

[5] The Rephaites were part of the same giant-sized race as the Anakites, but Moses tells us in Deuteronomy 2:9–12, 19–22 that they were no match for God's grace towards the descendants of Esau and Lot.

Joshua 2:8–11 tells us the Canaanites were afraid because they had seen God the Saviour through his People.

Second, the ten spies argued that the land was already so full of different people groups that there was no more room for the Hebrews to settle there. Note again how blind this argument is. Either the land *"devours those living in it"*, or it is so fertile that it produces invincible giants, but both cannot be true at the same time! The fact that the nations they found dwelling in the land were the same ones God predicted would be there in Genesis 15:20–21 and Exodus 13:5 should have whetted their faith for victory. The only people group they discovered there that God had not explicitly promised they would conquer in Genesis 15 were the Amalekites, but God had already granted victory over them in Exodus 17. They should have treated this as a down payment on all the others.

Only Joshua and Caleb opened their eyes to trust God's promises on the basis of what they saw. The rest of the Israelites followed the ten blind spies, as a terrible reminder that it is unbelief, not faith, which is truly blind. They closed their eyes to the promise of 14:9 that *"the Lord is with us"*; to the fact that the Lord had already trounced Egypt's gods ten-nil; to the memory of him wiping out the world's largest standing army at the Red Sea, as well as the Amalekites at Rephidim; and to the way he had provided his People with manna, quail and water in the desert. This blind unbelief was what angered the Lord in 14:22, not their refusal to take a blind leap of faith. They *"saw my glory and the miraculous signs I performed in Egypt and in the desert,"* God complained as he struck the ten spies down dead with a plague. Those forty days of blindness to the facts had earned the Israelites forty years of squinting under the fierce desert sun. The New Testament warns us not to be like those *"whose bodies fell in the desert...because of their unbelief... For we also have had the gospel preached to us, just as they did; but the message they heard was of no value to them, because those who heard did not combine it with faith."*[6]

Richard Dawkins' idea that Christian faith is blind is proved even more wrong by a tragic epilogue at the end of chapter 14. When the Israelites see how much God hates their blind unbelief, they try to work themselves up into blind faith instead. The Lord has told them they can no longer enter the land but they launch a presumptuous attack without any facts in their favour. This is the "blind leap of faith" Richard Dawkins seeks to counter, but the Lord tells us that this isn't what he is after either. Presumption is nothing like the wide-eyed faith displayed by God's obedient People. It is simply blind unbelief wearing religious clothes, and it leads just as surely to death and destruction.

There is nothing new about Richard Dawkins' delusion. Mark Twain said before him that *"Faith is believing something you know ain't true."*[7] The Lord tells Richard Dawkins, Mark Twain and every other reader of Numbers to stop talking and start learning the lesson behind these two tragic chapters. True faith in God the Faithful One comes not through mimicking the ten blind spies but through the wide-eyed wisdom of Joshua and Caleb. They alone would survive the forty years in the desert and enter the Promised Land, because they rejected blind unbelief and feasted their eyes on the evidence God gave them. Facts are what should teach us to be sceptical of Dawkins and Twain and any other blind spy, and what should teach us to have faith in God the Faithful One.

---

[6] Hebrews 3:17, 19; 4:2. Hebrews does not tell us that the Israelites were not saved, but that they missed out on their inheritance by ignoring the facts which would have given them faith to inherit the land.

[7] Mark Twain, *Following the Equator* (1897). Contrast 13:31, 33 and 14:8–9 to Dawkins and Twain's real problem. The blind spies focus on *"we, we, we"*, but Joshua and Caleb focus on *"the Lord, the Lord, the Lord"*.

Run into the Flames
(14:11–38)

If you put these people to death all at one time, the nations who have heard this report about you will say, "The Lord was not able to bring these people into the land he promised them."

(Numbers 14:15–16)

Ryan Cooper was kissing his wife goodbye in his driveway when a Cessna 310 aeroplane crash-landed on the roof of a house across the street. Burning aviation fuel immediately engulfed two houses, and he instinctively began to run. Not away from the inferno, as might have been expected, for Ryan Cooper was an off-duty firefighter and had been taught to run into the flames. He heard screams which told him that people were inside, people who desperately needed his help.

Cooper pushed through the door of the first burning house and pulled a ten-year-old boy outside with his clothes on fire. He doused the burning clothes before going back into the building to retrieve the boy's disorientated father. Even though Ryan Cooper was almost overcome by the thick black smoke, he burst through the door of the second house and checked that there was no one trapped in the downstairs rooms. He emerged to take deep lungfuls of oxygen, then made a fourth trip into the flames to try to check upstairs. By the time the ambulances reached the inferno and found Cooper administering first aid to the father and son outside, they were forced to treat him for serious heat exhaustion and smoke inhalation. They hailed him as a hero, but he shrugged off any honours, claiming that

"Everybody that goes to work every twenty-four hours at every fire station across the country – it's their job to do it."[1]

The Lord was very pleased with Moses when he acted like Ryan Cooper, and he wants to teach us to be Ryan Coopers too. Having judged Nadab and Abihu with fire and burned the outskirts of the Israelite camp, he was now burning with anger again towards the faithless Hebrews. The cloud of God's presence turned into a glorious blaze, and he told Moses in verse 12 that *"I will strike them down with a plague and destroy them, but I will make you into a nation greater and stronger than they."* It was a similar moment to the Golden Calf in Exodus 32, but the Israelites were a year wiser and knew that the fire of God's judgment was not just a metaphor.[2] Moses had much to gain personally from letting Israel burn, and he took great risks in running into the flames to save them. Yet like a spiritual Ryan Cooper, he ran to meet God's judgment and dragged a burning nation back from the brink through his prayers. The Israelites had sinned through their blind unbelief, but God only needed one man with his eyes open to set things right.

You are God the Faithful One, Moses tells God, *and you want to be seen as the Faithful One through your People.* The Egyptians and Canaanites know that you are God the Saviour (verse 13), God the Indweller (verse 14) and God the Faithful One who daily guides his People (verse 14). All this will be in jeopardy, though, if you eradicate the Israelites as you have threatened. Even though you would be entirely just to do so, it will make the Egyptians and Canaanites assume that you are not really the God the Faithful One. You are just a smooth-talking politician who makes promises he can't keep. They will assume that you slaughtered the Israelites because you overstretched your

---

[1] This event took place on 10th July 2007 in the city of Sanford, Florida. Ryan Cooper was interviewed on NBC's *Today Show* the following morning.

[2] Exodus 32 and Numbers 14 are very similar prayers. For example, both show that we must never plead with God on the basis of our own merits, but only on the underserved merits of Jesus.

power and panicked because you are not really God the Saviour at all (verses 15–16). If you want to be seen through your People, then killing the Israelites is a very bad idea.

Moses takes a second dash into the flames in verses 17–19. Not only would destroying the Israelites make the Lord appear weaker than the gods of Canaan, but it would also squander a positive opportunity to reveal himself as God the Faithful One through his People. The Egyptians and Canaanites did not worship gods who were gracious enough to forgive them if they behaved as unfaithfully as Israel, so this was a chance for the glorious Gospel preached at Sinai to be shouted to the world. Israel's God accepted the wicked as if they were righteous because of their faith in a blood sacrifice which was to come![3] The Israelites had offered the Lord the dark canvas of their sin on which he could paint the brilliant colours of his grace. *"If we are faithless, he will remain faithful, for he cannot disown himself,"* Paul would rejoice centuries later in 2 Timothy 2:13, but now the Lord had an opportunity to be seen as God the Faithful One throughout the entire Middle East through the way in which he responded to Israel's guilt.

Like Ryan Cooper, Moses was successful when he ran into the flames. The plague which looked set to wipe out Israel in verse 12 was diverted and only destroyed the ten blind spies in verse 37. The Exodus generation would still die in the desert, but they would do so during four more decades of walking closely with the Lord. They would even have the chance to train up a fresh generation of Israelites to trust God where they had failed. The Lord explains his change of mind in Ezekiel 20, telling us that *"For the sake of my name I did what would keep it from being profaned in the eyes of the nations in whose sight I had brought them out."*[4] That's what spiritual Ryan Coopers can achieve.

---

[3] This may be why God gives a long recap on how to offer blood sacrifices between the prayer of chapter 14 and the statement at the end of chapter 15 that *"I am the Lord your God"*.

[4] Ezekiel 20:9, 14, 22.

God wants to encourage you to look on the failures of your own church and to be a Ryan Cooper in prayer. The great intercessors who have prayed before every great move of God in history have always run into the flames and turned the very failure of God's People into further grounds to ask for grace. It was what marked Evan Roberts as he prayed before the great Welsh Revival of 1904 and 1905, writing later that:

> *For a long, long time I was much troubled in my soul and my heart by thinking over the failure of Christianity. Oh! It seemed such a failure – and I prayed and prayed, but nothing seemed to give me relief. But one night, after I had been in great distress praying about this... I found myself with unspeakable joy and awe in the presence of the Almighty God... I saw things in a different light, and I knew that God was going to work in the land, and not in this land only, but in all the world.*[5]

Evan Roberts ran into the flames and made the failure of Welsh Christianity the reason why the Lord needed to move and take hold of an opportunity to be seen through his People. Let's not simply be those who lament sin and failure in the Church, but those who take it back to God in prayer. God is still looking for spiritual Ryan Coopers who will see his fireball coming and run into the flames.

---

[5] Evan Roberts in an interview with W.T. Stead in *The Bruce Herald*, 28th March 1905.

Authority (16:1–19:22)

*They came as a group to oppose Moses and Aaron
and said to them, "You have gone too far! The whole
community is holy, every one of them, and the Lord is
with them. Why then do you set yourselves above the
Lord's assembly?"*

(Numbers 16:3)

The Israelites were a difficult nation to lead, even when their journey was the short one from Sinai to Canaan. When they realized that their travel plans now included four more decades of wandering in the desert, their simmering unruliness turned into outright mutiny. Moses covers thirty-eight years in only four chapters in Numbers 16–19, and those chapters are full of angry challenges to his authority.

It takes little time as a church member, and even less as a church leader, to discover that resentment and rebellion are still an issue for God's People today. God takes it so seriously that the New Testament writer Jude warns against *"grumblers and faultfinders"* who undermine their leaders. Such people have always been part of the history of God's People, and Jude tells us they have always *"been destroyed in Korah's rebellion"*.[1] He therefore warns us that these chapters were written for us, to teach church leaders the true basis for their spiritual authority, and to warn modern-day Korahs not to dare to rebel against it.

First, the Lord tells us that spiritual authority can never

---

[1] Jude 11, 16. Numbers 26:10 tells us that these rebels should serve as a *"warning sign"* for us.

be founded on *human democracy*. Korah's cry in 16:3 was "power to the people", but it was simply a pious veneer for his selfish agenda to manipulate the people into voting for him.[2] Democracy would not have chosen Moses as God's leader in Exodus 6:9, and it would have deselected him at almost every pitfall along the way. It would have chosen a new leader in Numbers 14:4 to abandon the pillar of cloud and lead them back to slavery in Egypt. The Lord responds to Korah's popular support in 15:41, when he tells Israel that *"I am the Lord your God, who brought you out of Egypt to be your God"*. Moses did not need to consult polling data as the leader of God's People, because the Lord's vote is the only one that actually matters. He wants to be seen through his People, and he gets to choose the leaders who will best make him visible.

Second, the Lord tells us that spiritual authority cannot be founded on *good connections*. Korah and his Levite supporters knew the workers at the Tabernacle every bit as well as Aaron and his sons, but their connections did not legitimize their desire to become priests in 16:10. The Reubenites were descended from Jacob's eldest son, but this connection did not justify their resentment towards the ascendant tribe of Levi in verses 12–14. The 250 officials who had been granted limited authority under Jethro's reforms viewed themselves literally as *"men of name"* in 16:2, but their fine reputations were no guarantee of spiritual authority. God chooses the leaders he chooses to choose, because one of the biggest things which stops him being seen through his People is the political manoeuvring of ambitious would-be leaders.

Third, the Lord tells us that spiritual authority does not even come through *gifting* or *impressive track record*. When Miriam touted her gifting as a prophetess in chapter 12, she ended up with leprosy instead of leadership. When the

---

[2] It is not unbiblical for congregations to vote to recognize the leaders God has appointed, but their authority comes from God and not the congregation's recognition of it (Deuteronomy 1:13; Acts 6:3–6).

Reubenites followed her lead in 16:12–14 by accusing Moses of incompetence and questioning his track record, the Lord silenced their wagging tongues by swallowing them up in an earthquake as a deadly reminder that true competence is always a grace gift from God.[3] When the Israelites as a whole accused Moses of murdering the rebels in 16:41, the Lord vindicated his much-maligned leader by striking down almost 15,000 of his accusers with a plague. No one can earn their way to spiritual authority through gifting or track record alone, since the Lord states clearly in 16:5 that *"the man he chooses he will cause to come near him."*

No. The lesson of these four chapters is that spiritual authority can only come through *God's sovereign choice*. Before the Lord commissioned Moses, a mere slave could send him running in Exodus 2:14 with the question *"Who made you ruler and judge over us?"* Once the Lord commissioned him, he could stand up to Pharaoh and face down each of these rebellions because he knew deep down that *"the Lord has sent me... It was not my idea"* (16:28). He does not respond to Korah and the other rebels by calling for a vote of confidence, or by reminding them of his connections to the Egyptian royal family, or by listing his successful track record since the Exodus. He simply tells them that they are rebelling against the Lord's choice of leader, then stands back to give the Lord space to vindicate him. A man who follows the crowd will never be followed by a crowd, but a man who knows the Lord has chosen him to lead can respond to challenges gently but firmly.

Because Moses was so remarkably secure in his leadership, he continued to make God visible even when he was under attack. He saves the lives of the Israelites in 16:22 and 46 by asking God to forgive them and sending Aaron to appease his anger with the smell of smoke from the altar of blood sacrifice. He lets the Lord vindicate Aaron as his chosen high priest by

---

[3] 2 Corinthians 3:5.

causing his dead wooden stick to bear fruit in resurrection glory. He consolidates this lesson in chapters 18 and 19 by directing Israel's gaze to the one who would cleanse them through a mixture of blood, water, wood and hyssop, all of which feature strongly in John's account of Jesus' crucifixion.[4] When leaders derive their authority from the Lord's choice alone, it frees them to lead with such gentle assurance that they make the Lord visible even through his unruly People.

There is a sequel to this story in Psalm 84, which was written by the descendants of the executed rebel Korah.[5] Whereas he was dissatisfied with his calling to serve in the Tabernacle courtyard and coveted the priesthood, his descendants had learned the lessons of Numbers 16–19. *"My soul yearns, even faints, for the courtyards of the Lord,"* they write as an expression of their contentment to serve under the calling God had given them. *"Better is one day in your courtyards than a thousand elsewhere; I would rather be a doorkeeper in the house of my God than dwell in the tents of the wicked... No good thing does he withhold from those whose walk is blameless."*

If even Korah's descendants could learn to submit to God's choice and delight in the parameters of the authority he had given them, then there is hope for even the unruliest of churches. When we submit to God's choice of leaders without grumbling or complaining, he teaches us to enjoy our own calling like the children of Korah. When we each delight in the grace and calling he has given us, we allow the sovereign God to be seen through his People.

---

[4] See John 19:29, 34.

[5] We discover in Numbers 26:10–11 that by God's grace not all of Korah's descendants died with him. The children of Korah wrote twelve of the Psalms.

Moses' Moment of Madness (20:1–13)

The Lord said to Moses and Aaron, "Because you
did not trust in me enough to honour me as holy
in the sight of the Israelites, you will not bring this
community into the land I give them."

(Numbers 20:12)

The warship *Mary Rose* was the perfect weapon for the English
King Henry VIII when she sailed out of Portsmouth harbour to
fight the French fleet in 1545. She was one of the few purpose-
built warships of her era, and one of very few vessels able to
fire a full broadside of cannons. After four decades of service,
she had recently been modified with below-deck gun ports to
shield her heavy artillery, but she was about to make history
on that July morning for all the wrong reasons. As she turned to
fire a volley at one of the French galleys, she listed too far to one
side and dipped her gun ports under the water. Her captain's
moment of madness undid forty years of glory. Within minutes
she had sunk with over 500 men on board.

Almost four decades had passed since the Israelites left
Egypt, and Moses' track record was even more impressive
than that of the *Mary Rose*. The constant refrain in both Exodus
and Leviticus is that *"Moses did everything just as the Lord
commanded him."* We are told over a dozen times in Numbers in
the run-up to this chapter that Moses ensured that the Israelites
followed God's commands to the letter,[1] and even here we are

---

[1] He even took up the census of Israel on the very same day that he received
the command in 1:1, 18.

told in 20:9 that *"Moses took the staff from the Lord's presence, just as he commanded him."* Yet Moses was about to have a *Mary Rose* moment, and the Lord wants to teach us through his tragic fit of disobedience.

It was the first month of Israel's final year in the desert, and they had arrived back at Kadesh Barnea where the ten spies had reaped the reward of their blind unbelief thirty-eight years earlier. Almost all of the Exodus generation had died in the meantime, and the death of Moses' sister Miriam reinforced that the nation was stepping into a new beginning. When Moses saw that the new generation of Israelites were as complaining and rebellious as their sinful parents, it finally proved too much for the ever-patient leader.

As usual Moses took the People's complaining to the Lord, but notice the change in his tone as he addresses them in verse 10: *"Listen, you rebels, must we bring you water out of this rock?"* He lacks his normal concern to identify himself with the Israelites, and treats the problem as something which he and Aaron have to solve. He is so consumed with Israel's unfaithfulness that he forgets the Lord is God the Faithful One. Thirty-nine years earlier at Rephidim in Exodus 17, the Lord had commanded him to hit a rock with his staff in order that water might gush out for the Israelites, but this time the Lord simply told him to *"Speak to that rock before their eyes and it will pour out its water."* Moses was as distracted as the captain of the *Mary Rose*, and was about to shipwreck his own hope of leading the new generation of Israelites into the Promised Land. He angrily struck the rock twice with his staff in direct disobedience to God's command.

Many readers struggle to understand why the Lord took Moses' sin so seriously. Why should it matter whether Moses spoke or struck the rock? What they forget is that the Lord wants to preach the Gospel through his People, and Paul tells us that the Israelites *"drank from the spiritual rock that accompanied them, and that rock was Christ".*[2] Let's backtrack over the story with this Gospel perspective to see why little acts of disobedience make such a massive difference.

Do you remember the Gospel lessons the Lord displayed through the Israelites in the first few days after the Exodus? He told them to sacrifice a Passover lamb as a picture of Jesus' death on the cross as God's Redeemer. He showed the power of water baptism to take off the spiritual handbrake when he led them through the Red Sea and drowned their former masters. He taught them the importance of the cross when he healed the bitter waters of Marah, then provided them with manna from heaven as a picture of Jesus, God's Word, who would be broken to feed his People. This culminated in the rock of Rephidim, where the Lord gave them a picture of the gift of the Holy Spirit which the risen and ascended Lord Jesus would pour out on his People.

Moses needed to strike the first rock at Rephidim with his wooden staff in Exodus 17, because the outpouring of the Holy Spirit is linked to Jesus' sacrifice at Calvary. *"If anyone is thirsty, let him come to me and drink,"* Jesus explained in John 7:37–39. *"Whoever believes in me, as the Scripture has said, streams of living water will flow from within him."*[3] John clarifies for us that *"by this he meant the Spirit"*, but then tells us that the Spirit could not be poured out until Jesus had suffered on the cross and been glorified. When Moses hit the rock at Kadesh Barnea in the same way as at Rephidim,[4] he unwittingly twisted this Gospel message. He did not trust the Lord to grant this blessing again and again through the once-for-all sacrifice he had already enacted thirty-nine years previously.

God still wants to be seen through his People, and he still

---

[2] 1 Corinthians 10:4.

[3] Jesus expected the Jews to see this promise in Scriptures such as Exodus 17 and Numbers 20.

[4] Moses renamed both the rock at Rephidim and the one at Kadesh Barnea *"Meribah"*, which means *Quarrelling* (Exodus 17:7; Numbers 20:13).

takes it seriously when we display a doctored Gospel to the world. If we doubt the finality of Jesus' work on the cross; if we deny the importance of Christians being filled with the Holy Spirit; if we treat a charismatic experience in the past as a one-off blessing instead of something to be spoken into being all along our Christian journey; if we do anything similar to Moses' *Mary Rose* moment, then such little modifications of the Gospel become massive barriers to us inheriting all that God intends to give us. The Lord wanted to make himself visible through the obedience of Moses and Aaron in verse 12, but instead he would make himself visible by judging their disobedience in verse 13. Neither of them would enter the Promised Land.[5]

It therefore doesn't really matter if our track record as Christians is as impressive as that of Moses or of Henry VIII's great warship *Mary Rose*. The Lord warns us that he wants his Gospel to be seen unimpeded through his obedient People. He urges us to learn from Moses' moment of madness and not repeat it ourselves. Let's do nothing to distort the message of the crucified, risen and ascended Saviour, who still freely pours out God's Spirit on his People whenever they ask him today.

---

[5] The Lord includes both Moses and Aaron in verse 12 by using the *"you plural"* form of the verb in Hebrew.

Snakebite (21:4–9)

So Moses made a bronze snake and put it up on a pole. Then when anyone was bitten by a snake and looked at the bronze snake, he lived.

(Numbers 21:9)

Aaron was dead. His *Mary Rose* moment of madness had cost him dearly. He had gone the same way as the 600,000 Israelites who had been counted in the census of Numbers 1 but had failed to trust in God the Faithful One only a few days later on the border of the Promised Land. The corpses of almost all that generation were now rotting in the desert outside the Promised Land they had refused. Now, as he installed Aaron's son Eleazar as the new high priest of Israel, the Lord decided it was time to teach the new generation of Israelites what it truly meant to place their faith in him to save them.

First, he convinced them that *sin is always fatal without the Gospel.* He deliberately tested them by guiding them south towards the Red Sea and away from the border of the Promised Land to test them. Moses tells us literally in 21:4 that *"the people became impatient because of the way"*,[1] and rebelled against God and his servant Moses because of their route, their lack of food and water, and the monotony of eating manna every day. They sinned by accusing the Lord of being an unfaithful murderer, so he punished them with a plague of poisonous snakes. The Greek historian Herodotus tells us that *"the vipers and the winged serpents"* which infested that region possessed the ability to coil

---

[1] Green's Literal Translation.

and spring through the air, so no protective footwear could save them.[2] The new generation of Israelites had sinned like the old one, and God must teach them that the wages of sin is always death.

Next, the Lord revealed that *the Gospel is the one and only remedy for sin.* When the Israelites grasped that fatal venom was in their veins, they cried out to the Lord and he answered their prayer. He told Moses to make a bronze model of a snake and raise it up on a pole to deliver them.[3] The Hebrew word *nes* in verse 8 means *pole* or *banner* and is the same word Moses used when he held up his wooden staff at Rephidim in Exodus 17 and worshipped God as *Yahweh-Nissi,* the *Lord My Banner.* It is also the word used in Isaiah 11:10 in the prophecy that Jesus the Messiah would be the *banner* to which the nations would rally so that the Lord could be seen through his People. The cross of Jesus is the only antitoxin that can deal with sin.

The Lord deliberately chose to use a bronze snake because no other object looked less likely to heal a snakebite. Human wisdom would rush after fleshly patch-up jobs and man-made serums, and would despise God's message about a snake on a stick. It still despises the message about a Saviour who died on a cross to atone for our sin,[4] but Jesus prophesied in John 12:32 that *"I, when I am lifted up from the earth, will draw all people to myself."* He saves anyone who believes in God's foolish message of salvation.

Next, the Lord taught the Israelites that *faith by itself has no power to save anyone.* If an Israelite looked at the Tabernacle in faith that God would heal him, he died. If he looked at the pillar of cloud and fire with great faith, he also died. Faith in

---

[2] Herodotus in his *Histories* (3.109.1–3), written in the late fifth century BC. See also Isaiah 14:29.

[3] The serpent Satan hates the Gospel so much that he later convinced the Israelites to worship the bronze snake as an idol instead of the Lord (2 Kings 18:4). He wants to turn our worship aids into distractions too.

[4] 1 Corinthians 1:18–25.

God in general has never saved anyone, but only faith in the means of salvation he has provided. It didn't matter if an Israelite doubted that looking at the bronze snake could heal his snakebite at all, he would be healed just so long as he looked at it with the faltering faith he possessed. What matters is never the measure of our faith, but the power of the object in which our faith is placed. If you lend me money, it matters little what you believe about my character; what matters is whether I am genuinely faithful. The bronze snake showed the Israelites that their hope of salvation lay in a forthcoming sacrifice from God the Faithful One.

Next, the Lord taught the Israelites that *salvation comes through faith, but true saving faith will always lead to action.* They didn't need to bring anything, be anything, say anything or achieve anything to be healed. God's way of salvation is disarmingly simple. But talking about faith in the Lord and his bronze snake could not deliver anyone, because *"faith by itself, if it is not accompanied by action, is dead".*[5] If an Israelite spoke much about the bronze snake but never actually turned to look at it, he died. If another Israelite could not explain the bronze snake half as eloquently yet looked at it, he lived. In the same way, God encourages each of us to examine our lives to see evidence for our faith. Faith always changes how we live, just as true faith in the bronze snake would always lead to going and looking.

Finally and most importantly, the Lord taught the Israelites that *nobody can be bitten by sin's venom to a point at which they are beyond the power of the Gospel to save them.* Moses tells us in verse 8 that God promised to heal *anyone*, and repeats in verse 9 that *anyone* who looked at the bronze snake was healed. Jesus quoted from this passage to make the same point when he taught the Gospel to Nicodemus many centuries later in John 3:

---

[5] James 2:17.

*Just as Moses lifted up the snake in the desert, so the Son of Man must be lifted up, that **everyone** who believes in him may have eternal life. For God so loved the world that he gave his one and only Son, that **whoever** believes in him shall not perish but have eternal life... **Whoever** believes in him is not condemned, but **whoever** does not believe stands condemned already.*[6]

These "whoevers" remind us that we must respond to the Gospel like this new generation of Israelites, not like their apathetic fathers. If you are not sure that you have truly been saved through Jesus, the one this bronze snake pointed to, it is time for you to turn your eyes to his cross and ask him to forgive your sin. If you know you have been saved, it is time for you to share this Gospel with every sin-bitten unbeliever who is dying from the bite of *"that ancient serpent, who is the devil, or Satan."*[7]

The Lord reminded the new generation of Israelites that this is the Gospel which would lead them into the Promised Land in spite of their sin. He reminds us that this Gospel still saves anyone in our own generation who looks up at Jesus' cross and puts their trust in God the Faithful One.

---

[6] John 3:14–18.

[7] Revelation 12:9; 20:2.

Genocide (20:14–21:35)

Then Israel made this vow to the Lord: "If you will deliver these people into our hands, we will totally destroy their cities." The Lord listened to Israel's plea and gave the Canaanites over to them. They completely destroyed them and their towns.

(Numbers 21:2–3)

In my house we have the strangest children's Bible. It has only two pages in which to cover Israel's forty years in the desert, so it places the Sixth Commandment – *"You shall not murder"* – on the same page as God's order to annihilate the Canaanites. When I recently read those pages to my children at bedtime, my four- and six-year-olds started laughing and assumed that I was playing a trick on them. *"Stop it, Daddy. Read it properly!"* they objected. But I was reading it properly. That causes me a problem.

Frankly, it should cause you a problem too. The Americans and Soviets agreed on virtually nothing in the year of the Berlin Blockade, but even they found common ground to assert together that year that *"genocide is a crime under international law, contrary to the spirit and aims of the United Nations and condemned by the civilised world."*[1] How can God therefore order the Israelites to annihilate whole nations and see this as an important part of him being seen through his People? As the story of the Pentateuch turns towards the conquest of the

---

[1] Quoted from the UN General Assembly's Resolution 260 against genocide in December 1948.

Promised Land, we cannot simply ignore the question which provoked Richard Dawkins to assert that *"The God of the Old Testament is arguably the most unpleasant character in all fiction:... A vindictive, bloodthirsty ethnic cleanser, a misogynistic, homophobic, racist, infanticidal, genocidal, filicidal, pestilential, megalomaniacal, sadomasochistic, capriciously malevolent bully."*[2] Thankfully Moses, himself a genocide survivor, foresaw this objection and answers it head on with some commentary in Deuteronomy 7. Why did the Lord order Israel to wipe out the indigenous inhabitants of Canaan, and what does this tell us about his character?

Moses explains in Deuteronomy 7:1–6 that this was simply the outworking of the Lord being *God the Holy One*. When we object to the judgment that the Lord decreed for the Canaanites, Amorites and Midianites in these final chapters of Numbers, we simply prove that we have not yet fully grasped the message of Leviticus that sin is deadly serious. We forget that these people groups were gang-rapists, baby-murderers, drunkards, idolaters and incestuous sexual perverts.[3] The Lord tells us in Leviticus 18 that such practices defiled the Promised Land, so he ordered the Israelites to perform a spiritual spring clean. This was not ethnic cleansing, as is demonstrated by the opposite fates of Rahab and Achan in Joshua 7. Rahab the Gentile prostitute converts to Yahweh and is saved, whereas Achan the Hebrew chooses idols and must die. The Lord wants us to be shocked by the annihilation of the sinful Canaanite nations, because it is a picture of a greater Judgment Day which is coming to the whole world. Unless we repent of our objections and turn away from sin, we will have an even greater problem with God the Holy One when he comes to end world history with fire.

Moses tells us in the rest of Deuteronomy 7 that this was

---

[2] Richard Dawkins, *The God Delusion* (2006).

[3] For example, Genesis 19:4–9, 30–38; Leviticus 18:1–30; 20:1–6; Deuteronomy 9:5. God wants us to feel the same horror against these sins as Phinehas in Numbers 25:6–13. Tolerance is not always a virtue.

simply the outworking of the Lord being *God the Indweller*. We tend to forget how easily the Israelites were led astray, like an insecure teenager caving in quickly to peer pressure. They worshipped Canaanite idols before God took them down to Egypt, then swapped them for Egyptian idols during their years of slavery. They even started worshipping Moabite idols during the few days they spent camping near Moabite territory in Numbers 25![4] *"Do not defile the land where you live and where I dwell, for I, the Lord, dwell among the Israelites"*, the Lord warned, and then told them that they would find this command harder to obey than they imagined. Their only hope of steering clear of pagan idolatry was to *"destroy all the peoples the Lord your God gives over to you. Do not look on them with pity and do not serve their gods, for that will be a snare to you."*[5]

That's why Moses also tells us in Deuteronomy 7 that this was simply the outworking of the Lord being *God the Faithful One*. We must not forget his statement in Deuteronomy 7:9–10 that there are two aspects to the fact that *"the Lord your God is God; he is the faithful God"*. We tend to be happy that it means *"keeping his covenant of love to a thousand generations of those who love him"*, but rather less comfortable that it also means that *"those who hate him he will repay to their face by destruction"*. Remember that this problem was much closer to home for Moses than for us, since he was married to a Midianitess and had lived for forty years in Midian. We cannot fathom the depth of his agony in Numbers 31 when the Lord tells him to slaughter the Midianites who had rejected the Gospel preaching of Jethro, the Lord's missionary-priest to their nation.[6] His own sons were half-Midianite, and he had no doubt preached Yahweh in the Midianite language himself, but he knew that those who

---

[4] Genesis 31:19; 38:15, 21; Numbers 25:1–3; Joshua 24:14; Ezekiel 20:7–8.

[5] Numbers 35:34; Deuteronomy 7:16. See also Numbers 33:55–56.

[6] Exodus 2:15–22; 18:1–12. Even so, Moses told the soldiers in 31:14 to go even further in their slaughter than they intended. He understood that compromise would lead to the situation of Judges 6:1–2.

reject God the Saviour must ultimately encounter him as God the Judge. *"He is patient with you, not wanting anyone to perish, but everyone to come to repentance. But the day of the Lord will come like a thief."*[7]

Perhaps that's why Moses is sure to fill these chapters of judgment with plenty of reminders that the Lord is *God the Saviour*. God forbids the Israelites from fighting the Edomites in Numbers 20, despite their rudeness, because he still had plans to save many of Esau's descendants in the future. He forbids them from fighting the Moabites in Numbers 21, because he had similar plans to save many of Lot's descendants too.[8] He only commands them to destroy the Amorites after they choose to respond aggressively to Israel's kind overtures, and he only tells them to destroy the Midianites in Numbers 31 when they conspire with King Balak of Moab to corrupt God's holy People. Before we complain about these chapters of fierce judgment, we should note the inclusion of Hobab the Midianite, Rahab the Canaanite and Ruth the Moabitess among God's People.

Seven centuries earlier, the Lord had told Abraham in Genesis 15:16 that *"the sin of the Amorites has not yet reached its full measure"*. As we read how he finally judged them when they failed to repent, we must not shrink back in embarrassment or complain against the Lord. This judgment is what it means for the Lord to be God the Holy One, God the Indweller and God the Faithful One. If anyone ignores his tender message that he is God the Saviour, they will reap his fierce destruction when he comes as God the Judge.

---

[7] 2 Peter 3:9–10.

[8] Deuteronomy 2:5, 9; 23:7–8; Ruth 1:4, 15–17.

Permissive (22:1–25:18)

> *God came to Balaam and said, "Since these men*
> *have come to summon you, go with them"... But*
> *God was very angry when he went.*
>
> (Numbers 22:20, 22)

"Lord, do not take the least notice of any petition of mine if I ask for anything that is not for thy glory and for my own and others' good!" That's what Charles Spurgeon taught the people at his prayer meetings to pray.

> Be so good as to thwart me when I want that which would
> do me harm. Be so kind as to be cruel to me sometimes.
> Understand that this proviso of mine shall override all
> the petitions that I may put up when I am suffering from
> fever. Do not mind what I say then; do not give heed to
> me when I talk nonsense; but let me have only what I ask
> for when I am in my right senses, when I am my inmost,
> truest, healthiest self.[1]

If we need any encouragement to pray Charles Spurgeon's prayer ourselves, then we have only to look at the tragic fate of Balaam.

Balaam son of Beor was an Aramaean soothsayer who made his living as a self-appointed spokesman for the gods. Archaeologists have unearthed an inscription in primitive Aramaic at Deir Alla in Jordan, which records an ancient

---

[1] From one of Charles Spurgeon's nineteenth-century messages recorded in *Only A Prayer Meeting* (2010).

prophecy of *"Balaam son of Beor, the man who was a seer of the gods"*. He was King Balak of Moab's natural choice of helper, since any nation he cursed would be unable to annihilate the Moabites as the Israelites had the Amorites.

Balaam knew something of Israel's God, but he assumed he could manipulate him like a common idol. Although he addressed him as *Yahweh*, he refused to submit to him by praying the words of Charles Spurgeon's prayer. When he saw the size of Balak's fee for divination, he asked the Lord for permission to take it and curse the Israelites, and he was bitterly disappointed when the answer came back: *"Do not go with them. You must not put a curse on those people, because they are blessed"*. When Balak sent fresh messengers who offered him an even greater fee, he didn't send them packing but tried to change God's mind. He addressed him in 22:18 as *"the Lord my God"*, but rebelled by even asking the question. He discovered the hard way that God has a permissive will for our lives which is far less pleasant than his perfect will.[2] *"Go with them,"* the Lord conceded, but he *"was very angry when he went"*. Balaam's example teaches us to trust in the faithfulness of God, even when his will crosses our own.

Moses does not tell us whether there was anything genuine about Balaam's faith in the Lord.[3] What he tells us is that God was still merciful to Balaam and sent an angel to block his path three times to stop him from riding into danger. Three times Balaam's donkey saw what the so-called seer was too money-blind to notice, and the Lord even opened the donkey's mouth so it could rebuke him. Beasts of burden *"which have no understanding but must be controlled by bit and bridle"* are more able to see the difference between God's perfect will and his permissive will than a person who thinks he can manipulate the

---

[2] See also Deuteronomy 5:29.

[3] He simply hints that Balaam was a spiritual phoney by telling us that he was a sorcerer who was just as at home on the high places of Baal as he was at the Lord's altar (22:40–23:6; 24:1).

Lord.[4] The angel followed this miracle by appearing to Balaam and warning, *"I have come here to oppose you because your path is a reckless one before me."*[5]

Surely Balaam would finally learn his lesson? *"If you are displeased, I will go back,"* he said, still resisting the Lord's unambiguous rebuke. *"Go with the men, but speak only what I tell you,"* God conceded, and the foolish Balaam rode onwards into God's permissive will. There is something worse than praying to the Lord and not being answered. It is praying with such arrogant insistence that he grants your request but lets you stray from his perfect will.

Things do not work out for Balaam as he hoped in chapters 23 and 24. Every time he asks the Lord to inspire him to curse Israel, he finds himself speaking blessings instead. He forfeits Balak's divination fee in 24:11, but by then his heart has already been fatally corrupted. He tries to set off home in 24:25, but we discover in 31:8 that he quickly makes a U-turn on his donkey. In 2 Peter 2:15 and Jude 11 we are told that he *"loved the wages of wickedness"*; he is an object of warning for any modern-day dreamer who hopes to make God dance to his tune. He was so out of tune with the Lord's perfect will that he tried a new approach with King Balak. We discover in 31:16 and Revelation 2:14 that Balaam devised the honey trap of chapter 25.

Balaam had evidently discovered that Leviticus 26 put curses on Israel if they disobeyed God's Law. He therefore figured that if God would not allow him to curse Israel, he could still earn his fee by seducing them into cursing themselves! He invaded Israel's camp with some beautiful Moabite and Midianite women who were far more dangerous than an army of men. Their offer of free sex quickly won the weak-willed

---

[4] Psalm 32:9. It was no harder for God to speak through a donkey than for Satan to speak through a snake in Genesis 3:1.

[5] The Hebrew word for *adversary* in 22:22, 32 is the root of the English word for *Satan*, the great adversary of all Christians. Balaam's greed had placed him on the wrong side of the spiritual battle.

Hebrews over into sleeping with them and worshipping their god Baal. God's permissive will had run its full course. It was now time for Balaam to pick up his pay cheque.

The message of Numbers is that God is always faithful, and that he even uses his permissive will in order to fulfil his perfect plans for his People. Phinehas, grandson of Aaron and son of the new high priest Eleazar, was so committed to making God visible through his People that he led a faithful remnant of Hebrews in turning back the tide of wickedness. They slaughtered their Israelite brothers in the way that the Lord had commanded them to slaughter their wicked neighbours, and their passionate zeal for God's holiness halted the plague, which had already taken 24,000 lives. Moses then led the reconsecrated Israelite nation in slaughtering Balaam's Midianite allies, and he tells us in 31:8 that *"They also killed Balaam son of Beor with the sword."* When we refuse to pray Charles Spurgeon's prayer and try to manipulate God's will to our own, we are effectively idolaters and cannot marvel when we feel the fierce heat of his judgment.

So rather than insist on receiving God's permissive will like Balaam, let's follow Paul's encouragement in Romans 12:2: *"Do not conform any longer to the pattern of this world, but be transformed by the renewing of your mind. Then you will be able to test and approve what God's will is – his good, pleasing and perfect will."*

Four Blessings (23:1–24:25)

When Balaam looked out and saw Israel encamped tribe by tribe, the Spirit of God came upon him and he uttered his oracle.

(Numbers 24:2–3)

The Lord has a clever way of emphasizing that his plan to be seen through his People cannot be thwarted. When the soothsayer Balaam stood on the cliff top to look out on the Israelites and curse them for Balak's fee, something happened to him which must have come as quite a surprise. Probably for the first time in his career as a professional prophet, the Holy Spirit came on him and inspired him to prophesy from the Lord. Some of the clearest descriptions in Numbers of God's plan to be seen through his People are actually given through this would-be opponent of his will. Let's look at the four blessings that Balaam spoke over Israel's future, and which summarize the message of the Pentateuch so far.

Balaam gave his first blessing in 23:7–10. Although he came from the high places of Baal in 22:41, it was the Lord who put these words of blessing in his mouth. Their theme is that the Israelites make God visible as *The Holy One* by the way in which they live in separation from their sinful neighbours. Rebels like Balaam might normally need a donkey to point out God's invisible glory, but even he could see God's holy character through a People devoted to modelling a different way of living. Whenever God's People refuse to act like Egyptians, Canaanites or twenty-first-century Westerners, they shine in the darkness like the stars which represent them in Genesis 15:5. When they consider themselves set apart to transform and redeem their cultures through the Gospel, they become as numerous as the dust which represents them in Genesis 13:16.[1]

Balaam changes his vantage point over Israel, in the hope that a new location might enable him to curse them. However, *"the Lord met with Balaam and put a message in his mouth"* which was just as full of blessing as the first one. The second oracle of 23:18–24 declares that the Israelites make God visible as *The Faithful One* by the way in which he treats them in spite of their repeated sin. Balaam uses the Hebrew words *'āven* and *'āmāl* to declare in verse 21 that their *wickedness* and *mischief* have been covered over by God's grace.[2] Despite their endless sinning, their lives cry out to the nations, *"See what God has done!"* Their very survival as a nation is proof to the world that the Lord is faithful even when his People are unfaithful. *"God is not a man, that he should lie, nor a son of man, that he should change his mind,"* Balaam prophesies, and he would have been wise to have taken heed of his own words himself. *"Does he speak and then not act? Does he promise and not fulfil?"* This second viewpoint, like the first one, simply revealed the character of the God who wants to be seen through his People.

Balaam tries a third vantage point, but he still can't earn his fee because *"the Spirit of God came upon him"* and inspired him to prophesy the blessing of 24:3–9. He builds on his statement in his second blessing that *"The Lord their God is with them; the shout of the King is among them"*,[3] and declares that the Israelites make God visible as *The Indweller* by the way that

---

[1] Numbers 23:10 deliberately uses the same Hebrew word *'āphār*, or *dust*, as was used in the promises of Genesis 13:16 and 28:14.

[2] Balaam is not talking about Israel being protected from *misfortune*. The word *'āven* is the same word for wickedness that is used in 1 Samuel 15:23 to describe King Saul's rebellion, disobedience and idolatry.

[3] Unlike Moab or any of the Canaanite nations, Israel had no flesh-and-blood king. Balaam is declaring in 23:21 that the Lord is the true King of Israel and that he is made visible by the People of his Kingdom.

they camp around the Tabernacle. *"How good are your tents, O Jacob, your tabernacles, O Israel"*, he literally exclaims, using the word *mishkān*, which is used over 100 times in the Pentateuch to refer to the Tabernacle. Balaam prophesies that so far the world has only seen the start of God's plan to turn his People into a nation of Spirit-filled tabernacles. More than that, he predicts that *"Water will flow from their buckets"*, which is a precursor of Jesus' promise in John 7:38 that *"Whoever believes in me, as the Scripture has said, streams of living water will flow from within him."* The Holy Spirit reveals to Balaam that God's plan is bigger than the magnificent Tabernacle he sees below. God the Indweller wants to be seen through his People by turning each one of them into a living, breathing tabernacle.

At this point Balak loses his temper and refuses to pay Balaam any of his fee, but the prophet is now on a roll and speaks a fourth blessing for free in 24:15–24. This is the greatest blessing of them all, since it prophesies that the Lord will reveal himself more and more through Israel as *God the Saviour*. The same God who had delivered the Hebrew slaves from Egypt would raise up a Hebrew Messiah who would be an even greater ruler than mighty King Agag of the Amalekites.[4] Balak's scheming would fail and the Lord would raise up King David to slaughter the Moabites, Edomites, Amalekites and any other nation wicked enough to resist God's Kingdom rule.[5] In time, even this great victory would be eclipsed by his greater heir, Jesus the Messiah, when he defeated Satan and his demons: *"Having disarmed the powers and authorities, he made a public spectacle of them, triumphing over them by the cross."*[6]

---

[4] Balaam mentions this brutal Amalekite king in his third oracle. The Agag who was defeated by Saul and Samuel in 1 Samuel 15:32–33 must have been named after his great predecessor.

[5] 2 Samuel 8:1–15. *Sheth* is probably another name for Moab since several ancient texts refer to them as the *Shutu*. *Kenites* was another name for Midianites, and is used to describe Jethro in Judges 1:16.

[6] Colossians 2:15.

Balaam tried to thwart the Lord's plan to be seen through his People by demanding that God grant him his permissive will instead. Far from thwarting his plan, however, the soothsayer found himself the means through which the Lord announced his unstoppable plan. Moses records these four prophecies which the Holy Spirit gave to Balaam, so that every believer in each succeeding generation can know the utter invincibility of God's sovereign plan. God wants to be seen through his People as the Holy One, the Faithful One, the Indweller and the Saviour.

And there is absolutely nothing that Satan can do to stop him.

The Next Generation
(26:1–36:13)

Not one of them was among those counted by Moses and Aaron the priest when they counted the Israelites in the Desert of Sinai... Not one of them was left except Caleb son of Jephunneh and Joshua son of Nun.

(Numbers 26:64–65)

The Israelites must have felt like the Karate Kid during their forty long years in the desert.[1] In both the original 1984 movie and in its 2010 remake, the Karate Kid is forced to perform menial tasks by his teacher. He must wax a fleet of cars, sand a wooden floor, paint a fence, and repeatedly take on and off his jacket. It is tediously dull and appears to be doing nothing to advance his karate. In fact, it seems about as pointless as four decades in the desert.

If you've watched *The Karate Kid*, you'll know what happens next. When he complains in frustration, his teacher reveals that these menial tasks have been the making of him as a fighter. His waxing, sanding and painting have taught him perfect muscle memory to perform blocking and striking moves. As we come to the end of Israel's forty years in the desert, the Lord gives his People their own Karate Kid moment. However perplexing those years in the wilderness may have been, he reveals that they have forged a different character in this new generation of Israelites. It was a twist so surprising that Moses urged them to *"Remember how the Lord your God led you all the way in the*

---

[1] *The Karate Kid* (Columbia Pictures, 1984 and 2010).

desert these forty years, to humble you and to test you...to teach you...as a man disciplines his son."[2] We must look out for this same kind of twist in the confusion of our own lives, for the God we serve is far wiser than the Karate Kid's teacher.

The last eleven chapters of Numbers show us a *new kind of leadership*, which God had created within this next generation of Israelites. The number of fighting men counted in the census of chapter 26 is almost the same as in the census of chapter 1, but only two individuals were counted on both occasions. Not only had the ten unbelieving spies been killed instantly at the end of chapter 14, but their entire unbelieving fan base had died slowly during the chapters in between. Caleb had been promoted to lead the tribe of Judah, and he tops the list in chapter 34 alongside eleven other tribal leaders who share his thirst to cross the Jordan and start conquering. As for Joshua, he is chosen to succeed Moses in chapter 27, and to work alongside the new high priest Eleazar who has already made a promising start. His young son Phinehas led the resistance to Balaam's seduction in chapter 25, and *"this was credited to him as righteousness for endless generations to come."[3]* Forty years of stern discipline in the desert had created a new generation of godly leaders within Israel.

Phinehas' zeal was not an isolated factor. We can also see in these chapters that a *new kind of zeal* had gripped this next generation. All of Israel's judges had followed Moses and Phinehas in picking up their swords with shared passion in 25:5. The Simeonite tribe, long guilty of spiritual compromise, had shrunk to a third of its former size and a new spiritual

---

[2] Deuteronomy 8:2–5.

[3] Psalm 106:28–31. The Midianite woman killed by Phinehas was called Cozbi, or *Deceit*. When the Lord says that he *"made atonement for the Israelites"* by killing her, he is treating his action as a prophetic picture of Jesus destroying the great Deceiver in his own zeal later.

zeal had gripped the reconstituted Israel.[4] They slaughter the Midianites in chapter 31 and offer more of the spoils to the Lord than he requested, and they ready themselves in chapter 33 to do the same to the Canaanites as well. This is a generation who will turn from sin and compromise so that nothing will prevent God from being seen through his People.

These chapters also reveal a *new kind of faith* in this next generation. Their fathers had sent spies into the Promised Land but they had shrunk back in fear when they heard about its challenges. Now their children look back on the Amorite giants they have killed already and plan how to divide the land in chapter 34 before they have even set foot inside its borders! They promise cities and pasture land to the Levites in chapter 35, and plan to make some of them cities of refuge for the innocent, mindful of God's warning to them in 35:34: *"Do not defile the land where you live and where I dwell, for I, the Lord, dwell among the Israelites"*. Their faith over the Promised Land is so different from their fathers' that even when they squabble over who should inherit the land in chapters 27 and 36, the Lord is delighted with their faith and grants the daughters of Zelophehad's request. They are eager to lay hold of all the Lord has allocated to them. Their confusing years in the desert are finally paying off.

That's why these chapters also include long sections of legislation, which resemble the description of holiness we found in Leviticus. This next generation had a *new kind of commitment* to live by the pledges that their parents had made to the Lord, but had broken. They are eager to be reminded in chapters 28 and 29 about the Sabbath, the Passover and the other national feasts which spoke of their salvation. They seek clarification from Moses in chapter 30 about the making of vows so that they will not anger the Lord like their insincere

---

[4] The Simeonites shrank from 59,300 men in 1:23 to only 22,200 men in 26:14. Examples of their compromise are in Exodus 6:15 and Numbers 25:14. They are the only tribe not blessed in Deuteronomy 33.

parents.[5] These chapters are not a digression from the plot of Numbers. They form a natural part of this new generation's commitment to let God be seen through the wholehearted obedience of his People.

The Lord wants to use this to answer your confusion if your life is as hard and frustrating as the Karate Kid's. He wants to show you through these chapters that he is working godly character in you, *to humble and to test you so that in the end it might go well with you.*[6] Everybody loves the end of the movie when the Karate Kid wins the big fight because of the unconventional methods of his master. We just find it harder in practice to do the spiritual equivalent of waxing, sanding and painting today in order to become the great fighters of tomorrow.

A few weeks ago, one of my young friends discovered he had cancer. After his initial shock, he began his chemotherapy and surprised me by displaying the same faith as these Israelites. *"I warmly embrace this trial that will help purify my faith and develop my godliness, patience and perseverance,"* he wrote, *"and I trust make me a better Christ-follower, wife-lover, father and pastor."* Now that is a man who has learned the lesson of Numbers 26–36. That is a man like Joshua, Caleb or Phinehas – one of God's Karate Kids that he is training for the future.

---

[5] This clarification is not so much about men and women making vows as it is about how an individual's vows work in the context of a family (30:9). Vows had to be ratified by the head of the home.

[6] Deuteronomy 8:16.

Don't Cash Out Too Early
(32:1–42)

Let this land be given to your servants as our
possession. Do not make us cross the Jordan.

(Numbers 32:5)

Not all of the Israelites had learned the lessons of a Karate Kid. By way of contrast and as a call for us to respond to God the Faithful One at the end of Numbers, Moses also introduces us to some who were slower learners. Two and half tribes were much more like the contestants on the TV show *Who Wants to Be a Millionaire?*

For a programme which promises to make its contestants fabulously rich, *Who Wants to Be a Millionaire?* has made a surprising amount of money. The makers of the most successful TV game show of all time use human psychology to load the prize money to ensure that competitors cash out too early. Get all five final questions right, and you go home with a million, but get just one of them wrong and you lose all but a tiny fraction. Contestants are forced to balance risk against safety, and most of them crumble under the glare of the TV cameras. In its first twelve years on British television, only five people held their nerve to go home with a million.

In the middle of these last eleven chapters of Numbers, at the heart of their celebration of the new generation of Israelites, two of the tribes spoil the party. The Reubenites and Gadites approach Moses at the start of chapter 32 and ask for permission to settle for a smaller prize than God has promised. They point to the land that Israel has captured from the kings of the Amorites on the east side of the Jordan in chapter 21, and they argue that it is good enough for them to settle in instead of crossing over to take the Promised Land. A bird in the hand is worth two in the bush, so they would rather cash out early than have to fight like Karate Kids.

They appear genuinely surprised by how furious this makes Moses. After all, the matter seemed perfectly logical. The land to the east of the River Jordan was very fertile and it was largely unoccupied after the slaughter of the Amorites. They *"had very large herds and flocks"*, so they point out to Moses in a very matter-of-fact manner that those lands *"are suitable for livestock, and your servants have livestock"*. What could be wrong with them settling to the east of the river and leaving a little more land for the other ten tribes? It is as logical as cashing out early on *Who Wants to Be a Millionaire?*, but Moses explains that their logic is also deadly.[1]

First, he accuses them of using fine-sounding logic as a substitute for obedience. They are acting like the previous generation of Israelites at Kadesh Barnea, when they did evil by choosing to stay in the desert instead of entering the Promised Land. It does not matter that this time round the Amorite territory is fertile instead of a wasteland. They are still turning away from wholehearted obedience to the Lord, and exchanging his glorious promises for the lazy comforts of a man-made home. Even the fact that they ask *"Do not make us cross the Jordan"* betrays their sinfulness. Entering the Promised Land was not an irksome duty but the fulfilment of a destiny promised to the patriarchs! *"Here you are, a brood of sinners,"* Moses fumes at them in verse 14, *"standing in the place of your fathers and making the Lord even more angry with Israel."* When we settle

---

[1] Christian leaders need to call out the seriousness of sin to spare their people from delusion. People tend to assume that their sins are *small*, *limited* and *secret*. Moses exposes all three assurances as lies in verses 14, 15 and 23. This story links back to the chapter on "The Next Best Thing to Winning".

for Christian lives that are less than what God promises, he doesn't call it logical but utterly sinful.

Moses also warns them that if they cash out too early, their compromise will be contagious and will undo what the Lord has taught the other ten tribes during their years in the desert. *"You will be the cause of their destruction,"* he predicts in verse 15, and in verse 33 his prediction comes to pass. Half of the tribe of Manasseh suddenly enter the story, encouraged by the Reubenites and Gadites to make a similar request themselves. Manasseh was the tribe that had grown by two-thirds between the censuses of chapters 1 and 26, so it looked poised for a brilliant future serving the Lord.[2] Suddenly the tribe splits in two between *Karate Kid* fighters and *Millionaire* quitters. The no-risk religion of modern-day Reubenites and Gadites is still as destructive to churches. When we cash out too early and give up on God's promises, those around us suffer too.

Moses further warns that this present compromise will make it ever harder to follow the Lord wholeheartedly in the future. *"Shall your countrymen go to war while you sit here?"* he asks them in verse 6 with an eye to the days ahead. They have such an obligation to the other tribes in verses 22 and 23 that to fail to go to war would mean *"sinning against the Lord; and you may be sure that your sin will find you out"*. Sure enough, although they promise to play their part in conquering Canaan, only a third of them would ever actually follow through and go.[3]

These two and a half tribes reaped terrible disaster by cashing in God's promises too early. Those who crossed the Jordan were separated from their loved ones for several years until the Israelite army was finally disbanded in Joshua 22,

---

[2] Numbers 1:35; 26:34. Manasseh was Joseph's oldest son, but like Esau his descendants despised God's blessing and endorsed the Lord's decision to name Ephraim as the true spiritual firstborn (Genesis 48:8–20).

[3] Compare the number of warriors in Numbers 26 with the number who actually crossed the Jordan in Joshua 4:12–13.

because whenever we idolize comfort over obedience, the Lord destroys our idol anyway. Not only are compromised Christians even more miserable than out-and-out non-Christians, but it almost cost the two and a half tribes their very lives. They had such a reputation for compromise by the time they returned home that it took Phinehas' intercession to stop the nine and half tribes misinterpreting one of their actions and annihilating them like pagans in Joshua 22.[4] They bore the brunt of Israel's centuries of invasion from the east, being occupied in turn by the Moabites, Ammonites, Midianites and Aramaeans. Their land was annexed by the Aramaeans in about 815 BC, and after a brief reprieve was annexed again by the Assyrians in 732 BC.[5] Those who managed to survive the slaughter in these waves of invasion were taken into exile, never to return.

We have now reached the end of Numbers, so the Lord takes this opportunity to ask us, do we trust him as God the Faithful One? He tells us not to cash out on his promises too early and swap them for missed dreams and painful disappointment. Instead, he invites us to step forward in faith as a gutsy and well-trained conquering generation.

"We do not want you to become lazy," warned the writer to a much later generation of Hebrews, *"but to imitate those who through faith and patience inherit what has been promised."*[6]

---

[4] Once again they had compelling logic to justify their action, but this time Phinehas believed them.

[5] 2 Kings 10:32–33; 15:29; 1 Chronicles 5:18–26.

[6] Hebrews 6:12.

Deuteronomy:

God the Covenant Keeper

Covenant Part One
The Preamble (1:1–5)

These are the words Moses spoke to all Israel in the desert east of the Jordan…in the fortieth year, on the first day of the eleventh month.

(Deuteronomy 1:1, 3)

Moses was about to die and he knew it. It was mid-January, only ten weeks until the fortieth anniversary of the Exodus, and the time had come for the Israelites to enter the Promised Land. Moses' moment of madness at Meribah meant that he could never enter the Promised Land with them.

His sister Miriam was dead. So was his brother Aaron. Every one of the adults he had led out of Egypt, except for Joshua and Caleb, were all dead too.[1] The time had come for Israel to cross the River Jordan and start conquering the land, so it was time for Moses to exit the stage of world history. That's why Deuteronomy records the two-week-long goodbye that Moses gave to the Israelites on the plains of Moab to the east of the Jordan,[2] and ends with the death of their great founder-leader.

But Moses' famous last words were much more than just a tearful farewell. The word *Deuteronomy* means literally *Second*

---

[1] Moses was aged 120, Joshua and Caleb were both aged about 80, but all the other Israelites aged 20 or over at Mount Sinai had since died in the desert (Deuteronomy 2:14–16; 34:7; Joshua 14:7).

[2] Joshua 4:19 and 1 Kings 6:1 tell us that the Israelites crossed the Jordan in late March in c.1406 BC. Deuteronomy 1:3 tells us that Moses spoke these words in late January and early February.

Law,[3] because it repeated the covenant the Lord had made with their parents at Sinai and gave God's guarantee that its terms were still in force.[4] That's why the Holy Spirit inspired Moses to speak the words of Deuteronomy in the familiar structure of an ancient suzerainty treaty.[5] It was time for the Lord to reveal himself to Israel as God the Covenant Keeper.

One of the greatest surviving examples of an ancient suzerainty treaty was drawn up by King Mursili II of the Hittites. He had just restored peace to his empire by defeating an offshoot of the Amorites called the Amurru, and had installed over them a docile puppet ruler named Duppi-Tessub. Although the treaty was formed in about 1315 BC, ninety years after Moses wrote Deuteronomy, there is a remarkable similarity between the structure of the two covenants.

King Mursili began his treaty with a **preamble**: *"These are the words of the Sun, Mursili, the great king, the brave king of the Hittites, the favourite of the storm-god."* Moses begins Deuteronomy with a more humble preamble, but he follows exactly the same formula: *"These are the words Moses spoke... in the fortieth year, on the first day of the eleventh month... all that the Lord had commanded him."*

Next, King Mursili recounted the **past**: *"Duppi-Tessub, your grandfather Aziras rebelled against my father but submitted again... He brought three hundred shekels of refined, purest gold every year, never refusing the tribute my father imposed on your grandfather... When your father died, I did not drop you... I, the Sun, put you in the place of your father."* Moses follows the same

---

[3] The name actually comes from a slight mistranslation of 17:18 in the Greek Septuagint. The translators misinterpreted *"copy of this Law"* to mean *deuteronomion*, which means literally *"repetition of the Law"*.

[4] Although 29:1, 12 treats Deuteronomy as an extra covenant, 5:2–3 clarifies that it reiterated the covenant already made with Israel at Sinai, formally extending it to the next generation of Israelites and beyond.

[5] A suzerainty treaty was made between an emperor and one of his local puppet rulers. Deuteronomy is not structured as a treaty between equals, because the Lord is Almighty and we are not.

format by summarizing the Lord's past dealings with Israel in four chapters of history in 1:6–4:43.

By far the largest part of King Mursili's treaty with Duppi-Tessub consists of the detailed ***provisions*** of the treaty. Although he promises that *"I, the king, will be loyal towards you, Duppi-Tessub; when you take a wife, and when you beget an heir, he shall be king in the land of Amurru"*, he also states at considerable length what he expects his puppet ruler to do for him in return. He must not neglect to pay his tribute, he must never make a pact with Egypt and he must promote the interests of the Hittites in many specific ways. Moses also spends the bulk of Deuteronomy in listing the detailed provisions of God's Covenant with Israel from 4:44–26:19. He repeats and expands on the Law of Sinai, because the new generation needed to know what the Lord expected of them.

King Mursili then moved into ***promises and penalties***, giving a series of blessings and curses in the names of his Hittite gods: *"If Duppi-Tessub fails to honour the words of the treaty and oath inscribed on this tablet, may these gods we swear by destroy Duppi-Tessub together with his body, his wife, his son, his grandson, his house, his land and everything he owns. But if Duppi-Tessub honours the words of the treaty and oath inscribed on this tablet, may these gods we swear by protect him together with his body, his wife, his son, his grandson, his house and his country."* Moses ends Deuteronomy in a similar way in chapters 27–30, by listing a series of blessings if the Israelites keep the treaty and a series of curses if they break it. He urges them to choose to abide by God's Covenant, which he has given them for their good and not to harm them.

The final four chapters of Deuteronomy emphasize that this covenant will last longer than any human suzerainty treaty. They stress that it will last for ***posterity*** and apply to each succeeding generation of Israelites. Before Moses dies in the final chapter, he hands over leadership to Joshua and sings a song about the covenant blessings which will fall upon the generations to come. He blesses each tribe by name and leaves them in no doubt that *God the Saviour*, *God the Indweller* and *God the Faithful One* is also *God the Covenant Keeper*. He will never renege on his promises in Deuteronomy, and its final verses hint that he will send his Messiah to upgrade this Old Covenant with an even better one.

The Israelites instinctively recognized this structure, so we need this background history to grasp the message of Deuteronomy. Moses spent his last two weeks dictating God's suzerainty treaty with the People he had chosen and redeemed. The *preamble* and recap of the *past* reminded them that they could trust what he wrote, and the *provisions* reminded them to heed the fences that separated the unclean, clean and holy. It was now up to them to choose between his *promises and penalties*, and to respond to God's appeal to let him be seen through the obedience of his People.

As you read these final chapters of the Pentateuch, the Lord still wants to use them to win your heart to complete surrender. Will you be wise enough to bow the knee and serve the Sovereign Lord with full devotion, or will you try to rebel against his mighty rule? That is the question the Lord asks you through Deuteronomy. God the Covenant Keeper wants to be seen through his People.

Only be careful, and watch yourselves closely so that you do not forget the things your eyes have seen or let them slip from your heart as long as you live. Teach them to your children and to their children after them.

(Deuteronomy 4:9)

Napoleon Bonaparte had created the largest army in human history. He would have to do something very stupid to prevent his French Empire from dominating Europe for the next hundred years. That's exactly what he did when he took his Grande Armée of 700,000 men on the reckless invasion of Russia in 1812, and discovered that sub-zero temperatures can defeat the strongest army. Only 40,000 frostbitten soldiers ever made it back to France from a freezing retreat in the face of the Russian winter. The Napoleonic Wars were lost through one rash decision.

The philosopher George Santayana argued that *"Those who cannot remember the past are condemned to repeat it."*[1] On that basis, Adolf Hitler should have listened more in history class. By June 1941, his Nazi armies controlled Europe from Norway to North Africa and from France to Crete. Hitler had all but won the Second World War. But then he made the same mistake as Napoleon. He took the best of his Wehrmacht and invaded Russia, discovering the hard way that winter hadn't got any warmer. Over 4 million of Hitler's soldiers were killed in a

---

[1] George Santayana in volume 1 of *The Life of Reason* (1905).

carbon copy of Napoleon's blunder. I'm mentioning this to warn you that we forget the lessons of the past at our peril.

That's why God began his covenant with the new generation of Israelites with a recap on the past forty years of their history. He observed this normal convention for a suzerainty treaty because he knew only too well that the Israelites needed it. They were more forgetful than Jason Bourne on a bad day. Sixteen times in Deuteronomy he urges them to *"Remember!"* Eight times more he pleads with them *"Do not forget!"* Their greatest protection from disaster in the future was to look back on their nation's past history with Yahweh. Nothing else would keep them walking on the narrow path of blessing which the Lord would lay out for them in the rest of the peace treaty.

A firm grasp of their past would teach them *to believe in God's promises.* It would remind them in 4:20 that God chose them long ago *"to be the people of his inheritance".*[2] It would remind them in 1:8 and 21 that he had sworn to give the land of Canaan to their forefathers and that they were marching to take possession of what was already theirs by right. As they feasted their minds on God's promise to Abraham and Isaac that he would make their descendants as numerous as the stars in the night sky, they could look around at their 2-million-strong campsite and agree with Moses' statement in 1:10 that *"The Lord your God has increased your numbers so that today you are as many as the stars in the sky."* Their faith to cross the Jordan and conquer the Promised Land would be nourished by looking back on the miracles their nation had already seen: a son to Abraham's post-menopausal wife, protection in Egypt and during forty years in the desert, and the reminder in 3:11 that the Lord had already granted them victory over the giant King Og and his Amorite army as a foretaste of what he would do to

---

[2] Although Deuteronomy focuses on the Israelites receiving the Promised Land as their inheritance, it also stresses in 4:20, 9:29 and 32:9 that the Israelites were the Lord's inheritance.

all the rest.[3] Instead of succumbing to the discouragement of 1:28, history would teach them in 3:21 that *"You have seen with your own eyes all that the Lord your God has done to these two kings. The Lord will do the same to all the kingdoms over there where you are going."*

A firm grasp of their past would also teach them *to trust in God's character.* For all their grumbling, it would remind them in 1:31 that *"The Lord your God carried you, as a father carries his son, all the way you went until you reached this place."* It would back up Moses' statement in 2:7 that *"He has watched over your journey through this vast desert. These forty years the Lord your God has been with you, and you have not lacked anything."*[4] It didn't matter that their challenges were going to get harder. If they remembered that God had hardened Pharaoh's heart to deliver them from Egypt, they would trust him to harden the hearts of the Canaanite kings in the same way to destroy them.[5] If they remembered how the Lord had been their Faithful One in 4:31, their Saviour in 4:32–34, their Holy One in 4:35–36 and their Indweller in 4:37–38, they would find it easy to trust him as they moved to the next stage.

A firm grasp of their past would teach them *to choose the path of God's blessing.* If they remembered what happened to their parents when they listened to the ten spies' blind unbelief, then it would help not to anger the Lord with similar unbelief themselves.[6] If they remembered what had happened more

---

[3] Og was one of the last surviving Rephaite giants, whose bedstead or sarcophagus was super-size (the Hebrew word *'eres* in 3:11 simply means *resting place* and could refer to either).

[4] In fact, Moses points out in 3:26 out that God is so committed to answering prayer that he had to tell Moses to stop praying for something he knew must not be given.

[5] Note the deliberate link between Moses' description of God hardening Sihon's heart in 2:30 to grant Israel his land, and hardening Pharaoh's heart in Exodus 7:3 to grant Israel freedom.

[6] Moses describes the human side of the decision to send out the twelve spies in 1:22–23, but he clarifies in Numbers 13:1–2 that God initiated it.

recently through Balaam at Baal Peor, it would convince them beyond doubt that disobedience is always madness. Since God's Law is perfect, they would grasp in 4:2 that adding to it is as a sinful as subtracting from it. Moses' survey of the past would prepare them to listen to the treaty provisions which were to come next.

Therefore a firm grasp of their past would persuade them *to surrender to God's plan* to be seen through his People. It would make them sit up and listen to the command of 4:6–8:

> *Observe [these laws] carefully, for this will show your wisdom and understanding to the nations, who will hear about all these decrees and say, "Surely this great nation is a wise and understanding people." What other nation is so great as to have their gods near them...? What other nation is so great as to have such righteous decrees and laws...?*

This is where you and I step into the story. God still wants to be seen through us, his modern-day People. He wants us to look back on the spiritual milestones of our past and give us similar faith from our personal histories in God's promises, person, path and plans. He doesn't want us to be as foolish as the historically challenged Hitler, who forgot the lessons of the past and reaped disaster for the future. God still wants to make himself visible. So let's retrace our past like Moses and, by looking back on our yesterdays, be ready to respond to God's new challenges today.

Joshua 2:1 shows us that the sin was not sending spies, but unbelief.

Covenant Part Three: The Provisions (4:44–26:19)

Hear, O Israel: The Lord our God, the Lord is one.
Love the Lord your God with all your heart and with
all your soul and with all your strength.

(Deuteronomy 6:4–5)

Dear John, I want a man who knows what love is all
about. You are generous, kind, thoughtful. People who
are not like you admit to being useless and inferior. You
have ruined me for other men. I yearn for you. I have no
feelings whatsoever when we're apart. I can be forever
happy – will you let me be yours? Gloria.

Now let's read that text message again with different punctuation, to show that where we place our emphasis makes a world of difference.

Dear John, I want a man who knows what love is. All
about you are generous, kind, thoughtful people, who
are not like you. Admit to being useless and inferior. You
have ruined me. For other men, I yearn. For you, I have no
feelings whatsoever. When we're apart, I can be forever
happy. Will you let me be? Yours, Gloria.

When many Christians read the detailed provisions of Deuteronomy, they place their emphasis on the first three words of 6:4 – *"Hear, O Israel"*. They assume that these laws applied to the Israelites but have very little relevance for us today. What use is the command in 14:21 not to cook a young goat in its mother's milk?[1] What use are the instructions in 21:10–14 on how to go about marrying a pretty prisoner of war? What meaning can there possibly be for us today in the command that a woman who grabs a man's private parts in the heat of a fight must have her hand amputated?[2] If Jesus called time in Mark 7:19 on the food laws of chapter 14, surely the rest have reached their use-by date as well? What this emphasis forgets is that Deuteronomy is quoted as much in the New Testament as Exodus, Leviticus and Numbers put together. The detail of these provisions may seem out of date, but the principles remain vitally relevant today.

The Pharisees read Deuteronomy and placed the emphasis on 6:25 – *"If we are careful to obey all this law… that will be our righteousness."* They treated these twenty-two chapters of detailed provision as a spiritual to-do list for getting right with God. They forgot that the Lord only gave the Law at Sinai *after* he had saved them through the death of the Passover lamb, or that he gave these commands on the plains of Moab at the *end* of Israel's wandering in the desert. They treated it as a formula through which people could be saved, instead of as a description of how saved people ought to live. The Pharisees added Deuteronomy to Exodus, Leviticus and Numbers in order to divide the Law into 248 commands, 365 prohibitions and 1,521 amendments. They built synagogues and preached that obedience to these treaty provisions was the path to being righteous. They were very offended when Jesus confronted them and told them that they had got their emphasis wrong.

Jesus gave the proper emphasis when one of them asked him to identify the greatest commandment in the Law. He

---

[1] Cooking a young goat in its mother's milk may have been a Canaanite fertility rite, but if not then this stands alongside 22:6–7 as a command not to be cruel to animals. See also Leviticus 22:28 and Proverbs 12:10.

[2] At the very least, this is a forceful reminder that the end never justifies the means.

identified the command of 6:5 as the pivotal verse: *"Love the Lord your God with all your heart and with all your soul and with all your strength."* Adding it together with its companion command in Leviticus 19:18 to *"Love your neighbour as yourself"*, Jesus explained that *"All the Law and the Prophets hang on these two commandments."*[3]

This meant rewriting the Pharisees' handbook.[4] It meant that these twenty-two chapters were actually a detailed explanation of what loving God and our neighbours truly meant in practice. They begin by repeating the Ten Commandments already listed in Exodus 20, which set God's standards so far beyond our reach that we might as well attempt the Labours of Hercules. The provisions continue with a stark reminder in 9:6 that *"it is not because of your righteousness that the Lord your God is giving you this good land to possess, for you are a stiff-necked people."* Then, after the general principles of chapters 5–11, they become frighteningly specific in chapters 12–26. When we read them with an emphasis on them explaining in practice what it means to truly love God, they drive us to our knees with a humble cry for mercy. *"Cursed is everyone who does not continue to do everything written in the Book of the Law,"* warns the Lord in 27:26.[5] These chapters are not a to-do list for Pharisees but a reminder that we can never make ourselves righteous before God, no matter how hard we try.

That makes these chapters in Deuteronomy as relevant to us today as they were to the Israelites on the plains of Moab. We also need to be stripped of our fatal self-confidence, because when boasting is silenced we can finally hear Jesus speak. *"Do not think*

---

[3] The Pharisees knew this was the right emphasis in Luke 10:25–27. They simply forgot to read the Law that way in daily practice. Note that Jesus adds the reference to loving with the *"mind"* himself.

[4] In fact, the way these provisions flit from one topic to another is a warning that God's Law defies codifying.

[5] Paul quotes this Septuagint rendering of the verse in Galatians 3:10. See also Romans 3:19–21.

that I have come to abolish the Law or the Prophets; I have not come to abolish them but to fulfil them," he explains. *"I tell you the truth, until heaven and earth disappear, not the smallest letter, not the least stroke of a pen, will by any means disappear from the Law... For I tell you that unless your righteousness surpasses that of the Pharisees and the teachers of the law, you will certainly not enter the kingdom of heaven."*[6] Jesus wants us to recognize that we can never become righteous by loving the Lord and each other as God commands. Our only hope is to admit that we have failed, and to look to the one who has fulfilled this Law on our behalf. When we place the emphasis rightly on 6:5, the command of 6:25 comes into its proper perspective. Because Jesus obeyed all these treaty provisions, yet died under the curse which our lawbreaking deserves, God is able to declare us righteous through the one that Deuteronomy prepares its readers to receive.[7]

With this right emphasis, we remember that the same Jesus who cancelled these treaty provisions in Colossians 2:14 now commands us to live out the principles behind them under the New Covenant *"Law of Love"*.[8] These chapters are vital because they carefully describe the five love languages which characterize how God's People should still love him. Some detail requires more explanation than others, but could there possibly be anything more important for us to learn?

So let's take a trip through these five love languages together, neither ignoring these pages like many Christians nor getting lost in the detail like the Pharisees. These chapters remind us how much we cannot save ourselves, and how we should express our gratitude that God saved us through his Son. When Christians understand the five love languages of Deuteronomy, God delights to be seen through his People.

---

[6] Matthew 5:17–20. A few verses later, Jesus reinforced and intensified the provisions of Deuteronomy by quoting them and saying *"You have heard that it was said…but I tell you…"*

[7] Galatians 3:10, 13, quoting Deuteronomy 21:23 and 27:26. See also Galatians 3:24.

[8] 1 Corinthians 9:21; Galatians 6:2; Romans 13:8–10; James 2:8.

First Love Language: Trust (8:1–20)

*Remember how the Lord your God led you all the
way in the desert these forty years, to humble you
and to test you in order to know what was in your
heart.*

(Deuteronomy 8:2)

The nation of Israel had done a lot of waiting. This new
generation had done little else. So it is fitting that the first of the
five love languages in the provisions of Deuteronomy is *trust*
in the midst of our day-to-day confusion. The acid test of the
Israelites' love for the Lord was their trusting him with their
past, their present and their future. Our own love still faces the
same acid test today.

The Israelites needed to trust God with their *past*, after
four confusing decades of wandering in the desert. They needed
to grasp what Winston Churchill did when he forgave his long-
term critics as soon as he became British Prime Minister: *"Of
this I am quite sure, that if we open a quarrel between the past
and the present, we shall find that we have lost the future."*[1] This
new generation needed to draw a line under their questions
and decide not to let bitterness and disappointment rob them
of what lay ahead. They needed to stand at the crossroads and
believe Moses when he told them that *"the Lord led you all the
way in the desert these forty years...so that in the end it might
go well with you."* To help them, he did more than simply ask

---

[1] Churchill spoke these words in his "Their Finest Hour" speech to the House
of Commons after the fall of France to the Nazis on 18th June 1940.

them to find closure on their past. He shed fresh light on their history.

He tells the Israelites that the Lord did not merely permit them to suffer the trials of the previous forty years. He deliberately engineered it for their own long-term good, because it *"humbled you, causing you to hunger and then feeding you with manna...to teach you that man does not live on bread alone but on every word that comes from the mouth of the Lord"*. Their greatest danger was spiritual pride and self-reliance, but four desert decades had prepared them for great victory. They must rejoice that he had led them through that *"vast and dreadful desert, that thirsty and waterless land, with its venomous snakes and scorpions"*, because he did it *"to test you in order to know what was in your heart"*. They must recognize the character their trials had forged inside them, and do what Paul did centuries later when he told the Corinthians that *"I delight in weaknesses, in insults, in hardships, in persecutions, in difficulties. For when I am weak, then I am strong."*[2]

The Israelites also needed to trust the Lord with their *present* and to pass the test their parents had failed four decades earlier. Would they trust the Lord enough to cross the River Jordan and conquer the land by faith? Moses asks this question in chapters 7 and 9, emphasizing that in the next few days they must attack *"seven nations larger and stronger than you...with large cities that have walls up to the sky. The people are strong and tall – Anakites!"* He does not want the Israelites to close their eyes to the facts, but to open them to the greater facts which the ten spies failed to see. Despite the overwhelming odds stacked against them, they must *"remember what the Lord your God did to Pharaoh and to all Egypt"*, and believe that *"the Lord will do the same to all the peoples you now fear."* Heaven's facts were

---

[2] 2 Corinthians 12:10, as demonstrated by Paul's singing in Acts 16:22–25.

more than able to transform the situation, since *"The Lord your God, who is among you, is a great and awesome God".*[3]

If you are a Christian, God wants you to face facts. He has called you to make disciples of nations,[4] cast out demons, heal the sick and bring his Kingdom to bear in every corner of the earth.[5] If you don't feel out of your depth like the Israelites, then you probably haven't grasped the scale of your task. Like the Israelites, God calls you speak his first love language by trusting him and crossing over to take the land. As Charles Spurgeon pointed out in a sermon on the Great Commission: *"You have a factor here that is absolutely infinite, and what does it matter as to what other factors may be? 'I will do as much as I can,' says one. Any fool can do that! He that believes in Christ does what he cannot do, attempts the impossible and performs it."*[6]

The Israelites also needed to trust the Lord with their *future*, since the Lord warns them in 7:22 that it will take them many years to conquer the Promised Land. The Israelites were not ready to handle overnight victory, as the land would be overrun by weeds and wild animals before they could settle in it. Moses warned that *"The Lord your God will drive out those nations before you, little by little. You will not be allowed to eliminate them all at once."* They needed to trust the Lord even when it took them five years to conquer the land in the early chapters of Joshua, and to trust him when a fifth of the land held out 400 more years until the reign of King David. Like us, the Israelites were prone to grow impatient, but they could prove their love for God by trusting him with their frustration.

---

[3] The word for *hornet* in 7:20 means literally *the scourger* and is linked to the Hebrew word for *leprosy*. They could trust the Scourge of Egypt forty years ago to be the Scourge of Canaan at the present time too.

[4] Note that Matthew 28:19 does not merely send us to make disciples *in* all nations, but *of* all nations.

[5] Mark 16:15–18.

[6] Quoted by Samuel Zwemer, the early twentieth-century pioneer missionary to Muslim Arabia and Egypt, in his missionary classic *The Unoccupied Mission Fields of Africa and Asia* (1911).

Perhaps you accepted Jesus' mission at conversion and crossed your own "River Jordan" to capture the "land". Perhaps the years of disappointment and failure have taken the edge off your radical love. If you have stopped sharing the Gospel, praying for the sick or speaking out for the Kingdom of God, the Lord wants to teach you to speak his first love language again. He wants to remind you of the example of the missionary William Carey, who worked for seven barren years in late eighteenth-century India without seeing a single convert in return. He confessed:

> When I left England my hope of India's conversion was very strong; but amongst so many obstacles, it would die, unless upheld by God. Well, I have God, and His Word is true. Though the superstitions of the heathen were a thousand times stronger than they are, and the example of the Europeans a thousand times worse; though I were deserted by all and persecuted by all, yet my faith, fixed on the sure Word, would rise above all obstructions and overcome every trial. God's cause will triumph.[7]

Sure enough, the breakthrough came in his eighth year and by the time he died three decades later there were half a million believers in his part of India.

If we meet the disappointments of the past, the anxieties of the present and the frustrations of the future with greater love for the Lord, then we can see a similar end to our own stories. When we speak words of *trust*, then the world sits up and listens, for it sees we are a People who truly love our God.

---

[7] Quoted from his diary in S. Pearce Carey's book *William Carey* (1923).

Second Love Language: Obedience (10:12–22)

SECOND LOVE LANGUAGE: OBEDIENCE (10:12–22)

Circumcise your hearts, therefore, and do not be stiff-necked any longer.

(Deuteronomy 10:16)

When God made his covenant with Abraham, he told him to do something surprising and painful. He told him to take a flint knife and cut off his foreskin, before doing the same to every male in his household. God's covenants are free but they are never cheap. Every circumcised Hebrew knew that only too well.

But something had happened during the centuries in Egypt which was almost as surprising as the original command. Despite the fact that circumcision was the non-negotiable mark of participation in God's Covenant, the Hebrews had silently dropped the tradition. Their bodies looked no different from those of the Egyptians, and they never felt the sharp pain of a flint knife as commanded. For the moment, God bided his time and said nothing.

When Moses began his journey back to Egypt after the burning bush, the Lord decided it was time to force the issue with his new messenger. He ambushed Moses as he settled down for the night in Exodus 4:24–26, and made as if to kill him. It took Zipporah, herself a descendant of Abraham through Midian, to guess why the Lord was so angry with her husband and to take drastic action to save his life. She reached for her saddlebag, found a flint knife and quickly circumcised their young son Gershom.[1] If Moses were going to lead Israel into a fresh covenant at Sinai, he would need to be leading his family with integrity according to the previous one made with Abraham.

The Lord reiterated his command for the Hebrews to be circumcised on the first Passover night in Exodus 12:48, and reissued it a second time in Leviticus 12:3.[2] Nevertheless, in Joshua 5:2–9 we discover that they only finally did so a month after Deuteronomy at the grimly named *Gibeath Haaraloth*, which means *Hill of the Foreskins*. Although the Lord wanted every male Israelite to be a circumcised, he didn't force the issue until he had taught them what circumcision really meant. *"Circumcise your hearts... and do not be stiff-necked any longer,"* he commands them in Deuteronomy 10:16. A "stiff-necked" person is someone who refuses to bow their head to obey, and circumcision was an outward expression God's second love language in these chapters. It was an outward symbol of humble *obedience*.

The Hebrew word *shāma'*, meaning either *to listen* or *to obey*, occurs almost ninety times in Deuteronomy. The word *shāmar*, meaning *to keep* a command, is used almost the same number of times. God gave the Israelites twenty-two chapters of treaty provisions, rarely bothering to explain why those commands actually mattered, because he wanted to give them an opportunity to show that they loved him by doing as he said even when they didn't understand why. Circumcision was *intimate* because it spoke of utter nakedness before God, and it was *bloody* because it spoke of a man letting his own will die.[3] Until the Israelites understood that this was an outward sign

---

[1] Exodus 4 only mentions one son, but she presumably circumcised both Gershom and Eliezer. Ironically Moses may well have been circumcised already, since it was common practice for the Egyptian royal family.

[2] He also referred to *"uncircumcised hearts"* in Leviticus 26:41.

[3] Colossians 2:11–12 says it particularly pointed to us dying and being raised to new life in Jesus.

of his second love language, he would not press them to make their grisly hill of foreskins.

This was brought home to me last month when I helped an Arab friend to break his Ramadan fast with an *iftar* evening meal. He makes much of being descended from Abraham's son Ishmael, much of his Muslim circumcision and much of the fact that *Islam* is the Arabic word for *submission*. Yet when he disappeared after dinner and I found him bowed prostrate on his prayer mat, he quickly betrayed that his obedience was external. When I asked him what he hoped to achieve through his month of prayer and fasting, he confessed that he actually lives a very sinful life. He hoped to offset his life of sin with thirty days of religion, as if outward signs could buy him some much-needed forgiveness.

These treaty provisions in Deuteronomy warn us not to think that outward religion can ever be a substitute for inward obedience. As the New English Translation of Jeremiah 4:4 puts it: *"Just as ritual circumcision cuts away the foreskin as an external symbol of dedicated covenant commitment, you must genuinely dedicate yourselves to the Lord and get rid of everything that hinders your commitment to me."* The Lord commanded the Israelites to circumcise their hearts because he didn't want their walk with him to be as empty and self-deluded as my friend's Islam. *"Neither circumcision nor uncircumcision means anything,"* Paul explains. *"What counts is a new creation...faith expressing itself through love."*[4] Obedience is not the way to curry God's favour but the way to express our love and gratitude that, despite not deserving it, we have it already.

These treaty provisions also warn us not to think that profession of faith can ever be a substitute for inward obedience. If you find these twenty-two chapters excessively long and detailed, you are probably closer to understanding them than you think. The Lord wants you to grasp that professions of

---

[4] Galatians 5:6; 6:15.

faith must be examined under the microscope of day-to-day obedience. The person who sings loudly on Sunday but lives like a non-Christian from Monday to Saturday shows he is a foreigner to God's People by not speaking his love language. *"If you love me, you will obey what I command,"* Jesus explained. *"If anyone loves me, he will obey my teaching... He who does not love me will not obey my teaching."*[5] The Lord wanted the Israelites to know from the start that being part of his People meant getting rid of their idols, their high places, their greed, their deception and their sexual immorality. Flint knives or no flint knives, without dead-to-self obedience, professions of faith are nothing more than painful lies.

These treaty provisions also teach us that obedience is as much a gift through the Gospel as forgiveness itself. The Israelites did not need to grit their teeth and try harder to conquer sin, because he promised in 30:6 that *"The Lord your God will circumcise your hearts and the hearts of your descendants, so that you may love him with all your heart and with all your soul, and live."* Paul explains that Old Covenant circumcision always pointed to Jesus' cross, where we have died to sin and been raised to new life. True *"circumcision is circumcision of the heart, by the Spirit"*, he teaches, *"the putting off of the sinful nature... done by Christ."*[6]

So let's learn the lesson of these chapters and not fool ourselves that outward religion or loud professions of faith can ever save anyone. God's true People are those who prove their profession of faith is genuine by letting him crucify their sinful desires and shape their heart for obedience by the power of his Spirit.

---

[5] John 14:15, 23–24. This echoes the way that Deuteronomy 5:10 and 7:9 equate *loving* God with *obeying* him.

[6] Romans 2:28–29; Colossians 2:11. Ezekiel 11:19–20 and 36:26–27 call this a *new heart of flesh* from the Spirit.

Third Love Language: Family Life (11:1–21)

Teach [my words] to your children, talking about them when you sit at home and when you walk along the road, when you lie down and when you get up.

(Deuteronomy 11:19)

One of my friends watched *The Lord of the Rings* on DVD and enjoyed it so much she asked if anyone had ever thought to make a book of the film. Topsy-turvy, uneducated, call it what you like – we do exactly the same thing when we treat God the *Father*, Jesus the *Son* and Jesus the *Bridegroom* as clever human metaphors. God did not look at fathers, sons, husbands and wives, and decide that they offered a useful picture to describe himself. He deliberately created humankind to reflect him this way because it is one of the ways he wants to be seen through his People. When we follow his plan in our family lives, we find that we are speaking his third love language.

The treaty provisions of Deuteronomy are full of instruction on how to build healthy, committed marriages. Moses told us in Genesis 1:27 that God created humans male and female in order to reflect his three-in-one nature. In Genesis 2:24, he gave us sex as the wedding present through which a man can *"be united to his wife, and they will become one flesh"*. Genesis catalogued some of the ways in which sex can be abused – lust, incest, rape, homosexuality, prostitution, adultery and unwise marriage[1] – and warned in 34:3 that even casual sex unites people together.

---

[1] Genesis 6:2; 19:5, 31–36; 34:2; 35:22; 38:8–10, 15–18; 39:7. Genesis 34:3 says literally *"his soul was stuck to her"*.

Therefore the Law – remember, the word *Torah* in Hebrew means literally *Instruction* – teaches those who love the Lord how they can use this gift properly. Don't be surprised by God's command that those who have unnatural or pre-marital sex should be punished as severely as blasphemers. Sexual sin is one of blasphemy's disguises, since God gave marriage as a major way for us to make his nature visible.

More positively, these treaty provisions encourage us to make God visible by following his plan. Since God is under no false illusions about how sinful humans are, he permits divorce in certain circumstances in 24:1–4,[2] but his main emphasis is on a call to make him visible by building loving, God-glorifying marriages. He tells us in 22:5 that men must not act like women and women must not act like men, because we are called to reflect the diverse unity of the Trinity. He encourages men in 21:10–14 that they can reflect the grace God shows his People by redeeming a woman captured in war and turning the slave-girl into a beloved wife instead.[3] He encourages women to express their love towards the Lord by loving their husbands, even if they don't deserve it.[4] This is the Old Covenant equivalent of Ephesians 5:22 and 25: *"Wives submit to your husbands as to the Lord... Husbands, love your wives, just as Christ loved the church."*

If you are unfamiliar with God's third love language, expressed in our family lives, you may point out that marriage is *two* and the Trinity is *three*. Of course you are right, which is why Deuteronomy also focuses on the third aspect of family life. It talked early on in 1:31 about the way *"the Lord your God carried you, as a father carries his son"*, and its treaty provisions

---

[2] Jesus offers his own commentary on these verses in Matthew 19:7–9.

[3] These instructions also prevented Hebrew soldiers from raping after battle, as other armies did.

[4] Shockingly, the Lord even suggests a rape victim may choose to marry her attacker in 22:23–29. The context is 22:13–14, which tells us that this protected her from a culture that deemed rape victims unmarriageable.

continue the same theme of loving God through the way we reflect him as parents and as children.

The twenty-two chapters begin by repeating the Ten Commandments, one of which is *"Honour your father and your mother"*. How we act as children towards our parents is a reflection of the Trinity, which is why the Lord commands that grown-up children who curse their parents must be punished like blasphemers in 21:18–21.[5] More positively, the Lord encourages children to reflect him through their faithful obedience in 5:16, *"so that you may live long and that it may go well with you."*

Parents can also find plenty of instruction here on how they can reflect God the Father through their parenting. Parents are responsible in 5:14 for their children's behaviour, so they must not shrink back from exerting physical authority to shape their lives. Moses encourages them in 8:5 that *"As a man disciplines his son, so the Lord your God disciplines you"*, and this is the Old Covenant equivalent of Ephesians 3:15, which tells us that God is *"the Father, from whom every family in heaven and on earth is named."*[6] The simplest and greatest parenting guide is to treat our children the same way that God treats us.

Furthermore, we are to train our children to put the Lord at the centre of their lives. We can start in 13:6–8 by making it clear to them that God comes first in the family, not them,[7] and by making God's Word the constant topic of family conversation in 6:6–9 and 11:18–20 – from morning to evening, at home and away. We can use feasts, household ornaments and everyday tasks as object lessons in 6:7 through which to *shānan* – literally *sharpen* – our children by chiselling away at their false thinking

---

[5] See also Exodus 21:17 and Leviticus 20:9. The reference to *"a profligate and a drunkard"* shows that this is not referring to young children, since 1:39 points out that they may not know any better.

[6] Ephesians 3:15 (English Standard Version).

[7] When we do this, God promises to bless our family life all the more. See Genesis 22:15–18 and Exodus 32:29.

and replacing it with a razor-sharp understanding of the Gospel.[8] Ronald Reagan claimed that *"Freedom is never more than one generation away from extinction. We didn't pass it on to our children in the bloodstream. It must be fought for, protected, and handed on for them to do the same, or one day we will spend our sunset years telling our children what it was once like in the United States when men were free."*[9] The Lord told the Israelites that in a similar fashion he had placed their nation's fate in the hands of each generation of parents.

So whether you are single, a husband, a wife, a son, a daughter, a parent or a grandparent – whichever life stage the Lord has led you into for the moment – the question is how are you speaking God's third love language in your family life? Are you conscious of being single or of loving your spouse to the glory of God? Are you conscious of honouring your parents or shaping your children for the glory of God too? Do you talk to your children throughout the day about Jesus, and teach them the daily discipline of family Bible study and prayer? This is what it means to speak God's third love language in our families, and to make the Lord visible through our day-to-day lives.

Let's take the encouragement of Martyn Lloyd-Jones:

> *If you love your children; if you would bring down the blessing of heaven upon your families; if you would have your children make their houses the receptacles of religion when they set up in life for themselves; if you would have religion survive in this place, and be conveyed from age to age; if you would deliver your own souls – I beseech, I entreat, I charge you to begin and continue the worship of God in your families from this day to the close*

---

[8] See also Exodus 12:26–27; 13:8–9, 14–16. Many Jews still obey the literal commands of Deuteronomy 6:8–9 and 11:18–20 through mezuzahs and phylacteries containing snippets from the Law.

[9] Future US President Ronald Reagan in an address to the Phoenix Chamber of Commerce in March 1961.

of your lives... Consider family religion not merely as a duty imposed by authority, but as your greatest privilege granted by divine grace.[10]

---

[10] Quoted by Donald S. Whitney in *Family Worship* (2006).

Fourth Love Language: Generosity (14:22–15:11)

> *Bring all the tithes...so that the Levites...and the aliens, the fatherless and the widows who live in your towns may come and eat and be satisfied, and so that the Lord your God may bless you in all the work of your hands.*
>
> (Deuteronomy 14:28–29)

A few days ago I took my young children blackberry picking. Mainly, I just wanted some ingredients for a pie, but I also saw an opportunity to apply the message of the previous chapter. When the Lord turned this new generation of Israelites from desert nomads to settled farmers, he took harvest time as a chance to teach them how to speak his fourth love language. He gave them lavish provision and then asked them to make him visible through displaying similar generosity themselves. There isn't much opportunity to go harvesting in London, so blackberry picking was as good as I could get.

Harvesting reminds us that God's grace is *lavish and overflowing*. That's why it didn't matter that my children ate far more blackberries than they collected in their baskets. God provided so much fruit that we could cram our mouths with berries and still have more than enough to take home for the pie. As we did so, I talked to my children about the God who is so wealthy that we can never run his resources dry. Each blackberry bush proclaims to the world that the Lord is not a reluctant giver. He delights to meet our needs and to surprise us with even more than we could ever have imagined.

Harvesting also reminds us that God's grace is *completely undeserved*. My children and I didn't plant the blackberry bushes, nor did we water them or do anything to provide them with sunlight. All we did was turn up at the very end of the process and reap the fruit of God's work on our behalf, quite regardless of our own. I could remind my children that God is not like Santa Claus, holding back his gifts until he has checked whether we have been naughty or nice. *"He causes his sun to rise on the evil and the good, and sends rain on the righteous and the unrighteous,"* Jesus tells us, so we should reflect God's undifferentiating generosity in order *"that you may be sons of your Father in heaven"*.[1]

Harvesting also provides us with an opportunity to *rejoice and praise God*. Everyone is happy when they find a bargain in the sales or if they receive a surprise present. As we feasted on blackberries, I encouraged my children to speak thankful prayers between mouthfuls and to celebrate God's goodness towards us.

In the context of the agricultural economy of Canaan, the Lord taught Israel through these treaty provisions to speak his fourth love language of *generosity*. Sadly, most of the discussions in the commentaries on these chapters are on tithing versus not tithing, or on differentiating between the "deserving" and "undeserving poor". That treats these chapters as nothing more than a long list of regulations, not a detailed expression of what it means to love the Lord. If read properly, they reveal our kind and generous God, and they tell us that he wants to be seen through his satisfied and grateful People.

For a start, Deuteronomy warns us that tithing isn't the issue. To clear that up, God actually mentions three different tithes in the Pentateuch: first a general tithe to the Levites from the people, then a second tithe to the Levites from any worshipper eating a sacred meal, then finally a third tithe paid

---

[1] Matthew 5:43–48.

every three years to the poor.[2] Deuteronomy tells us that giving a 10-per-cent cut of our income to God has never been a full expression of our love. What matters is the key principle of 16:17, which urges us to reflect God's lavish and overflowing generosity by *"giving a freewill offering in proportion to the blessings the Lord your God has given you"*. Like the Israelites, we are to recognize that all our wealth has come from God for us to steward for his glory.[3] Jesus unpacked these chapters when he taught in Luke 21:1–4 that what matters is not how much we give, but how much we have left.

John Wesley referred to this love language when he wrote that *"If I leave behind me ten pounds, you and all mankind bear witness against me that I lived and died a thief and a robber."*[4] He was true to this pledge throughout his life, earning £1,500 a year in his old age but still keeping only £30 for himself. *"You know the grace of our Lord Jesus Christ, that although he was rich, he became poor for your sakes, so that you by his poverty could become rich"*, Paul told the Corinthians without mentioning tithing. We are simply to reflect God's lavish generosity and to *"excel in this grace of giving"*.[5] Whenever we give to others as generously as the Lord gives to us, we speak his fourth love language and make him visible through our actions.

Furthermore, Deuteronomy warns us not to turn our backs on the so-called "undeserving poor". It concedes in 15:11 that *"there will always be poor people in the land"*, but far from treating this as a reason to ignore certain groupings, that same verse urges us to be all the more generous as a result.[6] We must

---

[2] Numbers 18:21–32; Deuteronomy 14:22–27, 28–29. Some scholars assume that these are three ways of using the same tithe, but most understand them to be three separate tithes.

[3] Deuteronomy 8:17–18; 26:9–11.

[4] Wesley writing in 1744, quoted by J. Wesley Bready in *England Before and After Wesley* (1938).

[5] 2 Corinthians 8:7, 9. Read the whole of chapters 8 and 9.

[6] Jesus quotes from this verse in Matthew 26:11, Mark 14:7 and John 12:8. The Mark verse and Luke 12:33 make it clear that helping such poor people is

help widows and orphans and foreigners and casual workers, even at the risk of them taking advantage of our kindness.[7] Since undeserved grace is at the heart of every harvest and at the very heart of the Gospel, these are precisely the kind of gifts which put the Gospel on display. The last pagan Roman emperor, Julian the Apostate, blamed this fact for the conversion of his empire to Christianity: *"It is disgraceful that...while the impious Galileans support both their own poor and ours as well, everyone sees that our people lack aid from us!"*[8] God wants his grace to be seen through his People, as they refuse to turn their backs on others because the Lord refused to turn his back on them.

Finally, Deuteronomy warns us that the Lord wants cheerful givers. Nine times these chapters tell us to rejoice as we give, since we cannot out-give our generous God.[9] The more we give today, the more we make space for him to entrust us with more tomorrow. Small wonder, then, that the New Testament sums up this fourth love language with a call for us not to give *"reluctantly or under compulsion, for God loves a cheerful giver"*.[10]

In the fields of Canaan, in the blackberry bushes of London, or wherever you may find yourself today, the Lord wants to teach you to speak his fourth love language. He is the lavishly generous God, and he wants to be seen through his lavishly generous People.

---

at the very heart of Christianity.

[7] We are told to take risks to help the poor in 24:6–18, and are told to pay labourers' invoices promptly.

[8] Emperor Julian wrote this in 362 AD in a letter to Arsacius, pagan high priest of Galatia.

[9] Deuteronomy 12:7, 12, 18; 14:26; 16:11, 14, 15; 26:11; 27:7.

[10] 2 Corinthians 9:7 goes alongside Deuteronomy 15:10. Paul also uses Deuteronomy 25:4 to argue in 1 Corinthians 9:9 and 1 Timothy 5:18 that God hates churches begrudging proper salaries to their leaders.

Fifth Love Language: Justice and Mercy (16:18–20)

Do not pervert justice or show partiality... Follow justice and justice alone, so that you may live and possess the land the Lord your God is giving you.

(Deuteronomy 16:19–20)

If you find Deuteronomy brutal in places, then I recommend you take a trip to the Louvre Museum in Paris. There you will find the Law Code of King Hammurabi of Babylon, which he wrote for his subjects in about 1790 BC.[1] If you find some of God's commands offensive, Hammurabi is the perfect antidote. He reminds us that Bronze Age Middle Easterners were very different in their thinking from twenty-first-century Westerners. When we understand the context of the culture in which it was given, we can grasp that God's fifth love language in Deuteronomy is *justice and mercy*.

While we tend to be offended by the *severity* of some of the punishments in Deuteronomy, its original Hebrew readers were offended for precisely the opposite reason. Among Hammurabi's 282 commandments for Babylon are ones that a man who slanders his neighbour's wife must be branded on the forehead, that a son who hits his father must have both his hands amputated, and that an adopted child who is ungrateful to his new parents must have his tongue cut out. Hammurabi

---

[1] Hammurabi's Law Code is carved on a stele similar to the ones described in Deuteronomy 27:1–8.

commanded that a doctor whose patient died on the operating table must have his hands amputated, and that a wet nurse who allowed a baby to die through negligence must have her breasts cut off. Although Hammurabi's Law Code dates back to almost 400 years before Deuteronomy, it nevertheless gives a broad picture of the kind of culture into which the Lord spoke his covenant through Moses. The Hebrews were not offended by its severity, but by its order to judge with unprecedented mercy.

Take the *death penalty*, for example. Execution was Hammurabi's stock solution, not just for murder but also for theft and a host of other petty crimes. Had someone bought goods from a slave and forgotten to get a receipt? Execute him. Had a barmaid sold drink for less than the state-sanctioned price? Bind her hand and foot and then throw her in the river. Had a tavern been used to discuss a conspiracy? Find the poor landlord and execute him too. In contrast, the Lord reserves the death penalty for murder, black magic, blasphemy, Sabbath-breaking, gross sexual sin and rebellion. Crimes against property were punished less severely, and cities were designated throughout the land in which unwitting perpetrators of manslaughter could find protection. You may not like the idea of any death penalty at all, but it is a foolish anachronism to project those modern feelings backwards in time. In a culture where executions were commonplace and frivolous, the Lord told his People to limit them as an expression of his mercy. Only the most serious criminals must die.

Something similar is true for the *lex talionis* – the principle of *"eye for eye, tooth for tooth, hand for hand, foot for foot"* – which insists that a punishment should always fit the crime.[2] Hammurabi's Law Code used this principle to demand that the maximum penalty should always be exacted: *"If a man puts out the eye of another man, his eye shall be put out. If he breaks another man's bone, his bone shall be broken."* God's

---

[2] Exodus 21:24; Leviticus 24:20; Deuteronomy 19:21.

Law, however, uses this principle to set limits that prevented vengeful victims from overcompensating for a crime. Even the guilty were entitled to justice, and their victims could make God visible if they chose to grant mercy instead of exacting the letter of the law. *"You have heard that it was said, 'Eye for eye, and tooth for tooth,'"* Jesus explained as he taught on Deuteronomy. *"But I tell you, Do not resist an evil person. If someone strikes you on the right cheek, turn to him the other also."*[3] God wants to be seen through his People exercising a mercy and restraint that were alien to Hammurabi.[4]

Many people take offence at the fact that the Law of Moses appears to condone *slavery*. Again, Hammurabi helps us to see Deuteronomy in its historical context. A slave in Babylon who tried to resist his master would be punished by having his ear amputated, but a slave in Israel need only wait to be freed without paying any money at the Year of Jubilee.[5] A person who harboured a runaway slave in Babylon and championed his rights would be executed, but a person found kidnapping someone into slavery in Israel would be executed for committing a crime akin to murder.[6] William Wilberforce, Abraham Lincoln and Martin Luther King all derived principles, inspiration and imagery for their fight against slavery and racism from Moses' Law and the Old Testament prophets who preached from it. Despite the fact that slavery was deeply embedded in Bronze Age culture, Deuteronomy sowed the seeds for its later abolition.

There is a similar answer for those who are offended that the Law of Moses does not do enough to defend the *rights*

---

[3] Matthew 5:38–39. The Mosaic Law does not present the *lex talionis* in terms of *revenge*, but as part of the wider goal to *"purge the evil from among you"* so that God could be seen through his People.

[4] The Lord even commanded in 25:1–3 that anyone found guilty must still be treated fairly.

[5] In fact, Hebrew slaves would be freed within seven years under Exodus 21:2–6 and Deuteronomy 15:12–18.

[6] Exodus 21:16; Deuteronomy 24:7. See also Deuteronomy 23:15–16 and 1 Timothy 1:9–11.

of women. Hammurabi decreed that if a wife neglected her husband, he could take a new wife and enslave the old one to be their live-in servant. If he wanted to divorce her, he could do so easily by paying back her dowry, but if a woman left her husband she would be bound hand and foot and drowned in the river. In contrast, the Law of Moses affirms the rights of women by flouting the prevailing Middle Eastern culture and treating them as equally valued worshippers in God's sight.[7]

It was not just women's rights which the Lord protected in his Law as an expression of his fifth love language. Hammurabi punished a slave who struck a free man by cutting off his ears, a free man who struck a nobleman with *"sixty blows with an ox-whip in public"*, but a nobleman who punched a commoner with a simple fine. In contrast, the Lord refused to countenance partiality and set the same punishments regardless of class, wealth or race.[8] Hammurabi decreed that a swindler who swore his innocence in the name of Babylon's gods was unassailable, no matter how many witnesses stood against him, whereas the Lord called for two or three witnesses to settle any crime.[9] Hammurabi commanded that a man who caused a pregnant woman's death must be punished by his own innocent daughter being executed, whereas the Lord outlawed such vindictive injustice by decreeing that *"Fathers shall not be put to death for their children, nor children put to death for their fathers; each is to die for his own sin."*[10]

So if you have ever been embarrassed by some of these treaty provisions, a trip to the Louvre would make a world of difference. When we stop measuring all past cultures arrogantly against our own, and start comparing the Law of Moses with the other law codes of its day, we can see God's fifth love language

---

[7] For example, Exodus 15:20–21; 21:10; Numbers 6:2; 27:1–7; Deuteronomy 22:13–19.

[8] Deuteronomy 1:16–17; 10:17–19; 16:19; 24:17; 27:19; Numbers 35:31.

[9] Deuteronomy 19:15–19.

[10] Deuteronomy 24:16.

written on every page. The Lord loves justice and mercy and calls us to love them too. As we do so, he promises to be seen through us, his People.

Better Than Moses
(18:14–22)

I will raise up for them a prophet like you from among their brothers; I will put my words in his mouth, and he will tell them everything I command him.

(Deuteronomy 18:18)

The Lord has one more thing to say before he finishes talking about his five love languages. He wants to make sure we give our love to the right person. That may sound obvious, but it would actually prove to be Israel's biggest problem. They grew so attached to the memory of Moses as their founding father that they fell in love with his memory instead of his message.

In the movie *The Decoy Bride*, the former *Doctor Who* star David Tennant is engaged to be married to a beautiful film star.[1] She is an A-list celebrity, the cover-girl for every fashion magazine, and crowds of reporters follow her every move. When their constant harassment turns her plans for a dream wedding into a nightmare, her quick-thinking agent pays a lookalike to throw them off her scent. The plan unravels when the local girl does more than distract the attention of the paparazzi. David Tennant falls in love with the decoy bride and ditches the gorgeous film star for her lookalike instead.

When that happens in a movie, we call it romantic comedy. When it happens to God's People, we call it spiritual tragedy. Moses suspected that the Israelites might look back on his memory and let their glorious past rob them of their even better future. He was the one who had led them out of Egypt to Mount

---

[1] *The Decoy Bride* (CinemaNX, 2011).

Sinai, and had gone up the mountain to act as their mediator with God. He was the one who had looked after them in the desert, where they ate bread from heaven, drank water from the rock, and had clothes and shoes which miraculously never wore out.[2] He was the one who had given them the treaty of Deuteronomy. He held such a place in their affections that even fourteen centuries later the Jews still rejected Jesus by saying, *"We are disciples of Moses! We know that God spoke to Moses, but as for this fellow, we don't even know where he comes from."*[3] That's why Moses makes sure to remind them in chapter 18 that he is not the real superstar, and that they must not fall for the equivalent of David Tennant's decoy bride.

Moses made it clear that the Lord had something better in store for his People than the Law of Sinai. The Law was perfect but it wasn't God's last word. One day its endless blood sacrifices would be fulfilled by a once-for-all sacrifice, and its small caste of priests would expand to include all God's People. On that day they would no longer be forced to stand at a distance, because the Most Holy Place would be open to them all.

Moses also made it clear that the Lord had a better leader in store for them than he himself had ever been. He was a mere judge, whose sin meant he could not lead them into the Promised Land. Their better leader would be a King, he prophesied in chapter 17, and would be completely obedient wherever he had failed. Like Moses, this King would be a Jewish prophet who would mediate God's New Covenant with his People.[4] Chapter 18 warns the Israelites that *"The Lord your God will raise up for you a prophet like me from among your own brothers. You must listen to him."* If they imagined that

---

[2] This miracle is not mentioned in Exodus or Numbers, but only in Deuteronomy 8:4 and 29:5.

[3] John 9:28–29.

[4] Muslims argue that Moses was prophesying about Muhammad, but he was not a Jewish *brother* like Moses and Jesus.

Moses was the hero of the Pentateuch, they needed to read these chapters and think again.[5]

Sadly, the Israelites acted like David Tennant and were easily distracted from God's real superstar. When they saw John the Baptist leading their nation in revival, they asked *"Are you the Prophet?"*, but didn't listen to his reply. It took Philip, one of John's disciples, to take his words seriously when he pointed to Jesus of Nazareth as *"the Lamb of God, who takes away the sin of the world."*[6] *"We have found the one Moses wrote about in the Law... Jesus of Nazareth,"* Philip told a friend excitedly, and soon the Jewish crowds suggested *"Surely this is the Prophet who is to come into the world."*[7] God confirmed it when his voice boomed out on the Mount of Transfiguration as it had on Mount Sinai, quoting from Deuteronomy 18 that *"This is my Son, whom I have chosen; listen to him."*[8] The moment which Moses had predicted had finally arrived. It was time for the Israelites to exchange their memories for their Messiah.

Tragically, their love affair with Moses proved too powerful. *"The Law was put in charge to lead us to Christ"*, Paul tells us, but its traditions had become an end in themselves for the Jewish leaders. *"We have a Law, and according to that Law he must die,"* they insisted, invoking Deuteronomy's blasphemy laws.[9] As they connived with the Romans to crucify their Messiah, they didn't realize that they were offering a better Passover Lamb than Exodus, a better blood sacrifice than Leviticus, a better bronze snake than Numbers and a better mediator than Moses in Deuteronomy.[10] When they sent soldiers to guard Jesus' tomb

---

[5] The Lord was so concerned that Israel must not fall for a decoy that he ordered that false prophets be put to death. Acts 21:10–15 and 1 Corinthians 13:9 and 14:29 accept that today it is normal for us to *"prophesy in part"*.

[6] John 1:21, 29.

[7] John 1:45; 6:14; 7:40.

[8] Luke 9:28–36.

[9] Galatians 3:19–25; John 19:7.

[10] It was *good* for the Hebrews to recognize they needed a mediator between them and God in verse 17. We are told that Jesus is a better mediator of a

they didn't realize they were re-enacting the battle between the Devil and God's angels for Moses' corpse in Deuteronomy 34.[11] Whereas the Lord rescued Moses' body and hid it somewhere near Mount Nebo, he rescued Jesus' body by raising him from the dead and hid it with the clouds as he lifted him to heaven in front of his disciples.

So let's not fall for a decoy bride like David Tennant or like the first-century Jews who rejected the one better than Moses. Jesus warned them that *"Your accuser is Moses, on whom, your hopes are set. If you believed Moses, you would believe me, for he wrote about me."* Peter taught the same: *"Moses said, 'The Lord your God will raise up for you a prophet like me from among your own people; you must listen to everything he tells you. Anyone who does not listen to him will be completely cut off from among his People.'"*[12] Let's express our love for Moses and his Law by loving God's Messiah in all his five love languages.

---

better covenant in 1 Timothy 2:5 and in Hebrews 8:6, 9:15 and 12:24.

[11] Compare Deuteronomy 34:5–6 with Jude 9.

[12] John 5:45–46; Acts 3:22–23. See also Acts 6:13–14; 7:37; 28:23.

Covenant Part Four: Promises and Penalties (27:1–30:20)

I have set before you life and death, blessings and curses. Now choose life, so that you and your children may live.

(Deuteronomy 30:19)

Being part of God's People can be a mixed blessing. Just ask Tevye, the Russian-Jewish milkman in the musical *Fiddler on the Roof*.[1] At one point he lifts his troubled eyes to heaven and prays, *"I know, I know. We are your chosen People. But once in a while – can't you choose someone else?"* He is experiencing the fourth part of the treaty of Deuteronomy, when the Lord repeats and expands on the promises and penalties of Leviticus 26.

God's Plan "A" is to be seen through his People by blessing them as they obey him. That's why he commanded half of the Israelite tribes to climb Mount Gerizim after they had conquered the Promised Land to call out the blessings of obeying his covenant. In the first fourteen verses of chapter 28, he promises to make them fruitful at home and in the field, victorious in business and on the battlefield, and successful as a nation so that he can become visible. So long as they obeyed these treaty provisions and reflected God's true character, he would bless them and *"all the peoples on earth will see that you are called by the name of the Lord."*

But the Lord had not changed since Leviticus 26, and he

---

[1] *Fiddler on the Roof* was released as a movie by United Artists in 1971.

still had a terrible Plan "B" in reserve if they despised their calling as a nation. That's why he commanded the other six tribes to climb Mount Ebal to call out the curses that would fall on them if they broke his covenant.[2] He would make them barren at home and in the field, defeated in business and on the battlefield, and humiliated as a nation to make him visible in a different way. He would visit on them the plagues that he spared their parents from in Egypt, and would fill their lives with disease and drought and despair. He would thwart their wedding plans, their building plans, their business plans and their plans for their sons and daughters. He would hand them over to foreign invasion until they grew so crazed with hunger in their besieged cities that they would even kill and eat their own children. If they despised his Plan "A" and refused to make *"this glorious and awesome name – the Lord your God"* visible to the world, he would make himself visible by the way in which he judged and exiled them, as a warning to other nations to sit up and take him seriously.

Many readers misunderstand this fourth part of Deuteronomy, as if God were telling the Hebrews to earn their way to blessing through his covenant. They try to live life like a L'Oréal advert, hoping to attract God's blessing "because we're worth it". They forget that Moses tells us that

> *The Lord did not set his affection on you and choose you because you were more numerous than other peoples, for you were the fewest of all peoples. But it was because the Lord loved you and kept the oath he swore to your forefathers that he brought you out with a mighty hand and redeemed you from the land of slavery... He is the faithful God, keeping his covenant of love to a thousand generations.*[3]

---

[2] The Israelites followed through on these instructions at Gerizim and Ebal in Joshua 8:30–35.

[3] Deuteronomy 7:7–9.

That's why Moses reminds us that God's Covenant with his People is unconditional, and that they simply get to choose how he expresses it through them.

Whether Israel obeyed him or not, they would be his *segūllāh*, his *private treasure collection*. We looked at this word back in Exodus 19:5, but the Lord uses it again here in Deuteronomy 7:6, 14:2 and 26:18 to remind the Israelites that their worth derives from him. Even when they worshipped idols, lived like the Canaanites and chose the penalties described in chapter 28, he still viewed them as flawless, priceless jewels.[4] He simply shone his character differently through them to make himself visible through his People.

Whether Israel obeyed him or not, the Promised Land would belong to them as an unconditional inheritance. The Lord promises them repeatedly throughout Deuteronomy that *"I have given you the land"* as an *"everlasting possession"*,[5] but he also promises them repeatedly that they need to take possession of their possession! He warns them at the end of chapter 28 that *"If you do not carefully follow all the words of this law, which are written in this book...you will be uprooted from the land you are entering to possess. Then the Lord will scatter you among all nations, from one end of the earth to the other."* The Promised Land would not cease to be theirs, but the Lord would make himself visible through Plan "B" when he exiled them to show the world that he was not like Israel. If he punished even the Israelites when they disobeyed his rule, the nations must repent or suffer a similar fate.

I hope that you love the Jewish nation because of God's promises to Abraham in Genesis 12:2–3. I hope you love them enough to tell people like Tevye the milkman that there is a reason why being a modern-day Israelite is so painful. I hope you tell them that their troubles are a sign they have missed

---

[4] The clothing of the high priest in Exodus 28:9–21 looked forward to Revelation 21:9–21.

[5] Genesis 17:8; 48:4.

the better Prophet of chapter 18 and are reaping the curses of Mount Ebal. I hope you love them enough to tell them it will take more than a UN resolution to restore them to their land if they persist in rejecting Jesus, *"the hope of Israel"*, who has turned Calvary into a new Mount Gerizim.[6]

Tevye has no Christian friends in the musical to warn him that he has rejected the Messiah and is reaping God's Plan "B". He therefore clings to empty tradition and redoubles his passionate love affair with Moses: *"You may ask, how did this tradition start? I'll tell you. I don't know. But it's a tradition and because of our traditions every one of us knows who he is and what God expects him to do... Without our traditions, our lives would be as shaky as a fiddler on the roof!"*

God wants us to tell the Jews around us that their traditions must lead them to the promise of Deuteronomy 21:23 that *"anyone who is hung on a tree is under God's curse."* He wants us to imitate Paul who warned Tevye's countrymen that *"All who rely on observing the Law are under a curse, for it is written [in Deuteronomy 27:26]: 'Cursed is everyone who does not continue to do everything written in the Book of the Law'", yet "Christ redeemed us from the curse of the Law by becoming a curse for us, for it is written: 'Cursed is everyone who is hung on a tree.'""*[7]

God wants us to tell them that Jesus bore the curses and penalties of Deuteronomy so that Jew and Gentile can receive its blessings and promises together as God's New Covenant nation. He wants us to tell them that because one better than Moses has come, the Lord can now be seen by fulfilling his glorious Plan "A" through his People.

---

[6] Acts 26:6–7; 28:20.

[7] Galatians 3:10–13.

Covenant Part Five: Posterity (31:1–34:12)

When Moses finished reciting all these words to all Israel, he said to them, "Take to heart all the words I have solemnly declared to you this day, so that you may command your children to obey carefully all the words of this law."

(Deuteronomy 32:45–46)

"Success without a successor is failure". If that management mantra is true, then Moses was very successful. It was not enough for him to hand the treaty of Deuteronomy over to one generation of Israelites. After thirty chapters of preamble, past, provisions, and promises and penalties, the book ends with four chapters which extend its message for *posterity*. Moses wanted to make sure that every subsequent generation of Israelites knew that this treaty also applied to them, so he ended the Pentateuch with chapters that assured them that God the Covenant Keeper would not renege on his treaty.

First, Moses appointed a new *leader*, facing up to the fact that *"I am now a hundred and twenty years old and I am no longer able to lead you. The Lord has said to me, 'You shall not cross the Jordan.'"*[1] He sidestepped the trap that ensnares lesser leaders, by recognizing that his leadership was now a hindrance to God's People reaching the next stage in their history. For the past forty years he had been training Joshua as his apprentice, teaching

---

[1] Moses did not hand over to Joshua because he was old (Deuteronomy 34:7), but because God told him to. Moses' concern in Numbers 27:12–17 was not for his own future but for God's shepherdless People.

him how to experience God and how he must lead the Israelites to victory over their enemies.[2] Moses had taught him the heart of the Gospel by changing his name from Hoshea, meaning *Salvation*, to Joshua, meaning specifically *The Lord Saves*. He had also laid hands on Joshua to receive the same Holy Spirit as he himself.[3] The forty years in the desert had not just been the making of a new generation of Israelites. They had also been the making of their new leader.

Moses reminds Joshua that under his leadership the Lord will continue to be Israel's Saviour (31:5), Indweller (31:6), Covenant Keeper (31:7) and Faithful One (31:8). He does so in front of the Israelites as a public affirmation of his successor, and the Lord adds his own affirmation by appearing to Joshua at the entrance to the Tabernacle instead of (as usual) in the Tabernacle itself. As Moses passes this final test in his leadership, he paves the way for Israel to march behind Joshua to conquer the Promised Land. He ensures that under Joshua the Lord will continue to be seen through his People.

Second, Moses emphasized that the *Law* would apply to every succeeding generation of Israelites. Even after the Joshua generation died, their distant descendants would still live under this treaty. Moses wrote down the Law in chapter 31 – presumably a reference to him finishing writing the Pentateuch – and he gave it to the priests to be kept next to the Ark of the Covenant in the Most Holy Place. The priests would read the whole thing to all the People in every seventh year so that each new generation would understand that its provisions, promises and penalties applied to them too. We read in 2 Kings 22–23 that this copy of the Law was sometimes lost, but that whenever it was rediscovered it led to great revival and to God being seen through his People.

---

[2] Exodus 17:8–16; 24:13; 33:11.

[3] Numbers 13:16; 27:12–23; Deuteronomy 34:9. *Jesus* is the Greek for Joshua, so the name-change was also to make Joshua a picture of the great Conqueror to come.

Third, Moses gave the Israelites the *low-down* on what would happen to their descendants in the generations to come. He sang them a song in chapter 32 which prophesied that they would be unfaithful, but the Lord would remain faithful. While they grew fat, complacent and idolatrous, and naturally incurred the Lord's Plan "B" instead of his Plan "A", he would not reject them entirely as his People.[4] He would make them jealous by hiding from them and revealing himself to the Gentiles,[5] but he would never reject them because of *"the taunt of the enemy, lest the adversary misunderstand and say, 'Our hand has triumphed, the Lord has not done all this.'"* Even when he judged them, the Lord would remember mercy, so Moses gave them this prophecy in the form of a song so that each new generation could learn and sing it together in the centuries to come.

Fourth, Moses blessed the Israelites in chapter 33 by prophesying God's specific *legacy* for each of their tribes. He echoed Jacob's similar blessings in Genesis 49 by omitting the Simeonites whom Jacob had cursed, and by transforming Jacob's curse on the Levites into blessing because of Aaron and Phinehas' passion to make God visible in Exodus 32:25–29 and Numbers 25:7–13. Moses reminded the Israelites in verse 27 that the Lord is *"the eternal God"* who saved them and carries them in his *"everlasting arms"*. The God of Deuteronomy would never change in his affection towards Israel, and would cause the nations to exclaim in wonder in verse 29: *"Blessed are you, O Israel! Who is like you, a people saved by the Lord?"*

Fifth, Moses prepared the Israelites for their future in the manner of his *leaving*. He did not protest at God's plan when he climbed Mount Nebo in chapter 34 to view a Promised Land which he knew he could not enter. After forty years of service,

---

[4] *Jeshurun* in verse 15 is a poetic name for Israel (see 33:5, 26). It means *Upright One* and stresses the Israelites' true calling in spite of their sin.

[5] Paul quotes verse 21 in Romans 10:19, and Jesus gives specific examples of this in Luke 4:25–28. Paul quotes verse 43 in Romans 15:10 to explain that God's ultimate plan is to save Jews and Gentiles as one People together.

he was happy to pass on the baton whenever the Lord told him that his part in Israel's relay race was complete. This last chapter must have been written by Joshua or another of Moses' helpers, and they probably also inserted Numbers 12:3 and Deuteronomy 33:1, which is the only reference in the Pentateuch to Moses as *"the man of God"*.[6]

Finally, don't miss the promise that the Lord extends in the last three verses of Deuteronomy. At the end of these four chapters, which pledge that God's covenant treaty extends to every generation, we find a statement that no prophet has yet arisen in Israel to rival Moses. This is a reminder that the great Prophet predicted by Moses in Deuteronomy 18 has yet to appear, and that when the Messiah comes God will be seen through his People by better miracles, a better revelation of God and a better covenant to which the Law of Moses merely pointed the way.

The covenant of Deuteronomy would apply to each new generation, but – praise God – it would one day be fulfilled and superseded by God's Messiah. *"Christ is the mediator of a new covenant, that those who are called may receive the promised eternal inheritance,"* explains Hebrews 9:15. God the Covenant Keeper can never renege on this treaty, but he has upgraded it in Jesus and made it even more glorious for those who follow him today.

---

[6] The phrase is used elsewhere in Joshua 14:6; 1 Chronicles 23:14; 2 Chronicles 30:16; Ezra 3:2; Psalm 90:1.

Conclusion:
God Wants to Be Seen
Through His People

*Now may the Lord's strength be displayed, just as
you have declared.*

(Numbers 14:17)

In the movie *Welcome to the Jungle*, former wrestling star The
Rock plays a bounty hunter with an ultimatum.[1] He finds his
targets and asks them to co-operate or pay the price:

THE ROCK: I need you to make a choice for me.

TARGET: A choice?

THE ROCK: Option "A" or Option "B"?

TARGET: What's Option "A"?

THE ROCK: Option "A" is you and I walk out of here nice and
             easy, get in my jeep, we drive back to the airstrip,
             and then we begin the long journey back to Los
             Angeles. There'll be no blood, no broken bones and
             no problems.

TARGET: What's in Los Angeles?

THE ROCK: Your father.

TARGET: What's Option "B"?

THE ROCK: Pretty much the opposite of "A". But I wouldn't
             recommend that one.

---

[1] Universal Pictures distributed this 2003 movie in the USA as *The Rundown*,
but Columbia Pictures distributed it globally under the title *Welcome to the
Jungle*.

We can look back on the centuries since the giving of the Pentateuch and chart the way that God has made himself visible through his People. Like The Rock, he has always recommended Option "A", but very often they have insisted on receiving Option "B".

Joshua inspired the Israelites to go with Option "A", and they enjoyed the promised blessings of Deuteronomy together. They defeated giants, dispossessed mighty nations and settled in the Promised Land. Some Canaanites even begged them for peace and asked for a share in God's covenant, saying *"We have heard reports of...the fame of the Lord your God."*[2] Under Joshua, the Israelites served the Lord with all their hearts and he responded by revealing himself through blessing them as he had promised.

Sadly, the next few generations all chose Option "B". They incurred the penalties and curses of Deuteronomy when foreign troops invaded, occupied their land, and plundered what little harvest they could grow. From time to time, when they repented and called on God the Covenant Keeper to rescue them and help them return to Option "A", he raised up a judge who made him visible as God the Saviour and God the Faithful One. After every victory, once trouble had subsided, the Israelites quickly turned away again from God's Law and reaped the bitter fruit of Option "B". The Lord wanted to be seen through the way he blessed his People, but their actions made him visible as God the Father who disciplines his rebellious children.

Eventually the Israelites did as the Lord prophesied in Deuteronomy 17. They appointed Saul as their first king and were blessed when he chose Option "A" and led them to triumph over their enemies. Later, when he turned his back on the Lord and pursued Option "B", the Lord replaced his dynasty with that of godly David and Solomon. When David's dynasty also refused Option "A", he exiled them from the Promised Land to Babylon,

---

[2] Joshua 9:9.

as promised in Deuteronomy 28:63–64: *"You will be uprooted from the land you are entering to possess. Then the Lord will scatter you among the nations, from one end of the earth to the other."* As The Rock tells one of his very bruised targets: *"You should have chosen Option 'A'."*

God was merciful. Babylon was not the end of Israel's story. He brought them back from exile under Prince Zerubbabel and a godly priest who was aptly named Joshua. He revived them and settled them back in the Promised Land with a fresh resolution to choose his Option "A". When they turned away again, he handed them over to the Macedonians, then the Ptolemies, then the Seleucids and then the Romans. Finally, he sent the Prophet foretold by Moses in Deuteronomy 18, and asked for a definitive choice between Option "A" and Option "B". As Israel's destiny hung in the balance, Moses actually came from heaven to meet Jesus on the Mount of Transfiguration and encourage him as he forged a true and better Exodus for God's People.[3] Angels waited with bated breath to discover whether Israel would respond to this new Exodus with Option "A" or Option "B".

Tragically, they chose Option "B" and the curses of Deuteronomy 28. The Romans destroyed their nation, and the few survivors were scattered among the nations, but not before tens of thousands of Jews received their Messiah and formed a faithful community called the Church, which chose Option "A". They toured the nations persuading both Jews and Gentiles to join them in the discovery that God the Saviour still wants to be seen through his People. They told the world that God the Covenant Keeper had fulfilled the Law through his Messiah, that God the Holy One had crushed him as a sin offering and that God the Faithful One had raised him from the dead. They called the world to receive him as God the Indweller through his

---

[3] Moses and Elijah refer to Jesus' death and resurrection in Luke 9:31 by using the Greek word for *Exodus*. John also makes a similar link in Revelation 15:2–3.

Holy Spirit, and to choose Option "A" so he could reveal himself through his People.

The centuries of Church history have been as rocky as Israel's, but whenever Christians have chosen God's Option "A", he has blessed them and led the Church to great fruitfulness in Jesus. Whenever they have chosen Option "B", however, he has disciplined her, shrunk her membership and thwarted her at every turn.[4] That's why these books of the Pentateuch are not just ancient history about a People who have little in common with ourselves. These are our ancestors in the faith, and *"these things occurred as examples to keep us from setting our hearts on evil things as they did."*[5] Make no mistake. God wants to be seen through his People, and he will be seen through your life no matter which way you choose. As we end the Pentateuch, God turns to you and urges you to choose Option "A" like Jochebed, Moses, Joshua, Caleb or Phinehas, not Option "B" like the ten unbelieving spies, the Reubenites or the Gadites.

Since Jesus is the better Prophet that Moses predicted; since he entirely fulfilled the righteous requirements of the Law; since he died as the true sacrifice foreshadowed by the Pentateuch; and since he has signed a new and better covenant treaty with his blood; let's choose Option "A" and live under God's blessing.

Let's obey the message of the books that Moses wrote in the desert: God still wants to be seen through his People.

---

[4] God calls us to read Church history with the discernment recommended in Deuteronomy 32:28–30.

[5] 1 Corinthians 10:6.